FROUDE'S SPANISH STORY OF THE ARMADA

and Other Essays

FROUDE'S SPANISH STORY OF THE ARMADA

and Other Essays

Edited, and with an
Introduction by
A. L. Rowse

ALAN SUTTON
1988

ALAN SUTTON PUBLISHING
BRUNSWICK ROAD · GLOUCESTER

First published 1988

British Library Cataloguing in Publication Data

Froude, James Anthony, *1818–1894*
The Spanish story of the Armada.
1. England. War with Spain, 1588.
Spanish Armada
I. Title   II. Rowse, A.L. (Alfred
Leslie), *1903–*
942.05'5

ISBN 0-86299-500-0

Cover picture: The Spanish Armada in a Storm (detail) *by*
H.C. Vroom. *Private collection.*
Photograph: The Bridgeman Art Library.

Typesetting and origination by
Alan Sutton Publishing Limited
Printed in Great Britain by
The Guernsey Press Company Limited,
Guernsey, Channel Islands

To
Helen Mildmay of Flete
with fond memories of our
early Oxford days

Contents

Introduction

This volume contains three of James Anthony Froude's shorter, characteristic works. He was the leading historian of the Victorian age after Macaulay, the most controversial and the most controverted. Macaulay largely got away with his bias, Protestant, Parliamentarian, Whig: he had strong backing from his political party, the grand Whiggery, and always – right up to our time with the Trevelyans – from Cambridge. Froude had less than no support from Oxford: his point of view offended both the High Church Tractarians and the Liberals. Every volume of his great The *History of England* was attacked by the mean and irascible Regius Professor Freeman, and even Stubbs – the creator of the Oxford History School, and its exemplar up to our time – did not much hold with Froude.

> See ladling butter from alternate tubs,
> Stubbs butters Freeman, and Freeman butters Stubbs.

Those two were pure-blooded academics, and they thought that Froude was insufficiently academic. All the academics were against Froude. He wrote for the great wide public, his books sold in scores of thousands – theirs did not. He himself said, a generation after Macaulay, that he hoped to make his history as readable as a novel. He was a leading public figure in his time, who was familiar with the highest society, political and social. At the same time he was a reserved man whom people did not really know, and he was utterly, fearlessly independent, with no party backing. People said he was rather cynical – they meant sceptical; and, underneath his Protestant, patriotic line, he was sceptical, and had no use for Victorian illusions and humbug.

Altogether he was rather a paradox: people could not understand him – I do not think he wanted them to, for he never explained himself – and yet he was a best-seller:

> Though his sins were scarlet,
> Yet his books were *read*.

Ironically enough, the works of the two great Oxford academic historians have been totally superseded. No-one now sets store by Freeman's vast and laborious *History of the Norman Conquest*, with its idealisation of the Anglo-Saxons, and its hero Harold, last of the Saxons (he was half a Dane) as a kind of eleventh-century Mr Gladstone (a High Church Liberal, like Freeman). Stubbs' great *Constitutional History*, with its thesis of Lancastrian constitutionalism, is no less out of court.

In a double irony Froude's The *History of England* is not so out of date as the work of those two academics. Of course he is open to criticism, and our perspective has altered. He is much too enthusiastic about the Reformation, and sees things in terms of religious, or ideological, issues, where we see politics in terms of conflicts for power. We prefer Erasmus – as one side of Froude did – to Luther and Calvin. He was too favourable to Henry VIII, though he could be critical of him; he was consistently, and wrongly, critical of Elizabeth I. He did not like a *politique*: he preferred men of action – he was a man of action *manqué* himself. This is why he is so good on the Elizabethan seamen.

I

The first section of this book reprints his last work, the last lectures he gave at Oxford when he accepted the Regius Professorship after Freeman's death. He was over seventy, and told his daughter Margaret that it would kill him – and it did. Sir Charles Oman, historically a follower of Freeman, said that Froude's brief two years were 'a golden age of history lecturing in Oxford'. People crowded to hear the famous man. Only a handful had attended Freeman's lectures, and few came to listen to Stubbs, as he constantly complained. Again, after Froude, very few went to Sir Charles Firth's lectures in my time. Froude then was the exception – the odd man out, as in everything, for he was, as Stubbs had the magnanimity to admit, a man of genius.

One must remember then that the first work here consists of lectures; as such they give one an idea of Froude's lecturing style. I have retained his son's summing up of his father's life, above all for one sentence which gives us a clue to him. 'He was at home in any type of boat, from a racing eight to a trawler; but, when sailing, was rather apt to take chances with his life and his gear.'

Every man has the defects of his qualities, and perhaps some qualities that stem from his very defects. In reading Froude's work on the Elizabethan seamen, we have the advantage of reading an historian who knew all about sailing and seamanship, as few do. But he was all too ready to take risks. Froude was unfair to the Duke of Medina Sidonia, in command of the Armada of 1588 – true, the Duke was no sailor. He was equally unjust to Elizabeth I – no sailor either, though marvellously good at navigating the shoals and reefs of politics. Froude did not much appreciate that.

Then again, Froude was all too willing to regard Francis Drake and Hawkins as 'corsairs'. Of course the Spaniards regarded them as such, but that is no reason why we should. The Spaniards were bent on excluding everybody, except the Portuguese, from the New World of America. What sort of future would England have had if the Elizabethan seamen had been prepared to accept that sentence of exclusion? The Spaniards massacred all the French colonists who tried to set up a colony in Florida. Hawkins, who had been a servant of Philip's during his time in England, tried to establish trade with the West Indies by agreement with Spain then in alliance with England, and by collusion with the Spanish colonists. Elizabeth I contributed a ship to his semi-official voyage of 1567–8. All hope of that was overthrown by the Spaniards' pounce upon his ships at San Juan de Ulloa to his immense loss. Young Drake's successful *coup* at Nombre de Dios was by way of recouping himself and Hawkins for their losses: they regarded themselves as perfectly justified in getting their own back – and so did all the Elizabethan seamen. True, that was a private expedition; but after that Drake always regarded himself as the Queen's officer and cited her commission. So we must regard him as a privateer, and not a 'corsair', or pirate.

Froude did rather throw about words. Moreover he was a patriot, so he applauded the exploits of the seamen against the enemy, not minding whether they were corsairs or not. I do not think he much observed the distinction between pirates or privateers – he was not a careful writer – as a good modern sea-historian such as J.A. Williamson did.

Then too Froude was a Victorian rhetorician – like Macaulay. He was repetitive and he constantly exaggerated. He was apt to say 'thousands' when 'hundreds' would be nearer the mark, or 'hundreds' when scores or dozens would do. All historians, from Caesar onwards, exaggerate numbers. Froude says that the Armada carried some thirty thousand men, soldiers along with sailors, when twenty thousand would be nearer the number. It is true, however, that the ships were crowded with soldiers: the Armada, unlike the English squadrons, was not only a fleet, it carried an army.

'It was now or never for England,' he says, and this kind of thing must have made his lectures exciting for the young gentlemen of Oxford in the early 1890s, when people could be patriotic. Froude foresaw what the future would have been, without merchant fleets and a navy, without colonies or the Empire: just an island in the North Sea.

These last lectures of Froude's were never revised or corrected by him for the press, and were published posthumously. So it has fallen to me to revise and contract, slim them of repetitions and, very occasionally, correct a mistake or modernise the language. Anyway, here we have the essential Froude. I have placed this last work first, for it provides the historical perspective in which to see the more original two pieces, *Antonio Pérez* and *The Spanish Story of the Armada*.

II

Where Freeman, the academic *pur sang* prided himself on not using manuscript material, Froude was a pioneer in the use of archives. He spent years altogether working at original manuscripts in the British Museum, the Rolls Office and State Paper Office, precursors of the Public Record Office; he consulted the archives in Paris, Brussels, Vienna. I do not know of any English scholar who preceded him in working at the archives at Simancas, those beautiful rooms smelling of cedar wood which that good aesthete, Philip II, contrived in the old castle there not far from Valladolid. Froude now and again complains of the difficulty of Philip's hardly decipherable hand, but stuck to his last.

Though he was a patriotic English seaman himself, he had a proper appreciation of Spain's greatness, the magnitude of her achievement in the *siglo d'oro*; the country itself and its denizens, with a particular feeling for Cervantes and St Theresa of Avila. He paid tribute to Philip's conscientiousness, his life of hard labour – as the King himself wrote of the Escorial, 'this bare mountain-side from which I rule half the world'. What Froude could not bear was Philip's religiosity – as who can?

However, all this gave Froude a window into Spanish affairs in the sixteenth century such as no one else had. We see the profit he drew from this in the second piece. When he published it in 1883 he called it, '*Antonio Pérez: an Unsolved Historical Riddle*. Since then the riddle has been solved, and a great deal more has been found out, especially about Pérez in England. But Froude was on the right track, and the story is essentially right. The story created an immense sensation at the time: the prolonged duel between the first monarch in the world and his dismissed Secretary of State, formerly a favourite, and for some years a foremost figure on the European stage: Philip's dangerous opponent, in possession of a deadly secret. What was it?

At the time, and for centuries afterwards, people thought of it as an affair of the heart: the eternal triangle, with Philip and Pérez as rivals for the love of the Princess of Eboli, a hideous one-eyed Mendoza. There was nothing of that in it, of course: it was all politics. But over the centuries plays, operas and novels have been written on the basis of it being an emotional intrigue. It was vastly more important than that, and Froude got to the heart of it, though we have learned much more since.

Philip's illegitimate half-brother, Don John of Austria, victor of Lepanto – and hero of Chesterton's fine biased poem:

> Don John of Austria is going to the war –

was a glamorous figure, of wide and irresponsible ambitions. Among other flighty ideas, he would have invaded England from the Netherlands to put Mary Queen of Scots on the throne and marry her. He was encouraged in these rash ideas by his secretary, Escovedo; both he and his master were liabilities to the state in the eyes of the prudent King. Fortunately Don John died; Escovedo had been recalled to Madrid and was assassinated one night in the street. Philip had ordered it, and left it to Pérez to arrange it. Suspicion fell on Pérez. Philip could never quite clear himself of the guilt, but, like Henry VIII, the sacrosanct ruler had to appear above reproach.

Pérez was in and out of prison for years; parties formed, the Holy Inquisition was sympathetic to him and wanted to get to the bottom of the case. This made things difficult for the King: Pérez possessed his letters and could incriminate or blackmail him. At last, in 1590, Pérez escaped from prison in Madrid to Aragon. This kingdom enjoyed its *fueros*, its constititional rights, estates of its own, and came out in support of Pérez.

There was a revolt, which it took Philip many thousands of soldiers, and a couple of hundred hangings, to suppress. This ended the independent constitutional rights of Aragon. In the *mêlée* Pérez managed to escape across the Pyrenees to the court of Henry of Navarre's sister, the Princess Catherine, with her entourage of ladies. Henceforth he had the backing of Navarre, who was at war with Philip, and the support of Spain's enemies. He was for some years a prime figure on the international stage, not only for Henry of Navarre, now Henri IV of France, but also for Elizabeth I and the English.

Pérez journeyed up to Henry in the following of Princess Catherine. In April 1593 Henry speeded him on to England, with his strong recommendation, in the embassy of the Vidame de Chartres. With this French ambiance Pérez spent his first two months in the French embassy, but shortly graduated to Essex House, where he had the support of the whole Essex circle, on behalf of government and Court.

We now know a great deal more about Pérez in England, and the impression his personality made.[1] It was an unfavourable one. Of course he had Philip's secrets to reveal, information and advice to give. But he was extravagant and had expensive tastes and a group of young men to attend him. Although already in his fifty-third year – he was born in 1540 – he was notoriously fond of young men; at his age this made him something of a laughing-stock.

He had his uses, however. He had written up his story while in Pau with the French Princess; in London he published an augmented edition of his *Relaciones* under the pseudonym Raphael Peregrino. It was published by Richard Field, Shakespeare's fellow townsman, from his press in Blackfriars in 1594 – from which issued *The Rape of Lucrece* in the same year and *Venus and Adonis* in 1593. The Government – i.e. Queen Elizabeth and the Cecils – were willing to allow it to go forward in Spanish, as propaganda in Europe, but impeded its English translation.

Pérez became aligned with the forward group, the activists around Essex, to whom the book was dedicated, and among those to whom Pérez presented the book was Essex's close associate, Southampton. Pérez took a hand in running down Dr Lopez and his contacts with Spain in 1593–4, and that summer the Doctor, unwise enough to meddle in intelligence affairs, was brought to book by Essex. The poet of the circle refers to it, in his usual oblique way, in a sonnet he wrote for Southampton, his patron, at that time:

1. cf. G. Ungerer: *A Spaniard in Elizabethan England. The Correspondence of Antonio Pérez's Exile.* (2 vols).

The mortal moon hath her eclipse endured –

that is, the Queen had come through the shadow of the conspiracy against her.

Pérez's personality, as it revealed itself, was more and more of a liability, and as is the way with political exiles his usefulness gave diminishing returns. Even his closest associate in the circle, Anthony Bacon – another homosexual – became bored with him. Pérez was vain and conceited, an exhibitionist, gave himself patronising airs and graces, and had a great gift of the gab in Italian and Latin, as well as in his own ready tongue. He was a flatterer, who prided himself on the excessive compliments with which he larded his letters. As a rhetorician he was a proponent of a new Mannerist style of which he was the exemplar, and so proud of it that a few years later he published his fulsome *Letters* as models of their kind.

Here was a subject ready to hand for the poet-playwright of the circle to make fun of. Naturally, Shakespeare wrote *Love's Labour's Lost* for their private performance. The plot concerns the well-known theme of Southampton's reluctance to get tied down in marriage and his skittishness where women were concerned. Southampton himself is gently made fun of as Navarre, Shakespeare laughs at himself as Berowne (Biron) and the background is supposedly French, with the names familiar at the time, Longueville, Dumain (i.e. Mayenne). (These too had appeared in Field's publications.) It also features Princess Catherine of France, with her ladies, among whom appears Shakespeare's own dark mistress, well recognised now as the half-Italian, Emilia Bassano, young Mrs Lanier.

Along with these appears 'Don Adriano de Armado, a fantastical Spaniard':

> Our Court, you know, is haunted
> With a refinèd traveller[1] of Spain:
> A man in all the world's new fashion planted,
> That hath a mint of phrases in his brain.
> One who the music of his own vain tongue
> Doth ravish like enchanting harmony.

1. Note the preciseness with which Pérez is described: he put his work, his *Relacion*, forward as that of a *traveller*, *peregrino*, and Holofernes calls him 'too *peregrinate*'. And there was indeed a 'world's debate' about him: the affair created an international sensation.

A man of compliments, whom right and wrong
Have chose as umpire of their mutiny.
This child of fancy, that Armado hight,
For interim to our studies shall relate
In high-born words the worth of many a knight
From tawny Spain, lost in the world's debate . . .
But I protest I love to hear him lie,
And I will use him for my minstrelsy . . .
A man of fire-new words . . .

It took an historian, an authority on Spanish history, Martin Hume, to see the point and make the obvious identification: Pérez was being made fun of by the young men of the circle. None of the literary commentators or editors of Shakespeare, bogged down in superfluous notes on language, have seen the obviousness of the character, or for the most part the real character of the play.

Schoolmaster Holofernes is another who is made fun of (fairly certainly Florio, who was Southampton's Italian tutor). In the play Holofernes describes the Pérez character in recognisable terms: 'his humour is lofty, his discourse peremptory, his tongue filed, his eye ambitious, his gait majestical, and his general behaviour vain; ridiculous, and thrasonical [boastful]. He is too picked [refined], too spruce, too affected, too odd as it were, too *peregrinate*, as I may call it . . . He draweth out the thread of his verbosity finer than the staple of his argument. I abhor such fanatical phantasms, such insociable and point-devise [precise] companions . . .'

The clever dramatist goes on to parody the inflated, mannered style of letter writing, full of flattery and compliments, which Pérez affected and would exemplify as a new fashion. 'Great Deputy, the welk's Viceregent and sole dominator of Navarre, my soul's, earth's God and body's fostering Patron', etc, etc. We need go no further: the circle's poet and dramatist would know Pérez's style from the letters he wrote to Southampton. It was a good joke at the time to make the elderly homosexual fall for the simple country wench, Jacquenetta. Actually Pérez had been made to marry, very reluctantly, the faithful girl he had left behind him in Spain – as Southampton was to be made, just as reluctantly, to marry Essex's cousin a few years later.

All this, naturally enough, was unknown to Froude a hundred years ago, and we may doubt whether a conventional Victorian would much have appreciated its finer points. It is much to his credit, however, that he saw that the essence of the secret between Philip and Pérez was political, and not an amorous triangular intrigue. It is, however, true that Pérez encouraged people to think of it in terms of rivalry with his king for the 'favours' of a very grand princess: it satisfied his vanity, and it put fools off the scent.

We need follow his career no further. He retained Henri IV's support and backing so long as the war with Spain continued. Pérez came back to England for a second visit, and intrigues with Essex, in 1596–7. But when France made peace with Spain by the Treaty of Vervins in 1598, and with Philip's death in the same year, Pérez' usefulness ceased. His credit exhausted, he lapsed into poverty and obscurity, and died in Paris on November 4, 1611.

III

Our third piece, 'The Spanish Story of the Armada' was written in 1892. We are so used to hearing the story from the English point of view that it is fascinating, and useful, to have the other side. Put the two sides together and we can see with fair certainty what actually happened.

In the first place we have the advantage of Froude's seamanship, his life-long experience of sailing conditions, winds, tides, currents, coasts; his intimate knowledge of the English Channel and, for that matter, his familiarity with the North Sea and the Irish coast. On the other hand, we have his characteristic defects: his rash summary judgments of both the Duke of Medina Sidonia and Elizabeth I.

The Duke was no seaman, but he was no fool either. Neither was Philip II. The real mystery about the Armada was – what were Philip's intentions? We must not, as historians, enter into the realm of conjecture, but perhaps Philip's intentions were not altogether clear to himself. Did he mean a vast naval battle with the English fleet, a struggle *à outrance*: or did he mean the imposing show he put on rather as a threat?

We know now that Napoleon, in assembling his vast forces in Poland in 1812, did not really mean to invade Russia: he meant it as a threat, to overawe the Tsar, to force conditions upon him. It seems now that Hitler did not really intend to invade Britain in 1940: he expected her to come to terms. Was that, rather, Philip's intention? As a politician he was pragmatic. He had to allow lee-way for circumstances which were uncertain and changing. Peace negotiations were being carried on up to the last. Did he think that such a show of force might incline the English to give way? – as Hitler thought in 1940. It may well be that this is the reason for some uncertainty in Philip's detailed instructions to Medina Sidonia: they were in their nature contingent, Philip was allowing for uncertain contingencies.

Froude was all for action, not politics, and he condemns Medina Sidonia for not fighting his way into St Helen's and seizing a port of entry for the Armada. He says, as a seaman, that this was the Duke's best chance. We may doubt that. The Armada would have suffered great damage in the attempt, and failed. Moreover, it was contrary to the instructions the Duke had received, and to which he religiously adhered: he was above all to keep the Armada together, and secondly to join Parma's forces in Flanders. Parma was not ready, and in no position to deploy them. That was not the Duke's fault – at least he kept the Armada together. Of course, if a junction had been possible it would have increased the threat to England. Would it have forced her to concede without fighting? The fact that the Armada carried an army of soldiers looks like an intent to invade, if circumstances had permitted. In the event they did not: the English decided to fight.

The Duke was Philip's man, and suited his obscure purposes. The Marquis of Santa Cruz, though Spain's best seaman, victor at Terceira in 1583, was not. He was the aggressive Admiral who had originally proposed an Armada to conquer England, and was to have been in command. It was not until Philip annexed Portugal in 1582 and thereby acquired her ocean-going fleet, including the fine squadron of the twelve Apostles, that an Armada became a promising proposition. Then in 1587 Francis Drake raided Cadiz, where the merchant-ships were gathered to supply the Armada, inflicting so much damage that it held up the sailing of the Armada until the following year. This was the exploit which he called 'the singeing of the King of Spain's beard'. But Drake was not allowed to destroy the Armada itself, which was assembling at Lisbon – as yet all unprepared, as Santa Cruz admitted. That would have been going too far, and put an end to any hope of peace. In this interval Santa Cruz died, and Philip was free to make his own choice of the Duke. As commander he had the advice, and the services, of all Spain's ablest sea-captains.

Froude attaches importance to the inadequate provisioning and supplies, and the foulness and insufficiency of water, on board the Armada. Anyone who knows the documents will know the constant and regular stream of complaints against contractors in provisioning ships, the cheating, the short measures and the delays. Froude bemoans the sour beer in the English fleet; he as regularly attacked the 'parsimony' of the Queen, and holds her responsible for it – the insufficiency of ammunition, gunpowder, etc. This is all quite unfair and wrong[1] – though it has got into the history books and popular tradition.

The truth is that the English Government did the best it could as a small nation. Even Philip's resources were strained, with all the wealth of the Indies at his command; even so he twice went bankrupt. Elizabeth's government was the only one among the combatants to remain solvent. Yet the fleet that Sir John Hawkins built, on improved sea-going lines, was at its highest pitch of efficiency, and the whole country was keyed up for the test. Froude, as a Victorian, says that the whole fate of the Reformation was at stake. We may leave the Reformation, in many ways regrettable, to look after itself: it was enough that the country's future was in the balance.

A conflict such as took place that week in the Channel was unprecedented in history: we may take it as the first action in the subsequent naval warfare that made England's or, rather, Britain's fortune. In the conflict, which well merited the sensation it created all over Europe, and the attention it has properly received in history since, there was much that was new, as there were factors unknown to both combatants.

We now know that there was less disparity between the fleets than subsequent boasting has allowed. The Spanish ships were higher in build and shallower in draft, and, with their high forecastles and sterns, were less manoeuverable. The way that Lord Admiral Howard's fleet managed to warp out of Plymouth Sound and get to windward of the Spaniards was an unpleasant surprise to them from the beginning. In weight of guns the two fleets were fairly equal; but we now know – from Professor Lewis's study of the gunnery – that the English guns had longer range. Their firing was much more effective, since the Armada presented taller targets; and, since the ships were over-crowded with soldiers, far greater damage was inflicted. The English ships man-oeuvered so that the Spaniards could never come close enough to

---

1. cf. J.K. Laughton, ed. *The Defeat of the Spanish Armada*, (*Navy Records Society*), vol. I. lvii: 'From first to last, the Queen had nothing to do with the victualling of the fleet. No doubt she insisted on rigid economy in everything.' In that she was like her grandfather, Henry VII, not like her extravagant father, Henry VIII.

grapple and board, as Philip had hoped in his instructions. Altogether it does not appear that the English ships suffered much damage at all; only at the end of that week ammunition was exhausted on both sides so that there could not be any more fighting.

Bit by bit the Armada was defeated, and demoralised, on the route to Calais. The process is precisely described in Lord Howard's words: 'By little and by little we pluck them of their feathers'. The damage began early with the loss of one of the biggest and most powerful ships, *Nuestra Señora del Rosario*. This ship was damaged and got left behind by the Duke, who was severely criticised for deserting her. But he could not risk the whole fleet by turning round for the purpose, and his instructions were to go on. Drake, who was in command of the rear squadron, was detailed to see the big ship safely into Torbay, and take the surrender of her able and popular commander, Don Pedro de Valdez.

Drake kept his word: Valdez was given good treatment in England, as the English had not been by the Viceroy at San Juan de Ulloa. When Drake captured a Spanish Don off the coast of South America, he sent him off with a message to that same Viceroy: 'Tell him this is how an English gentleman keeps his word'. Another Spanish Don bore witness to Drake's humanity, and said that his men 'adored him'. Valdez remained in honourable confinement in England for five years, and on his departure was given a banquet by the friends he had made.

The losses to the Armada accumulated. Shortly the *San Salvador* blew up. Meanwhile the big *Santa Aña* lost her bearings and foundered on the French coast, near Le Havre. In the main action off Gravelines the *San Lorenzo* was taken. In this battle the Duke's flagship, the *San Martin*, was in the thick of the action; the Duke's ship battled bravely, but, crowded with soldiers, she had many killed and wounded. Later off the Flemish coast two fine ships of the Portuguese squadron, the *San Mateo* and the *San Felipe*, were 'driven on shore in a sinking state'.

'By little and by little' indeed the Armada was defeated, but it was not broken: the Duke managed at all costs to keep the fleet together. These losses, compounded by the dispatch of the galleys – accustomed to Mediterranean conditions, but of no use in British waters – turned the balance in favour of the English, who were now reinforced by Lord Henry Seymour's squadron from the Thames. Now luck, which had been with the English, definitely swayed with the greatest stroke of all

Now luck, which had been with the English, definitely swayed with the greatest stroke of all in the Duke's favour. He had sent urgent appeals for help to Parma, who was in no condition to give it. The Armada – after Gravelines and the fire-ships – was being driven by the prevailing wind upon the shoals of the Flemish coast. This would have meant a greater, and more general, disaster than what actually happened on the west coast of Ireland. Still more urgent prayers went up: the wind changed and enabled the Armada to keep clear of the shoals and to escape into the North Sea.

Here again Froude is critical of the Duke: he thinks that he would have had a better chance if he had tried to return by the English Channel. No one can say: the Duke was not to know that English ammunition was exhausted as well as his own – and the English were in a position to send out supplies from their own home coast, as they had done from Plymouth, where Hawkins' elder brother was Mayor.

So the Armada ploughed its way into the North Sea, the English fleet not in a condition to damage it further: as Drake characteristically put it, they 'put on a brag' to follow it up as far as the Forth and see it off.

It has not been my purpose to tell again the story of the defeat of the Armada,[1] but to put Froude's account of the Spanish side to it in historical perspective. There is no doubt that the Spaniards regarded it as the defeat it was, before the disaster that fell upon the Irish coast. The heaviest criticism of Medina Sidonia came from the Spanish side, though not from Philip whose instructions he had obeyed throughout to the letter. On his return to Spain the Duke was pursued and reviled by the populace in the streets, and even stoned. He did not lose the King's confidence, however, and was even promoted: he had kept the fleet together, and eventually brought back what was left of it – something more than a third – to serve Philip's purposes another day. What were these? The Duke was certainly closer to Philip's mind than we are – and may well have realised how contingent it was, so that he did not mean to risk all in one great sea-action, as Santa Cruz would have done. With Philip, as with Elizabeth, politics came first; Froude, like the seaman he was, and like the seamen on both sides, resented that.

We must make the point that there were persons of good judgment in

---

1. The standard work on the subject is by the American historian, Garrett Mattingly: *The Defeat of the Spanish Armada.*

Europe who doubted whether the Armada, for all its show of force and all its panoply, would succeed. Among these was the Pope himself, Sixtus V, a remarkable man. He was an unconditional admirer of Elizabeth I and of Drake and he expressed himself as such openly and frequently, much to the annoyance of his cardinals. The disaster to the Armada had immediate consequences in Europe. Of course it was good propaganda on the part of Elizabeth's government to ascribe it to God and the winds: 'He blew with his breath and his enemies were scattered', i.e. God was on their side. But in France, Henri III, who had havered and hovered, with the Catholic League of the Guises supported by Spain, switched sides, joining forces with Navarre against Philip's allies.

Spain's enemies everywhere were encouraged, especially in the Netherlands which had already revolted. There was now no hope that Spain would ever be able to recover the northern provinces. Before Philip died he came to recognise this, and set up his favourite daughter, Isabella, with her cousin the Archduke Albert, as rulers of the semi-independent, Catholic southern provinces, which eventually became Belgium. We may indeed conclude that the over-mighty effort of the Armada signalled, if it did not wholly register, the decline of Spain.

We are now able to add a few more details to Froude's exciting account of what happened to the Armada from the Spanish side. First, from the corroborative account of Juan Gomez de Medina.[1] Off Plymouth he learned that Sir William Winter was in command of one of the three squadrons under Lord Admiral Howard – the Queen's cousin, though not such a grandee as the Duke of Medina Sidonia. The second squadron was commanded by Hawkins, the third by Drake in the *Revenge*.

Of the first loss, of *Nuestra Señora del Rosario*, he tells us that 'the ship was taken away by the enemy that night, so we heard, and was more mercifully treated by them than by us. Don Pedro was sent to London to the Queen, and the rest of the prisoners distributed through the island, it was reported.' They were numerous, and a heavy burden for the West Country to feed. The abandonment of this fine ship was felt as a disgrace throughout the fleet, and 'within two hours', he tells us came the blowing up of the *San Salvador*. 'These two misfortunes

---

1. This is summarised from Fernandez Duro, *La Armada Invencible*, given by W.P. Ker in his 'The Spanish Story of the Armada', in *Collected Essays*, vol. II, 45ff.

[*desgracias*] were the announcement of our perdition. And happening within two hours weighed upon the thoughts of the whole Armada by its ill omen.'

Gomez notes the superiority of the English ships in sailing, and their constant care to keep the weather gauge windward of the Armada all the way up Channel. 'We sailed on with no certain knowledge of our destination.' Then came the Duke's order to throw the horses and mules overboard – there was no water for them. This must mean that he had given up hope of a landing, and may throw light on Philip's intentions. 'We saw many horses and mules swimming past: they kept on throwing them overboard; it was pitiful to see, because they all made for the ships, looking for help.' (My heart goes out to these poor creatures all through men's warfare, the victims of human folly. But I suppose the same may be said of the men themselves.)

On the last day of August, in the North Sea, 'one of the hulks gave in and called for help: the pumps had got choked with ballast. The men were taken off, but the weather was too bad to allow of any stores being taken.' During this time they were 'tacking to weather Clare [?] Island, but it pleased God not to allow us.' In a storm another hulk sprang a leak, and they were driven towards the coast of Norway. When the wind turned fair they came in sight of the Scottish islands, and they took their old course again with hope to see 'our dear Spain'. The leak got worse, but in a lull they managed to stop it with hides and planks and to keep going with one pump.

By the end of September they had 'great trouble at night in rough weather, finding islands ahead'. They were now in the Shetlands and made Fair Isle. It does not sound very fair. 'We found seventeen households there living in huts: wild people, their food is mostly fish, without bread, except for a little barley baked in cakes. Their only fuel was '*turba*', turf or peat. They have cattle of a sort, but seldom eat meat. They are not a clean people; neither Christians, nor yet utter heretics. They say they do not like the preachers who come to them yearly from another island,' evidently Orkney.

'We landed 300 men in the island, with no provision.' No wonder that by mid-November fifty had died, mostly of starvation. The weather was so bad that they were unable to send to Orkney for help until the end of October. By mid-November they had still not yet heard,' and there Gomez's story breaks off. Eventually Gomez reached Scotland, and his account, as far as that, has come down to us.

As for the reception of the wreckage of the fleet in Scotland, we have the tale from James Melvill, minister of Anstruther-Wester and other outlying places, if we may translate his Scots-Doric into English.[1] 'That winter the King was occupied in commenting of the Apocalypse [the Queen of England was otherwise engaged], and in setting out of sermons thereupon against the Papists and Spaniards.' When the news of the approaching Armada reached God's Elect, 'terrible was the fear, piercing was the preachings, earnest, zealous and fervent were the prayers, sounding were the sighs and sobs, and abounding was the tears at that Fast and General Assembly kept at Edinburgh.'

Still, 'the Lord of Armies, who rides upon the wings of the winds, the Keeper of his own Israel, was in the meantime conveying that monstrous Navy about our coasts and directing their hulks and galliasses to the islands, rocks and sands, whereupon He had destined their wreck and destruction.'

Some two or three months after this panic a Spanish ship arrived in the Forth, the commander 'a very reverend man of big stature, and grave and stout countenance, grey-haired and very humble-like, bowing down with his face near the ground and twitching my shoe with his hand, began his harangue.' He was the General of twenty hulks, which had been shipwrecked at Fair Isle, 'where so many as had escaped the merciless seas and rocks had more than six or seven hulks suffered great hunger and cold.' This bark had made its way from Orkney to seek relief: this was no other than Gomez.

He could speak some English, and Melvill could make out his Spanish from his knowledge of Latin. The minister was thus able to assure Gomez that, as against the Spaniards' habit of 'committing bodies to the cruel flaming fire for the cause of religion, they should find nothing among us but Christian pity and works of mercy and alms, leaving to God to work in their hearts concerning religion as it pleased Him.' So some 260 soldiers were suffered to land, 'for the most part young beardless men, silly, trauchled [?], and hungered, to whom a day or two kale, pottage and fish was given.' Melvill gives the names of the commanders as Juan Gomez, General of the twenty hulks; Captains Patricio, Lagorreta, Luffera, Mauritio, and Señor Serrano.

Gomez knew nothing of the wrecks of so many ships on the Irish coast, but 'supposed that the rest of the Army was safely returned'. When later he learned the truth, 'O then he cried out for grief, bursted and grat.' When Gomez eventually got home he was able to return the

---

1. Ker, op.cit., II. 48–52.

kindness he had received by taking a Scottish ship arrested at Cadiz under his protection, 'took the honest men to his house', and rode to Court to the King on their behalf, and 'inquired for the laird of Anstruther, for the minister, and his host, and sent home many commendations. But we thanked God with our hearts that we had seen them among us in that form.'

We may now leave the rest of the story to Froude.

Part I

Preface

The nine lectures now republished were delivered by James Anthony Froude at Oxford in the Easter Terms of 1893–4. They are pictures of the period to which the studies of his best years had been directed, with some of his last thoughts on the English Reformation, and on that 'Sea Cradle' which was to be the cradle also of England's greatness in subsequent centuries. He read the lectures from his own MS., and they created a sensation in Oxford the like of which had not been known since the days of Ruskin. They were attended by all sorts and conditions of men and women, and had to be given in the New Schools for lack of space in the ordinary lecture room.

They were published after his death, and only obvious corrections were made to the MS. Froude's literary life was not a summer cruise, but a long and arduous voyage through rocky and uncharted channels, rough seas, and adverse currents, not altogether unlike the difficulties which the early navigators had to meet and overcome.

The last two years of his life as Regius Professor of Modern History at Oxford, were to him a return to a harbour from which he had been driven forty-five years before. The feeling of rest and security thus gained gives these lectures a buoyant motion like that of a yacht in a whole sail breeze; while their matter represents the considered opinions of one who had devoted the greater part of his life to an exhaustive investigation of the events with which they deal, and who had a strong personal sympathy with the motives that inspired the actions recorded.

A deep sense of responsibility to a Supreme Controller of the Universe, a strong patriotism, and a fervent hatred of cant, hypocrisy, and their exponents, were the characteristics of Drake and his men. Froude's life was governed by like convictions. It is for this reason that these pages, when read and re-read, breathe life in every line, and the capture of Carthagena more than three centuries ago comes as vividly before us as the attack on Zeebrugge.

The first and the last great events in our naval history were the defeat of the Spanish Armada and the surrender of the German Fleet. Each occasion represented the overthrow of long years' preparation for world dominion. Possibly, in the next three hundred years, someone with a pen like Froude's will write an adequate description of the scene in the Firth of Forth on that November afternoon in 1918.

Froude was essentially a Devonshire man. He was born on April 23, 1818, at Dartington, where his father was rector, being also Archdeacon of Totnes, and a considerable landowner in the county. Anthony, as he was always called, was the youngest of a large family. His mother died when he was three, and his upbringing was left principally to his eldest brother, Hurrell, a fascinating genius, the intimate friend of Newman and Keble, and one of the pioneers of the Oxford movement: had he lived, he would probably have become a Cardinal. His educational methods were exceedingly harsh; but in spite of this, Anthony always spoke of his brother with admiration.

Hurrell Froude died in 1836. The only other brother who survived, and who, on the Archdeacon's death, inherited the family property, was William. He attained great eminence in scientific inquiries bearing on naval architecture, and his discoveries respecting the laws of ship-rolling and resistance were of the utmost value. He is remembered by those who knew him not only for his intellect but for his personal charm.

Of Anthony's education, all that can be said is that he survived it. At his first school, Buckfastleigh, he was taught Latin and Greek; for the latter he had a passion, and before he was eleven he had read twice both the *Iliad* and the *Odyssey*.

His natural delicacy as a boy was aggravated by the treatment which he received at home, and later at Westminster, where his health finally broke down. At fifteen he returned to Devonshire, and being considered to be an unworthy member of his family, was left largely to his own devices. He spent most of his days by the river, in the woods, or on Dartmoor, to the great benefit of his health; while in the long winter evenings he turned voraciously to the books in his father's excellent library. He became strong both in mind and body; he was permitted to go to Oxford, and matriculated at Oriel in 1836. For the first time in his life he was in a position to enjoy himself, and for a couple of years he took full advantage of the facilities for amusement which Oxford, and a good allowance, afforded.

But an intellect like Froude's could not long remain dormant. The influence of John Henry Newman, who was then in residence at Oriel, and who was kind to him for his brother's sake, and his own natural instincts, impelled him to exert himself. He started to read hard, his early love for the Greek classics revived, and by working day and night he obtained a second class in the final Classical Schools.

After taking his degree in 1840, he accepted a tutorship to the son of Mr Cleaver, a dignified Evangelical rector in County Wicklow. This experience showed him that there were other forms of faith besides that of Newman and his brother; the seeds of the strong Protestantism which ruled his after life were sown; and his visit to Ireland started the interest which he always felt for the sorrows of that unhappy country.

He returned to Oxford in 1842, and won the Chancellor's prize for an English essay. In the same year he was elected to a clerical Fellowship at Exeter College. He took deacon's orders, but soon found that he was unfitted for the work of a clergyman. He had, however, to bear this burden until released from it by the Act of 1870.

A study of Carlyle and Emerson confirmed his doubts as to the value of dogmatic teaching. In 1849, he published *The Nemesis of Faith*, a book which in modern times would only have been regarded as broad-minded, but which was then considered to be so heretical that it was publicly burnt in Exeter College by the senior tutor, the Rev. W. Sewell, afterwards Warden of Radley. Froude was compelled to resign his Fellowship, his father was furious and stopped his allowance, and he was thrown on his own resources for a living.

But by that time he had made many friends, including Charles Kingsley, who, realising his position, invited him to stay with him at Ilfracombe. He soon afterwards married Mrs Kingsley's sister, who possessed a small private fortune.

Although *The Nemesis of Faith* and some short novels he had published were of but little merit, Froude's style of writing had attracted considerable attention. He obtained work as a reviewer, which was well paid, and wrote himself for various periodicals. From that time, so far as the necessities of life were concerned, his troubles were at an end.

In the limited space available in this Introduction, it has only been practicable to mention the difficulties with which Froude had to contend in his early life.

Of the *History of England, The English in Ireland*, the many volumes of *Carlyle's Life and Letters*, and Froude's other published works, or of the controversies which arose concerning them, it is impossible to speak here. They are dealt with fully in the admirable biography written by Mr Herbert Paul in 1905, from which the two following extracts are given.

The first (p. 417) is a concise and remarkably accurate summary of Froude's style and character as a writer. 'He wrote, for all his scholarly grace, like a man of flesh and blood, and not a pedant nor a doctrinaire. Impartial he never was, nor pretended to be. Dramatic he could not help being, and yet his own opinions were seldom concealed. Three or four main propositions were at the root of his mind. He held the Reformation to be the greatest and most beneficent change in modern history. He believed the English race to be the finest in the world. He disbelieved in equality, and in parliamentary government. Essentially an aristocrat in the proper sense of the term, he cherished the doctrine of submission to a few fit persons, qualified for authority by training and experience. These ideas run through all Froude's historical writing.'

The second quotation (p. 328) deals with the storm which arose over the Carlyle Biography. It is an extract from a letter written to Froude in October 1884 by the fifteenth Earl of Derby, who, in the words of Mr Paul, was an omnivorous reader and a cool, sagacious critic, who was not led astray by enthusiasm, whose opinions were not lightly formed, and never said more than he felt.

After describing the Life of Carlyle as the most interesting biography in the English language, Lord Derby added: 'I think you have finally silenced the foolish talk about indiscretion, and treachery to a friend's memory. It is clear that you have done only, and exactly, what Carlyle wished done: and to me it is also apparent that he and you were right: that his character could not have been understood without a full disclosure of what was least attractive in it: and that those defects – the product mainly of morbid physical conditions – do not really take away from his greatness, while they explain much that was dark, at least to me, in his writings.'

To those to whom the reading of these accounts of British seamen has been of interest, Froude's *Short Studies on Great Subjects* can be commended. They deal with a great variety of subjects, and are often a help to the understanding of problems, both of this world and the next, by which so many of us are worried. The latest of them was written nearly forty years ago; but many of his predictions, and the hopes for the future that he expressed, have been realised. He foresaw the troubles that awaited British agriculturists if the large estates were broken up and sold; and his dream of the Federation of the South African States and of the Australian colonies has come true.

There were few notable people of his day with whom Froude was not acquainted. With many he was on terms of intimate friendship. To those from whose opinions he differed he was always courteous, an example not invariably followed by some of his critics.

With party politics Froude seldom interfered, and at various times he opposed both Liberals and Conservatives. He took a strong line against the suggested war with Russia in 1877, and I remember that he, the late Sir James Stephen, and I attended, as spectators, Mr Auberon Herbert's great anti-Jingo meeting in Hyde Park, and saw the last supporter of a peace policy brought down from a tree by a dead cat.

His opposition to Gladstone's Home Rule Bills was consistent, and the only occasion on which to my knowledge he took an active part in an election was in August 1886, when he spoke in support of the present Lord Mildmay of Flete, then a youthful but ardent Liberal Unionist contesting the Totnes Division.

From the time when he was first sent to South Africa by the late Lord Carnarvon in 1874, Froude always held that it was impossible to govern that country without the consent of the Dutch, and he was opposed strongly to the policy which led to the Boer War in 1880. But early in the following year he went on a health voyage to Madeira, in the same steamer as the late Lord Roberts, who was going out to take command of the British forces; at Madeira they received news of the armistice, and he shared Lord Roberts' view that surrender to the Boer claims after our defeat at Majuba, was not the magnanimity of a great empire to a small people, but was sowing the seeds of subsequent trouble.

Here again his forecast was correct.

The politician, both as a Radical and Liberal Unionist Leader, for whom Froude had the greatest respect and admiration was the late Mr Joseph Chamberlain.

Except that he shared his family's failing of being unable to follow any of the beaten tracks towards earning a living, my father was singularly devoid of the eccentricities of genius. He liked old clothes, but they were made by a good London tailor. Although as a child he was so delicate that he was not expected to survive, he grew to be a powerful man nearly six feet in height, with a strong and active constitution. He was a good shot and an expert fisherman, who made his own flies. He was at home in any type of boat, from a racing eight to a trawler, but when sailing was rather apt to take chances with his life and his gear.

One of the reasons for his influence over those with whom he came into contact was that he could adapt himself to any surroundings – as Mr Paul says, from Cabinet Ministers to Devonshire fishermen. He never talked above the capacity of his hearers, and on difficult questions he, like his brother William, could convey a wealth of information in a few words.

As his constant companion for nearly thirty years, in every variety of circumstance I always found him a more than trustworthy guide. This applied equally to catching my first fish, to accompanying him on walks or in omnibuses with Mr Carlyle, and later when staying in country houses, or when travelling abroad.

He never seemed to be instructing, but one had the feeling of an immensely superior knowledge to which one had only to refer for the immediate solution of a difficulty.

He rarely gave advice, but when I went to Oxford, suggested that it would be better not to play whist for more than sixpenny points, unless the conditions were exceptional.

Religious questions he seldom mentioned, but a few days before his death he said to me, 'Whether we shall meet again, only the Maker of all the world can tell.' And yet he was said to be unorthodox.

He died at Salcombe on October 20, 1894, and is buried in the cemetery overlooking the harbour he knew and loved so long.

The Sea Cradle of the Reformation

Jean Paul Richter, the German poet, said that God had given to France the empire of the land, to England the empire of the sea, and to his own country the empire of the air. The world has changed since Jean Paul's days. The wings of France have been clipped; the German Empire has become a solid thing; but England still holds her watery dominion; Britannia does still rule the waves, and in this proud position she has spread the English race over the globe; she has created the great American nation; she is peopling New Englands at the Antipodes; she has made her Queen Empress of India; and is in fact the very considerable phenomenon in the social and political world which all acknowledge her to be. And all this she has achieved in the course of three centuries, entirely in consequence of her predominance as an ocean power. Take away her merchant fleets; take away the navy that guards them: her empire will come to an end; her colonies will fall off, like leaves from a withered tree; and Britain will become once more an insignificant island in the North Sea, for the future students in Australian and New Zealand universities to discuss the fate of in their debating societies.

How the English navy came to hold so extraordinary a position is worth reflecting on. Much has been written about it, but little, as it seems to me, which touches the heart of the matter. We are shown the power of our country growing and expanding. But how it grew, why, after a sleep of so many hundred years, the genius of our forefathers suddenly sprang again into life – of this we are left without explanation.

The beginning was undoubtedly the defeat of the Spanish Armada in 1588. Until then the sea sovereignty belonged to the Spaniards, and

27

had been fairly won by them. The conquest of Granada had stimulated and elevated the Spanish character. The subjects of Ferdinand and Isabella, of Charles V and Philip II, were extraordinary men, and accomplished extraordinary things. They stretched the limits of the known world; they conquered Mexico and Peru; they planted their colonies over the South American continent; they took possession of the great West Indian islands, and with so firm a grasp that Cuba at least will never lose the mark of the hand which seized it. They built their cities as if for eternity. They spread to the Indian Ocean and gave their monarch's name to the *Philippines*. All this they accomplished in half a century, and, as it were, they did it with a single hand; with the other they were fighting Moors and Turks and protecting the coast of the Mediterranean from the corsairs of Tunis and Constantinople.

They had risen on the crest of the wave, and with their proud *Non suffict orbis* were looking for new worlds to conquer, at a time when the bark of the English water dogs had scarcely been heard beyond their own fishing grounds, and the largest merchant vessel sailing from the port of London was scarce bigger than a modern coasting collier. And yet within the space of a single ordinary life these insignificant islanders had struck the sceptre from the Spaniards' grasp and placed the ocean crown on the brow of their own sovereign. How did it come about? What Cadmus had sown dragon's teeth in the furrows of the sea for the race to spring from who manned the ships of Queen Elizabeth, who carried the flag of their own country round the globe, and challenged and fought the Spaniards on their own coasts and in their own harbours?

The English sea power was the legitimate child of the Reformation. It grew, as I shall show you, directly out of the new despised Protestantism. Matthew Parker and Bishop Jewel, the judicious Hooker himself, excellent men as they were, would have written and preached to small purpose without Sir Francis Drake's cannon to play an accompaniment to their teaching. And again, Drake's cannon would not have roared so loudly and so widely without seamen already trained in heart and hand to work his ships and level his artillery. It was to the superior seamanship, the superior quality of English ships and crews, that the Spaniards attributed their defeat. Where did these ships come from? Where and how did these mariners learn their trade? Historians talk enthusiastically of the national spirit of a people rising with a united heart to repel the invader, and so on. But national spirit could not extemporise a fleet or produce trained officers and sailors to match the conquerors of Lepanto.

One slight observation I must make here at the start, and certainly with no invidious purpose. It has been said confidently, it has been repeated, I believe, by all modern writers, that the Spanish invasion suspended in England the quarrels of creed, and united Protestants and Roman Catholics in defence of their Queen and country. They remind us especially that Lord Howard of Effingham, who was Elizabeth's admiral, was himself a Roman Catholic. But was it so? The Earl of Arundel, the head of the House of Howard, was a Roman Catholic, and he was in the Tower praying for the success of Medina Sidonia. Lord Howard of Effingham was no more a Roman Catholic than the present Archbishop of Canterbury or the Bishop of London. He was a Catholic, but an English Catholic, as those reverend prelates are. Roman Catholic he could not possibly have been, scarce anyone who on that great occasion was found on the side of Elizabeth. A Roman Catholic is one who acknowledges the Roman Bishop's authority. The Pope had excommunicated Elizabeth, had pronounced her deposed, had absolved her subjects from their allegiance, and forbidden them to fight for her. Few Englishmen who fought on that great occasion for English liberty were, or could have been, in communion with Rome. Loose statements of this kind, lightly made, fall in with the modern humour. They are caught up, applauded, repeated, and pass unquestioned into history. It is time to correct them a little.

I have in my possession a detailed account of the temper of parties in England, drawn up in the year 1585, three years before the Armada came. The writer was a distinguished Jesuit. The account itself was prepared for the use of the Pope and Philip, with a special view to the reception which an invading force would meet with, and it goes into great detail. The people of the towns – London, Bristol, etc. – were, he says, generally heretics. The peers, the gentry, their tenants, and peasantry, who formed the majority of the population, were Catholics. But this writer distinguishes properly among Catholics. There were the ardent impassioned Catholics, ready to be confessors and martyrs, ready to rebel at the first opportunity, who had renounced their allegiance, who desired to overthrow Elizabeth and put the Queen of Scots in her place. The number of these, he says, was daily increasing, owing to the exertions of the seminary priests; and plots were being continually formed by them to murder the Queen. There were Catholics of another sort, who were papal at heart, but went with the times to save their property; who looked forward to a change in the natural order of things, but who would not stir of themselves till an invading army actually

29

appeared. But all alike, he insists, were eager for a revolution. Let the Prince of Parma come, and they would all join him; and together these two classes of Catholics made three fourths of the nation.

'The only party.' he says (and this is really noticeable), 'the only party that would fight to death for the Queen, the only real friends she had, were the *Puritans* (it is the first mention of the name which I have found), the Puritans of London, the Puritans of the sea towns.' These he admits were dangerous, determined men. The numbers of them, however, were providentially small.

The date of this document is, as I said, 1585, and I believe it generally accurate. The only mistake is, that among the Anglican Catholics there were a few to whom their country was as dear as their creed – a few who were beginning to see that under the Act of Uniformity Catholic doctrine might be taught and Catholic ritual practised; who ahered to the old forms of religion, but did not believe that obedience to the Pope was a necessary part of them. One of these was Lord Howard of Effingham, whom the Queen placed in his high command to secure the wavering fidelity of the peers and country gentlemen. But the force, the fire, the enthusiasm came (the Jesuit saw) from the Puritans, from men of the same convictions as the Calvinists of Holland and Rochelle; men who, driven from the land, took to the ocean as their natural home, and nursed the Reformation in an ocean cradle. How the seagoing population of the North of Europe took so strong a Protestant impression it is the purpose of these lectures to explain.

Henry VIII on coming to the throne found England without a fleet, and without a conscious sense of the need of one. A few merchant hulks traded with Bordeaux and Cadiz and Lisbon; hoys and flyboats drifted slowly backwards and forwards between Antwerp and the Thames. A fishing fleet tolerably appointed went annually to Iceland for cod. Local fishermen worked the North Sea and the Channel from Hull to Falmouth. The Chester people went to Kinsale for herrings and mackerel: but that was all – the nation had aspired to no more.

Columbus had offered the New World to Henry VII while the discovery was still in the air. He had sent his brother to England with maps and globes, and quotations from Plato to prove its existence. Henry, like a practical Englishman, treated it as a wild dream.

The dream had come from the gate of horn. America was found, and the Spaniard, and not the English, came into first possession of it. Still, America was a large place, and John Cabot the Genoese with his son

30

Sebastian tried Henry again. England might still be able to secure a slice. This time Henry VII listened. Two small ships were fitted out at Bristol, crossed the Atlantic, discovered Newfoundland, looking for a passage to Cathay, but could not find one. The elder Cabot died; the younger came home. The expedition failed, and no interest had been roused.

With the accession of Henry VIII a new era had opened – a new era in many senses. Printing was coming into use – Erasmus and his companions were shaking Europe with the new learning, Copernican astronomy was changing the level disk of the earth into a revolving globe, and turning dizzy the thoughts of mankind. Imagination was on the stretch. The reality of things was assuming proportions vaster than fancy had dreamt, and unfastening established belief on a thousand sides. The young Henry was welcomed by Erasmus as likely to be the glory of the age that was opening. He was young, brilliant, cultivated, and ambitious. To what might he not aspire under the new conditions!

Henry VIII was all that, and looked about him. Europe was full of wars in which he was likely to be entangled. His father had left the treasury well furnished. The young King, like a wise man, turned his first attention to the broad ditch, as he called the British Channel, which formed the natural defence of the realm. The opening of the Atlantic had revolutionised war and seamanship. Long voyages required larger vessels. Henry was the first prince to see the place which gunpowder was going to hold in wars. In his first years he repaired his dockyards, built new ships on improved models, and imported Italians to cast him new types of cannon. 'King Harry loved a man,' it is said, and knew a man when he saw one. He made acquaintance with sea captains at Portsmouth and Southampton. In some way or other he came to know one Mr William Hawkins of Plymouth, and held him in especial esteem. This Mr Hawkins, under Henry's patronage, ventured down to the coast of Guinea and brought home gold and ivory; crossed over to Brazil; made friends with the Brazilian natives; even brought back with him a king of those countries, who was curious to see what England was like, and presented him to Henry at Whitehall.

A Bristol man, Robert Thorne, again with Henry's help, went out to look for the Northwest Passage which Cabot had failed to find. Thorne's ship was called the *Dominus Vobiscum*, a pious aspiration which, however, secured no success. A London man, a Master Hore, tried next. Master Hore, it is said, was given to cosmography, was a plausible talker at scientific meetings, and so on. He persuaded 'divers

31

young lawyers' (briefless barristers, I suppose) and other gentlemen –
altogether a hundred and twenty of them – to join him. They procured
two vessels at Gravesend. They took the sacrament together before
sailing. They apparently relied on Providence to take care of them, for
they made little other preparation. They reached Newfoundland, but
their stores ran out, and their ships went on shore. In the land of fish
they did not know how to use line and bait. They fed on roots and
bilberries, and picked fish bones out of the ospreys' nests. At last they
began to eat one another – careless of Master Hore, who told them they
would go to unquenchable fire. A French vessel came in. They seized
her with the food she had on board and sailed home in her, leaving the
French crew to their fate. The poor French happily found means of
following them. They complained of their treatment, and Henry
ordered an inquiry; but finding, the report says, the great distress
Master Hore's party had been in, was so moved with pity, that he did
not punish them, but out of his own purse made royal recompense to
the French.

Something better than gentlemen volunteers was needed if naval
enterprise was to come to anything in England. The long wars between
Francis I and Charles V brought the problem closer. On land the
fighting was between the regular armies. At sea privateers were let loose
out of French, Flemish, and Spanish ports. Enterprising individuals
took out letters of marque and went cruising to take the chance of what
they could catch. The Channel was the chief hunting ground, as being
the highway between Spain and the Low Countries. The interval was
short between privateers and pirates. Vessels of all sorts passed into the
business. The Scilly Isles became a pirate stronghold. The creeks and
estuaries in Cork and Kerry furnished hiding-places where the rovers
could lie with security and share their plunder with the Irish chiefs.
The disorder grew wilder when the divorce of Catherine of Aragon
made Henry into the public enemy of Papal Europe. English traders and
fishing-smacks were plundered and sunk. Their crews went armed to
defend themselves, and from Thames mouth to Land's End the
Channel became the scene of desperate fights. The type of vessel
altered to suit the new conditions. Life depended on speed of sailing.
The State Papers describe squadrons of French or Spaniards flying
about, dashing into Dartmouth, Plymouth, or Falmouth, cutting out
English coasters, or fighting one another.

After Henry was excommunicated, and Ireland rebelled, and
England itself threatened disturbance, the King had to look to his

security. He made little noise about it. But the Spanish ambassador reported him as building ships in the Thames and at Portsmouth. As invasion seemed imminent, he began with sweeping the seas of the looser vermin. A few swift well-armed cruisers pushed suddenly out of the Solent, caught and destroyed a pirate fleet in Mount's Bay, sent to the bottom some Flemish privateers in the Downs, and captured the Flemish admiral himself. Danger at home growing more menancing, and the monks spreading the fire which grew into the Pilgrimage of Grace, Henry suppressed the abbeys, sold the lands, and with the proceeds armed the coast with fortresses. You may see the remnants of Henry's work in the fortresses anywhere along the coast from Berwick to the Land's End.

Louder thundered the Vatican. In 1539 Henry's time appeared to have come. France and Spain made peace, and the Pope's sentence was now expected to be executed by Charles or Francis, or both. A crowd of vessels large and small was collected in the Scheldt, for what purpose save to transport an army into England? Scotland had joined the Catholic League. Henry fearlessly appealed to the English people. Catholic peers and priests might conspire against him, but, explain it how we will, the nation was loyal to Henry and came to his side. The London merchants armed their ships in the river. From the seaports everywhere came armed brigantines and sloops. The fishermen of the West left their boats and nets to their wives, and the fishing was none the worse, for the women handled oar and sail and line and went to the whiting-grounds, while their husbands had gone to fight for their King. Genius kindled into discovery at the call of the country. Mr Fletcher of Rye (be his name remembered) invented a boat the like of which was never seen before, which would work to windward, with sails trimmed fore and aft. A hundred and fifty sail collected at Sandwich to match the armament in the Scheldt; and Marillac, the French ambassador, reported with amazement the energy of King and people.

The Catholic Powers thought better of it. This was not the England which Reginald Pole had told them was longing for their appearance. The Scheldt force dispersed. Henry read Scotland a needed lesson. The Scots had thought to take him at disadvantage, and sit on his back when the Emperor attacked him. One morning when the people at Leith woke out of their sleep, they found an English fleet in the Roads; and before they had time to look about them, Leith was on fire and Edinburgh was taken. Charles V, if he had ever seriously thought of invading Henry, returned to wiser counsels, and made an alliance with him instead. The Pope turned to France. If the Emperor forsook him, the Most Christian King would help. He promised Francis that if he could win England he might keep it for himself. Francis resolved to try what he could do.

Five years had passed since the gathering at Sandwich. It was now the summer of 1544. The records say that the French collected at Havre near 300 vessels, fighting ships, galleys and transports. Doubtless the numbers are far exaggerated, but at any rate it was the largest force ever assembled to invade England, capable, if well handled, of bringing Henry to his knees. The plan was to seize and occupy the Isle of Wight, destroy the English fleet, then take Portsmouth and Southampton, and so advance on London.

Henry's attention to his navy had not slackened. He had built ship on ship. The *Great Harry* was 1,000 tons, carried 700 men, and was the wonder of the day. There were a dozen others scarcely less imposing. The King called again on the nation, and again the nation answered. In England altogether there were 150,000 men in arms in field or garrison. In the King's fleet at Portsmouth there were 12,000 seamen, and the privateers of the West crowded up eagerly as before. It is strange, with the notions which we have allowed ourselves to form of Henry, to observe the enthusiasm with which the whole country, as yet undivided by doctrinal quarrels, rallied a second time to defend him.

In this Portsmouth fleet lay undeveloped the genius of the future naval greatness of England. A small fact connected with it is worth recording. The watchword on board was, 'God save the King'; the answer was, 'Long to reign over us': the earliest germ discoverable of the English national anthem.

The King had come himself to Portsmouth to witness the expected attack. The fleet was commanded by Lord Lisle, afterwards Duke of Northumberland. It was the middle of July. The French crossed from Havre unfought with, and anchored in St Helen's roads off Brading Harbour. The English, being greatly inferior in numbers, lay waiting for them inside the Spit. The morning after the French came in was still and sultry. The English could not move for want of wind. The galleys crossed over and engaged them for two or three hours with some advantage. The breeze rose at noon; a few fast sloops got under way and easily drove them back.

But the same breeze which enabled the English to move brought a serious calamity with it. The *Mary Rose*, one of Lisle's finest vessels, had been under the fire of the galleys. Her ports had been left open, and when the wind sprang up, she heeled over, filled, and went down, carrying two hundred men along with her. The French saw her sink, and thought their own guns had done it. They hoped to follow up their success. At night they sent over boats to take soundings, and discover the way into the harbour. The boats reported that the sandbanks made the approach impossible. The French had no clear plan of action. They tried a landing in the island, but the force was too small, and failed. They weighed anchor and brought up again behind Selsea Bill, where Lisle proposed to run them down in the dark, taking advantage of the tide. But they had an enemy to deal with worse than Lisle on board their own ships, which explained their distracted movements. Hot weather, putrid meat, and putrid water had prostrated whole ships' companies with dysentery. After a three weeks' ineffectual cruise they had to hasten back to Havre, break up, and disperse. The first great armament which was to have recovered England to the Papacy had effected nothing. Henry had once more shown his strength, and was left undisputed master of the narrow seas.

So matters stood for what remained of Henry's reign. As far as he had gone, he had quarrelled with the Pope, and had brought the Church under the law. So far the country generally had gone with him, and there had been no violent changes in the administration of religion. When Henry died the Protector abolished the old creed, and created a new and perilous cleavage between Protestant and Catholic, and, while England needed the protection of a navy more than ever, allowed the fine fleet which Henry had left to fall into decay.

The spirit of enterprise grew with the Reformation. Merchant companies opened trade with Russia and the Levant; adventurous sea captains went to Guinea for gold. Sir Hugh Willoughby followed the phantom of the Northwest Passage, turning eastward round the North Cape to look for it, and perished in the ice. English commerce was beginning to grow in spite of the Protector's experiments; but a new and infinitely dangerous element had been introduced by the change of religion into the relations of English sailors with the Catholic Powers, and especially with Spain.

In their zeal to keep out heresy, the Spanish Government placed their harbours under the control of the Holy Office. Any vessel in which an heretical book was found was confiscated, and her crew carried to the Inquisition prisons. It had begun in Henry's time. The Inquisitors attempted to treat schism as heresy and arrest Englishmen in their ports. But Henry spoke up stoutly to Charles V, and the Holy

Office had been made to hold its hand. All was altered now. It was not necessary that a poor sailor should have been found teaching heresy. It was enough if he had an English Bible and Prayer Book with him in his kit; and stories would come into Dartmouth or Plymouth how some lad that everybody knew – Bill, or Jack, or Tom, who had wife or father or mother among them, perhaps – had been seized hold of for no other crime, been flung into a dungeon, tortured, starved, set to work in the galleys, or burned in a fool's coat, as they called it, at an *auto-da-fé* at Seville.

The object of the Inquisition was partly political: it was meant to embarrass trade and make the people impatient of changes which produced so much inconvenience. The effect was exactly the opposite. Such accounts when brought home created fury. There grew up in the seagoing population an enthusiasm of hatred for that holy institution, and a passionate desire for revenge.

The division of nations was crossed by the division of creeds; and each nation had allies in the heart of every other. If England went to war with Spain, Spain could encourage insurrection among the Catholics. If Spain or France declared war against England, England could help the Huguenots or the Holland Calvinists. All Governments were afraid alike of a general war of religion which might shake Europe in pieces. Thus individuals were left to their natural impulses. The Holy Office burnt English or French Protestants wherever it could catch them. The Protestants revenged their injuries at their own risk and in their own way.

Thus from Edward VI's time to the end of the century privateering came to be the special occupation of adventurous honourable gentlemen, who could serve God, their country, and themselves in fighting Catholics. Fleets of these dangerous vessels swept the Channel, lying in wait at Scilly, or even at the Azores – disowned in public by their own governments while secretly countenanced, making war on their own account on what they called the enemies of God. In such a business, of course, there were many mere pirates engaged who cared neither for God nor man. But it was the Protestants who were specially impelled into it by the cruelties of the Inquisition. The Holy Office began the work with the *autos-da-fé*. The privateers robbed, burnt, and scuttled Catholic ships in retaliation. One fierce deed produced another, till right and wrong were obscured in the passion of religious hatred. Vivid pictures of these wild doings survive in the English and Spanish State Papers. Ireland was the rovers' favourite haunt. Notorious

36

pirate captains were to be met in Cork or Kinsale, collecting stores, casting cannon, or selling their prizes – men of all sorts, from fanatical saints to undisguised ruffians. Here is one incident out of many to show the heights to which temper had risen.

'Long peace,' says someone, addressing the Privy Council early in Elizabeth's time, 'becomes by force of the Spanish Inquisition more hurtful than open war. It is the secret, determined policy of Spain to destroy the fleet, pilots, masters and sailors, by means of the Inquisition. The Spanish King pretends he dares not offend the Holy House, while we in England say we may not proclaim war against Spain in revenge of a few. Not long since the Spanish Inquisition executed sixty persons of St Malo, notwithstanding entreaty to the King of Spain to spare them. Whereupon the Frenchmen armed their pinnaces, lay for the Spaniards, took a hundred and beheaded them, sending the Spanish ships to the shore with their heads, leaving in each ship but one man to render the cause of the revenge. Since which time Spanish Inquisitors have never meddled with those of St Malo.'

A colony of Huguenot refugees had settled on the coast of Florida. The Spaniards heard of it, came from St Domingo, burnt the town, and hanged every man, woman, and child, leaving an inscription explaining that the poor creatures had been killed, not as Frenchmen, but as heretics. Dominique de Gourges of Rochelle heard of this fine exploit of fanaticism, equipped a ship, and sailed across. He caught the Spanish garrison which had been left in occupation and swung them on the same trees – with a second scroll saying that they were dangling there, not as Spaniards, but as murderers.

The genius of adventure tempted men of highest birth into the rovers' ranks. Sir Thomas Seymour, the Protector's brother and the King's uncle, was Lord High Admiral. In his time of office, complaints were made by foreign merchants of ships and property seized at the Thames mouth. No redress could be had; not restitution made; no pirate was even punished, and Seymour's personal followers were seen suspiciously decorated with Spanish ornaments. It appeared at last that Seymour had himself coveted the Scilly Isles, and if he could not have his way at Court, it was said that he meant to set up there as a pirate chief.

The persecution under Mary brought in more respectable recruits than Seymour. The younger generation of the Western families had grown with the times. If they were not theologically Protestant, they detested tyranny. They detested the marriage with Philip, which threatened the independence of England. At home they were power-less, but the sons of honourable houses – Strangways, Tremaynes, Staffords, Horseys, Carews, Killigrews, and Cobhams – dashed out upon the water to revenge the Smithfield massacres. They found help where it could least have been looked for. Henry II of France hated heresy, but he hated Spain worse. Sooner than see England absorbed in the Spanish monarchy, he forgot his bigotry in his politics. He furnished these young mutineers with ships and money and letters of marque.

The Huguenots were their natural friends. With Rochelle for an arsenal, they held the mouth of the Channel, and harassed the communications between Cadiz and Antwerp. It was a wild business: enterprise and buccaneering sanctified by religion and hatred of cruelty; but it was a school like no other for seamanship, and a school for the building of vessels which could outsail all others on the sea; a school, too, for the training up of hardy men, in whose blood ran detestation of the Inquisition and the Inquisition's master. The merchantmen went armed, ready for any work that offered; the Iceland fleet went no more in search of cod; the Channel boatmen forsook nets and lines and took to livelier occupations; Mary was too busy burning heretics to look to the police of the seas; her father's fine ships rotted in harbour; she lost Calais; she lost the hearts of her people in forcing them into orthodoxy; she left the seas to the privateers.

When Elizabeth came to the throne, the whole merchant navy of England engaged in lawful commerce amounted to no more than 50,000 tons. You may see more now passing every day through the Gulf Stream. In the service of the Crown there were but seven revenue cruisers in commission, the largest 120 tons, with eight merchant brigs altered for fighting. In harbour there were still a score of large ships, but they were dismantled; of artillery fit for sea work there was none. The men were not to be had, and, as Sir William Cecil said, to fit out ships without men was to set armour on stakes on the seashore. The mariners of England were otherwise engaged, and in a way which did not please Cecil. He was the ablest minister that Elizabeth had. He saw at once that on the navy the prosperity and even the liberty of England must eventually depend. If England were to remain Protestant, it was not by articles of religion or acts of uniformity that she could be saved without a fleet at the back of them. But he was old fashioned. He believed in law and order, and he has left a curious paper of reflections on the situation.

The ships' companies in Henry VIII's days were recruited from the fishing smacks, but the Reformation itself had destroyed the fishing trade. In old times, Cecil said, no flesh was eaten on fish days. Now to eat beef or mutton on fish days was the test of a true believer. The English Iceland fishery used to supply Normandy and Brittany as well as England. Now it had passed to the French. The Chester men used to fish the Irish seas. Now they had left them to the Scots. The fishermen had taken to privateering because the fasts of the Church were neglected. He saw it was so. He recorded his own opinion that piracy, as he called it, was *detestable*, and could not last. He was to find that it could last, that it was to form the special discipline of the generation whose business would be to fight the Spaniards. But he struggled hard against the unwelcome conclusion. He tried to restore the fisheries by Act of Parliament. He introduced a Bill recommending godly abstinence as a means to virtue, making the eating of meat on Fridays and Saturdays a misdemeanour, and adding Wednesday as a fish day. To please the Protestants he inserted a clause, that the statute was politicly meant for the increase of fishermen and mariners, not for any superstition in the choice of meats.

Events had to take their course. Seamen were duly provided in other ways, and such as the time required. Privateering suited Elizabeth's convenience, and suited her disposition. She liked daring and adventure. She liked men who would do her work without being paid for it, men whom she could disown when expedient; who would understand her, and would not resent it. She knew her turn was to come when Philip had leisure to deal with her, if she could not secure herself meanwhile. Time was wanted to restore the navy. The privateers were a resource in the interval. They might be called pirates while there was formal peace. The name did not signify.

After the war broke out in the Netherlands, they had commissions from the Prince of Orange. Such commissions would not save them if taken by Spain, but it enabled them to sell their prizes, and for the rest they trusted to their speed and their guns. When Elizabeth was at war with France about Havre, she took the most noted of them into the service of the Crown. Ned Horsey became Sir Edward and Governor of the Isle of Wight; Strangways, a red rover in his way, who had been the terror of the Spaniards, was killed before Rouen; Tremayne fell at Havre, mourned over by Elizabeth; and Champernowne, one of the most gallant of the whole of them, was killed afterwards at Coligny's side at Moncontour.

But others took their places: the wild hawks as thick as seagulls flashing over the waves, fair wind or foul, laughing at pursuit, brave, reckless, devoted, the crews the strangest medley: English from the Devonshire and Cornish creeks, Huguenots from Rochelle; Irish kernes with long skenes, 'desperate, unruly persons with no kind of mercy.'

The Holy Office meanwhile went on in cold, savage resolution. A note in Cecil's hand says that in the one year 1562 twenty-six English subjects had been burnt at the stake in different parts of Spain. Many more were starving in Spanish dungeons, from which occasionally by happy acccident, a cry could be heard like this which follows. In 1561 an English merchant writes from the Canaries:

'I was taken by those of the Inquisition twenty months past, put into a little dark house two paces long, loaded with irons, without sight of sun or moon all that time. When I was arraigned I was charged that I should say our mass was as good as theirs; that I said I would rather give money to the poor than buy Bulls of Rome with it. I was charged with being a subject to the Queen's grace, who, they said, was enemy to the Faith, Antichrist, with other opprobrious names; and I stood to the defence of the Queen's Majesty, proving the infamies most untrue. Then I was put into Little Ease again, protesting very innocent blood to be demanded against the judge before Christ.'

The innocent blood of these poor victims had not to wait to be avenged at the Judgement Day.

John Hawkins and the African Slave Trade

I begin this lecture with a petition addressed to Queen Elizabeth. Thomas Seely, a merchant of Bristol, hearing a Spaniard in a Spanish port utter foul and slanderous charges against the Queen's character, knocked him down. To knock a man down for telling lies about Elizabeth might be a breach of the peace, but it had not yet been declared heresy. The Holy Office, however, seized Seely, threw him into a dungeon, and kept him starving there for three years, at the end of which he contrived to make his condition known in England. The Queen wrote herself to Philip to protest. Philip would not interfere. Seely remained in prison and in irons, and the result was a petition from his wife, in which the temper which was rising can be read as in letters of fire. Dorothy Seely demands that 'the friends of Her Majesty's subjects so imprisoned and tormented in Spain may make out ships at their proper charges, take such Inquisitors or other Papistical subjects of the King of Spain as they can by sea or land, and retain them in prison with such torments and diet as Her Majesty's subjects be kept with in Spain, and on complaint made by the King to give such answer as is now made when Her Majesty sues for subjects imprisoned by the Inquisition. Or that a Commission be granted to the Archbishop of Canterbury and the other bishops word for word for foreign Papists as the Inquisitors have in Spain for the Protestants. So that all may know that Her Majesty cannot and will not longer endure the spoils and torments of her subjects, and the Spaniards shall not think this noble realm dares not seek revenge of such importable wrongs.'

Elizabeth issued no such Commission as Dorothy Seely asked for, but she did leave her subjects to seek their revenge in their own way, and they sought it sometimes too rashly.

In the summer of 1563 eight English merchantmen anchored in the Roads of Gibraltar. England and France were then at war. A French brig came in after them, and brought up near. At sea, if they could take her, she would have been a lawful prize. Spaniards under similar circumstances had not respected the neutrality of English harbours. The Englishmen were perhaps in doubt what to do, when the officers of the Holy Office came off to the French ship. The sight of the black familiars drove the English wild. Three of them made a dash at the French ship, intending to sink her. The Inquisitors sprang into their boat, and rowed for their lives. The castle guns opened, and the harbour police put out to interfere. The French ship, however, would have been taken, when unluckily Alvarez de Baçan, with a Spanish squadron, came round into the Straits. Resistance was impossible. The eight English ships were captured and carried off to Cadiz. The English flag was trailed under De Baçan's stern. The crews, two hundred and forty men in all, were promptly condemned to the galleys. In defence they could but say that the Frenchman was an enemy, and a moderate punishment would have sufficed for a violation of the harbour rules which the Spaniards themselves so little regarded. But the Inquisition was inexorable, and the men were treated with such brutality that after nine months only ninety of the two hundred and forty were alive.

Ferocity was answered by ferocity. Listen to this! The Cobhams of Cowling Castle were Protestants. One of them, Oldcastle, was famous in the Lollard martyrology. Thomas Cobham, one of the family, had taken to the sea like many of his friends. While cruising in the Channel he caught sight of a Spaniard on the way from Antwerp to Cadiz with forty prisoners on board, consigned, it might be supposed, to the Inquisition, for other offenders would have been dealt with on the spot. Cobham chased her down into the Bay of Biscay, took her, scuttled her, and rescued the captives. But that was not enough. The captain and crew he sewed up in their own mainsail and flung them overboard. They were washed ashore, wrapped in their extraordinary winding sheet. Cobham was called to account for this exploit, but he does not seem to have been actually punished. In a very short time he was out and away again at the old work. There were plenty with him.

After the business at Gibraltar, Philip's subjects were not safe in English harbours. Jacques le Clerc, a noted privateer, called Pie de Palo because of his wooden leg, chased a Spaniard into Falmouth, and was allowed to take her under the guns of Pendennis. The governor of the castle said that he could not interfere, because Le Clerc had a commission from the Prince of Condé. It was said that in the summer of 1563 there were 400 English and Huguenot rovers in and about the Channel, and that they had taken 700 prizes between them. The Queen's own ships followed suit. Captain Cotton in the *Phoenix* captured an Antwerp merchantman in Flushing. The harbour-master protested, Cotton sailed away with his prize. The Regent Margaret wrote in indignation to Elizabeth. Such insolence, she said, was not to be endured. She would have Captain Cotton chastised as an example to all others. Elizabeth measured the situation more correctly than the Regent; she preferred to show Philip that she was not afraid of him. She preferred to let her subjects discover for themselves that until Philip consented to tie the hands of the Holy Office she did not mean to prevent them from taking the law into their own hands.

Now and then, if occasion required, Elizabeth herself would do a little privateering on her own account. In the next story that I have to tell she appears as a principal, and her great minister, Cecil, as an accomplice. The Duke of Alva had succeeded Margaret in the Netherlands, and was drowning heresy in its own blood. The Prince of Orange was making a noble fight; but all went ill with him. His troops were defeated, his brother Louis was killed. He was still struggling, helped by Elizabeth's money. But the odds were terrible, and the only hope lay in the discontent of Alva's soldiers, who had not been paid their wages, and would not fight without them. Philip's finances were not flourishing, but he had borrowed half a million ducats from a house at Genoa for Alva's use. The money was to be delivered in bullion at Antwerp.

The Channel privateers heard that it was coming and went on the look-out for it. The vessels in which it was sent took refuge in Plymouth, but found they had run into the enemy's nest. Nineteen or twenty Huguenot and English cruisers lay round them with commissions from Condé to take every Catholic ship they met with. Elizabeth's friends thought that so rich a prize ought to fall to no one but Her Majesty. Elizabeth thought the same, but for a more honourable reason. It was of the highest consequence that the money should not reach the Duke of Alva at that moment. Even Cecil said so, and sent the Prince of Orange word that it would be stopped in some way.

But how could it decently be done? Bishop Jewel relieved the Queen's mind (if it was ever disturbed) on the moral side of the question. The bishop held that it would be meritorious in a high degree to intercept a treasure which was to be used in the murder of Protestant Christians. But the how was the problem. To let the privateers take it openly in Plymouth harbour would, it was felt, be a scandal. Sir Arthur Champernowne, the Vice-Admiral of the West, offered his services. He had three vessels of his own in Condé's privateer fleet, under his son Henry. As Vice-Admiral he was first in command at Plymouth. He placed a guard on board the treasure ships, telling the captain it would be a discredit to the Queen's government if harm befell them in English waters. He then wrote to Cecil.

'If,' he said, 'it shall seem good to your honour that I with others shall give the attempt for Her Majesty's use which cannot be without blood, I will not only take it in hand, but also receive the blame thereof unto myself, to the end so great a commodity should redound to Her Grace; hoping that, after bitter storms of her displeasure, showed at the first to colour the fact, I shall find the calm of her favour in such sort as I am most willing to hazard myself to serve Her Majesty. Great pity it were such a rich booty should escape Her Grace. But surely I am of that mind that anything taken from that wicked nation is both necessary and profitable to our commonwealth.'

Very shocking on Sir Arthur's part to write such a letter, so many good people will think. I hope they will consider it equally shocking that King Philip should have burned English sailors at the stake because they were loyal to the laws of their own country; that he was stirring war all over Europe. Spain and England might be at peace; Romanism and Protestantism were at war, and war suspends the obligations of ordinary life. Crimes were held to be virtues in defence of the Catholic faith. The Catholics could not have the advantage of such indulgences without the inconveniences. The Protestant cause throughout Europe was one, and assailed as the Protestants were with such ferocity, they could not afford to be scrupulous in the means they used to defend themselves.

Sir Arthur Champernowne was not called on to sacrifice himself in such peculiar fashion, and a better expedient was found to secure Alva's money. The bullion was landed and was brought to London by road on the plea that the seas were unsafe. It was carried to the Tower, and when it was once inside the walls it was found to remain the property of the Genoese until it was delivered at Antwerp. The Genoese agent in

London was as willing to lend it to Elizabeth as to Philip, and indeed preferred the security. Elizabeth calmly said that she had herself occasion for money, and would accept their offer. Half of it was sent to the Prince of Orange; half was spent on the Queen's navy.

Alva was of course violently angry. He arrested every English ship in the Low Countries. He arrested every Englishman that he could catch, and sequestered all English property. Elizabeth retaliated in kind. The Spanish and Flemish property taken in England proved to be worth double what had been secured by Alva. Philip could not declare war. The Netherlands insurrection was straining his resources, and with Elizabeth for an open enemy the whole weight of England would have been thrown on the side of the Prince of Orange. Elizabeth herself should have declared war, people say, instead of condescending to such tricks. Perhaps so; but also perhaps not. These insults, steadily maintained, shook the faith of mankind, and especially of her own sailors, in the invincibility of the Spanish colossus.

I am now to turn to another side of the subject. The stories which I have told you show the temper of the time, and the atmosphere which men were breathing, but it will be instructive to look more closely at individual persons, and I will take first John Hawkins (afterwards Sir John), a peculiarly characteristic figure.

The Hawkinses of Plymouth were a solid middle-class Devonshire family, who for two generations had taken a leading part in the business of the town. They still survive in the county – Achins we used to call them before school pronunciation came in, and so Philip wrote the name when the famous John began to trouble his dreams. I have already spoken of old William Hawkins, John's father, whom Henry VIII was fond of, and who brought over the Brazilian king. Old William had now retired and had left his place and his work to his son. John Hawkins may have been about thirty at Elizabeth's accession. He had witnessed the times of Edward VI and Mary, but, though many of his friends had taken to the privateering business, Hawkins appears to have kept clear of it, and continued steadily at trade. One of these friends, and his contemporary, was Thomas Stukely, afterwards so notorious – and a word may be said of Stukely's career as a contrast to that of Hawkins.

He was a younger son of a leading county family, went to London to seek his fortune, and became a hanger-on of Sir Thomas Seymour. Doubtless he was connected with Seymour's pirating scheme at Scilly, and took to pirating as an occupation like other Western gentlemen.

When Elizabeth became Queen, he introduced himself at Court and amused her with his conceit. He would go to Florida, found an empire there, and write to the Queen as his dearest sister. She gave him leave to try. He bought a vessel of 400 tons, got 100 soldiers to join him besides the crew, and sailed from Plymouth in 1563. Once out of harbour, he announced that the sea was to be his Florida. He went back to the pirate business, robbed freely, haunted Irish creeks, and set up an intimacy with the Ulster chief, Shan O'Neil. Shan and Stukely became bosom friends. Shan wrote to Elizabeth to recommend that she should make over Ireland to Stukely and himself to manage. Elizabeth not consenting, Stukely turned Papist, transferred his services to the Pope and Philip, and was preparing a campaign in Ireland under the Pope's direction, when he was tempted to join Sebastian of Portugal in the African expedition, and there got himself killed.

Stukely was a specimen of the foolish sort of the young Devonshire men; Hawkins was exactly his opposite. He stuck to business, avoided politics, traded with Spanish ports without offending the Holy Office, and formed intimacies and connections with the Canary Islands especially, where it was said 'he grew much in love and favour with the people.'

At the Canaries he naturally heard much about the West Indies. He was adventurous. His Canaries friends urged that blacks were great merchandise in the Spanish settlements in Española. He himself was intimately acquainted with the Guinea Coast, and knew how easily such a cargo could be obtained.

We know to what the slave trade grew. We have all learnt to repent of the share which England had in it, and to abhor everyone whose hands were stained by contact with so accursed a business. All that may be taken for granted; but we must look at the matter as it would have been represented at the Canaries to Hawkins himself.

The Carib races whom the Spaniards found in Cuba and St Domingo had withered before them as if struck by a blight. Many died under the lash of the Spanish overseers; many, perhaps the most, from the mysterious causes which have made the loss of freedom so fatal to the Red Indian, the Australian, and the Maori.

The natives perished out of the islands of the Caribbean Sea with a rapidity which startled the conquerors. The famous Bishop Las Casas pitied and tried to save the remnants that were left. The Spanish settlers required labourers for the plantations. It struck Las Casas that if blacks could be introduced into the West Indian Islands, the Indians might be left alone; the blacks could be made into Christians, and could be saved at worst from the horrid fate which awaited many of them in their own country.

The black races varied like other creatures: some were gentle and timid, some were ferocious. The strong tyrannised over the weak, made slaves of their prisoners, occasionally ate them, and those they did not eat they sacrificed at what they called their *customs* – offered them up at the altars of their idols. These customs were suspended while the slave trade gave the prisoners a value. They revived when the slave trade was abolished. When Lord Wolseley a few years back entered Ashantee, the altars were coated thick with the blood of hundreds of miserable beings who had been freshly slaughtered there. Still later similar horrid scenes were reported from Dahomey. Sir Richard Burton, who was an old acquaintance of mine, spent two months with the King of Dahomey, and dilated to me on the benevolence and enlightenment of that excellent monarch. I asked why, if the King was so benevolent, he did not alter the customs. Burton looked at me with consternation. 'Alter the customs!' he said. 'Would you have the Archbishop of Canterbury alter the Liturgy?' Las Casas and those who thought as he did are not to be charged with infamous inhumanity if they proposed to buy these poor creatures from their captors, save them from Mumbo Jumbo, and carry them to countries where they would be valuable property, and be at least as well cared for as the mules and horses.

The experiment seemed to succeed. The blacks who were carried to the Spanish islands proved docile and useful. Portuguese and Spanish factories were established on the coast of Guinea. The black chiefs were glad to make money out of their wretched victims, and readily sold them. The transport over the Atlantic became a regular branch of business. Strict laws were made for the good treatment of the slaves on the plantations. The trade was carried on under licence from the government, and an import duty of thirty ducats per head was charged on every black that was landed. The full consequences could not be foreseen; Las Casas, who approved of it, was one of the most excellent of men.

Our own Bishop Butler could give no decided opinion against black slavery as it existed in his time. It is absurd to say that ordinary merchants and ship captains ought to have seen the infamy of a practice which Las Casas advised and Butler could not condemn. The Spanish and Portuguese governments claimed the control of the traffic. The Spanish settlers in the West Indies objected to a restriction

47

which raised the price and shortened the supply. They considered that having established themselves in a new country they had a right to a voice in the conditions of their occupancy. It was thus that the Spaniards in the Canaries represented the matter to John Hawkins: if he liked to make the venture with a contraband cargo from Guinea, their countrymen would give him an enthusiastic welcome. It is evident from the story that neither he nor they expected that serious offence would be taken at Madrid. Hawkins at this time was entirely friendly with the Spaniards. It was enough if he could be assured that the colonists would be glad to deal with him.

I am not crediting him with the benevolent purposes of Las Casas. I do not suppose Hawkins thought much of saving black men's souls. He saw only an opportunity of extending his business among a people with whom he was already connected. The traffic was established. It had the sanction of the Church, and no objection had been raised to it anywhere on the score of morality. The only question which could have presented itself to Hawkins was of the right of the Spanish government to prevent foreigners from getting a share of a lucrative trade against the wishes of its subjects. And his friends at the Canaries certainly did not lead him to expect any real opposition. One regrets that a famous Englishman should have been connected with the slave trade; but we have no right to heap censures upon him, because he was no more enlightened than the wisest of his contemporaries.

Thus, encouraged from Santa Cruz, Hawkins on his return to England formed an African company out of the leading citizens of London. Three vessels were fitted out, Hawkins being commander and part owner. The size of them is remarkable: the *Solomon*, as the largest was called, 120 tons; the *Swallow*, 100 tons; the *Jonas* not above 40 tons. This represents them as inconceivably small. They carried between them a hundred men, and ample room had to be provided besides for the blacks. There may have been a difference in the measurement of tonnage. We ourselves have five standards: builder's measurement, yacht measurement, displacement, sail area, and register measurement. Registered tonnage is far under the others: a yacht registered 120 tons would be called 200 in a shipping list. However that be, the brigantines and sloops used by the Elizabethans on all adventurous expeditions were mere boats compared with what we should use now on such occasions. The reason was obvious. Success depended on speed and sailing power. The art of building big square-rigged ships which would work to windward had not been yet discovered. The fore- and aft-rig alone would enable a vessel to tack, as it is called, and this could only be used with craft of moderate tonnage.

The expedition sailed in October 1562. They called at the Canaries, where they were warmly entertained. They went on to Sierra Leone, where they collected 300 blacks. They avoided the government factories, and picked them up as they could, some by force, some by negotiation with local chiefs, who were as ready to sell their subjects as Sancho Panza intended to be when he got his island. They crossed without misadventure to St Domingo, where Hawkins represented that he was on a voyage of discovery; that he had been driven out of his course and wanted food and money. He said he had certain slaves with him, which he asked permission to sell. What he had heard at the Canaries turned out to be exactly true. So far as the governor of St Domingo knew, Spain and England were at peace. Privateers had not troubled the peace of the Caribbean Sea, or dangerous heretics menaced the Catholic faith there. The Inquisition had not yet been established beyond the Atlantic. The Queen of England was his sovereign's sister-in-law, and the governor saw no reason why he should construe his general instructions too literally. The planters were eager to buy, and he did not wish to be unpopular. He allowed Hawkins to sell two out of his three hundred blacks, leaving the remaining hundred as a deposit should question be raised about the duty. Evidently the only doubt in the governor's mind was whether the Madrid authorities would charge foreign importers on a higher scale. The question was new. No stranger had as yet attempted to trade there.

The profits were large. A ship in the harbour was about to sail for Cadiz. Hawkins invested most of what he had made in a cargo of hides, for which there was a demand in Spain, and he sent them over in her in charge of one of his partners. The governor gave him a testimonial for good conduct during his stay in the port; with this and with his three vessels he returned leisurely to England, having, as he imagined, been splendidly successful.

He was to be unpleasantly enlightened. A few days after he had arrived at Plymouth, he met the man whom he had sent to Cadiz with the hides forlorn and empty-handed. The Inquisition, he said, had seized the cargo and confiscated it. An order had been sent to St Domingo to forfeit the reserved slaves. He himself had escaped for his life, as the familiars had been after him.

Nothing shows more clearly how little thought there had been in Hawkins that his voyage would have given offence in Spain than the astonishment with which he heard the news. He protested. He wrote to Philip. Finding entreaties useless, he swore vengeance; but threats were equally ineffectual. Not a hide, not a farthing could he recover. The Spanish government, terrified at the intrusion of English adventurers into their Western paradise to endanger the treasure fleets, issued orders to close the ports there against all foreigners. Philip personally warned Sir Thomas Chaloner, the English ambassador, that if such visits were repeated, mischief would come of it. Cecil, who disliked all such semi-piratical enterprises, and Chaloner, who was an old companion in arms of Charles V, entreated their mistress to forbid them.

Elizabeth, however, had her own views in such matters. She liked money. She liked encouraging the adventurous disposition of her subjects, who were fighting the state's battles at their own risk and cost. She saw in Philip's reaction that the West Indies was his vulnerable point; if she wished to keep the Inquisition from burning her sailors, there was the place where Philip would be more sensitive. She thought that Hawkins had done nothing for which he could be justly blamed. He had traded at St Domingo with the governor's consent, and confiscation was sharp practice.

This was clearly Hawkins's own view of the matter. He had injured no one. He had offended no pious ears by parading his Protestantism. He was not Philip's subject, and was not to be expected to obey the instructions given by the Spanish government in the remote corners of their dominions. He held that he had been robbed, and had a right to indemnify himself at the King's expense. He would go out again. He was certain of a cordial reception from the planters. Between him and them there was the friendliest understanding. He meant to sell a fresh cargo of slaves, and the Madrid government should go without their 30 per cent duty.

Elizabeth approved. Hawkins had opened the road to the West Indies. He had shown how easy slave trading was, and how profitable; how it was also possible for the English to establish friendly relations with the Spanish settlers in the West Indies, whether Philip liked it or not. Another company was formed for a second trial. Elizabeth took shares, Lord Pembroke took shares, and other members of the Council. The Queen lent the *Jesus*, a large ship of her own, of 700 tons. Formal instructions were given that no wrong was to be done to the King of Spain, but what wrong might mean was left to the discretion of the commander. Where the planters were all eager to purchase, means of traffic would be discovered without collision with the authorities. This time the expedition was to be on a larger scale, and a hundred soldiers were put on board to provide for contingencies. Thus furnished, Hawkins started on his second voyage in October 1564. The autumn was chosen, to avoid the extreme tropical heats. He touched as before to see his friends at the Canaries. He went on to the Rio Grande, met with adventures bad and good, found a chief at war with a neighbouring tribe, helped to capture a town and take prisoners, made purchases at a Portuguese factory.

In this way he now secured 400 human beings, perhaps for a better fate than they would have met with at home, and with these he sailed off in the old direction. Near the equator he fell in with calms; he was short of water, and feared to lose some of them; but, as the record of the voyage puts it, 'Almighty God would not suffer His elect to perish,' and sent a breeze which carried him safe to Dominica. In the wettest of islands he found water in plenty, and had then to consider what next he would do. St Domingo, he thought, would be no longer safe for him, so he struck across to the Spanish Main to a place called Burboroata, where he might hope that nothing might be known about him.

In this he was mistaken. Philip's orders had arrived: no Englishman of any creed or kind was to be allowed to trade in his West Indies dominions. The settlers, however, intended to trade. They required only a display of force that they might pretend that they were yielding to compulsion. Hawkins said that he was out on the service of the Queen of England. He had been driven off his course by bad weather. He was short of supplies and had many men on board, who might do the town some mischief if they were not allowed to land peaceably and buy and sell what they wanted. The governor affecting to hesitate, he threw 120 men on shore, and brought his guns to bear on the castle. The governor gave way under protest. Hawkins was to be permitted to sell half his slaves. He said that as he had been treated so inhospitably he would not pay the 30 per cent. The King of Spain should have 7½, and no more. The settlers had no objection. The price would be the less, and with this deduction his business was easily finished off. He bought no more hides, and was paid in solid silver.

From Burboroata he went on to Rio de la Hacha, where the same scene was repeated. The whole 400 were disposed of, this time with ease and complete success. He had been rapid, and had the season still before him. Having finished his business, he surveyed a large part of the Caribbean Sea, taking soundings, noting the currents, and making charts of the coasts and islands. This done, he turned homewards, following the east shore of North America as far as Newfoundland. There he gave his crew a change of diet, with fresh cod from the Banks, and after eleven months' absence he sailed into Padstow, having lost but twenty men in the whole adventure, and bringing back 60 per cent to the Queen and other shareholders.

Nothing succeeds like success. Hawkins's praises were in everyone's mouth. Elizabeth received him at the palace. The Spanish ambassador, De Silva, met him there at dinner. He talked freely of where he had been and of what he had done, only keeping back the gentle violence which he had used. He regarded this as a mere farce, since there had been no one hurt on either side. He boasted of having given the greatest satisfaction to the Spaniards who had dealt with him. De Silva could but report to his master, and ask instructions how he was to proceed.

Philip was much disturbed. He saw in prospect his Western subjects allying themselves with the English; his treasure fleets in danger, all the possibilities with which Elizabeth had wished to alarm him. He read and re-read De Silva's letters, and opposite the name of Achines he wrote startled interjections on the margin: 'Ojo! Ojo!'

The political horizon was just then favourable to Elizabeth. The Queen of Scots was prisoner in Loch Leven; the Netherlands were in revolt; the Huguenots were looking up in France; and when Hawkins proposed a third expedition, she thought that she could safely allow it. She gave him the use of the *Jesus* again, with another smaller ship of hers, the *Minion*. He had two of his own still fit for work; and a fifth, the *Judith*, was brought in by his young cousin, Francis Drake, who was now to make his first appearance on the stage. I shall tell you by-and-by who and what Drake was. Enough to say now that he was a relation of Hawkins, the owner of a small sloop or brigantine, and ambitious of a share in a stirring business.

The Plymouth seamen were falling into dangerous contempt of Philip. While the expedition was fitting out, a ship of the King's came into Catwater with more prisoners from Flanders. She was flying the Castilian flag, contrary to rule, it was said in English harbours. The treatment of the English ensign at Gibraltar had not been forgiven, and Hawkins ordered the Spanish captain to strike his colours. The captain refused, and Hawkins instantly fired into him. In the confusion the prisoners escaped on board the *Jesus* and were let go. The captain sent a complaint to London, and Cecil – who disapproved of Hawkins and his proceedings – sent down an officer to inquire into what had happened.

52

Hawkins, confident in Elizabeth's protection, answered that the Spaniard had broken the laws of the port, and that it was necessary to assert the Queen's authority.

'Your mariners,' said De Silva to her, 'rob our subjects on the sea, trade where they are forbidden to go, and fire upon our ships in your harbours. Your preachers insult my master from their pulpits, and when we remonstrate we are answered with menaces. We have borne so far with their injuries, attributing them rather to temper and bad manners than to deliberate purpose. But, seeing that no redress can be had, and that the same treatment of us continues, I must consult my sovereign's pleasure. For the last time, I require Your Majesty to punish this outrage at Plymouth and preserve the peace between the two realms.'

No remonstrance could seem more just till the other side was heard. The other side was that the Pope and the Catholic powers were undertaking to force the Protestants of France and Flanders back under the Papacy with fire and sword. England's turn was to follow as soon as Philip's hands were free. Meanwhile he had been intriguing with the Queen of Scots; he had been encouraging Ireland in rebellion; he had been persecuting English merchants and seamen, starving them to death in the Inquisiton dungeons, or burning them at the stake. The Smithfield infamies were fresh in Protestant memories, and who could not tell how soon the horrid work would begin again at home, if the Catholic powers could have their way?

But spiritual tyranny had not yet learned its lesson, and the 'Beggars of the Sea' were to be Philip's schoolmasters in irregular but effective fashion. Elizabeth listened politely to what De Silva said, promised to examine into his complaints, and allowed Hawkins to sail.

53

Sir John Hawkins
and Philip the Second

My last lecture left Hawkins preparing to start on his third and, as it proved, most eventful voyage. I mentioned that he was joined by a young relation, of whom I must say a few preliminary words. Francis Drake was a Devonshire man, like Hawkins himself and Raleigh and Davis and Gilbert, and many other famous men of those days. He was born at Tavistock in 1541. He told Camden that he was of mean extraction. He meant merely that he made no idle pretentions to noble birth. His father was a tenant of the Earl of Bedford, and must have stood well with him, for Francis Russell, the heir of the earldom, was the boy's godfather. From him Drake took his Christian name. The Drakes were early converts to Protestantism. Trouble rising at Tavistock on the Six Articles Bill, they removed to Kent, where the father, probably through Lord Bedford's influence, was appointed a lay chaplain in Henry VIII's fleet at Chatham. In the next reign, when the Protestants were uppermost, he was ordained and became vicar of Upnore on the Medway.

Young Francis took early to the water, and made acquaintance with a ship-master trading to the Channel ports, who took him on board his ship and bred him as a sailor. The boy distinguished himself, and his patron when he died left Drake his vessel in his will. For several years Drake stuck steadily to his coasting work, made money, and made a solid reputation. His ambition grew with his success. The seagoing English were all full of Hawkins and his West Indian exploits. The Hawkinses and the Drakes were near relations. Hearing that there was to be another expedition, and having obtained his cousin's consent, Francis Drake sold his brig, bought the *Judith*, a handier and faster vessel, and with a few stout sailors from the river went down to Plymouth and joined.

De Silva had sent word to Philip that Hawkins was again going out, and preparations had been made to receive him. Suspecting nothing, Hawkins with his four consorts sailed, as before, in October 1567. The start was ominous. He was caught and badly knocked about by an equinoctial in the Bay of Biscay. He lost his boats. The *Jesus* strained her timbers and leaked, and he so little liked the look of things that he even thought of turning back and giving up the expedition for the season. However, the weather mended. They put themselves to rights at the Canaries, picked up their spirits, and proceeded. The slave catching was managed successfully, though with some increased difficulty. The cargo with equal success was disposed of at the Spanish settlements. At one place the planters came off in their boats at night to buy. At Rio de la Hacha, where the most imperative orders had been sent to forbid his admittance, Hawkins landed a force as before and took possession of the town, of course with the connivance of the settlers. At Carthagena he was similarly ordered off, and as Carthagena was strongly fortified he did not venture to meddle with it.

But elsewhere he found ample markets for his wares. He sold all his blacks. By this and by other dealings he had collected what is described as a large treasure of gold, silver, and jewels. The hurricane season was approaching, and he made the best of his way homewards with his spoils, in the fear of being overtaken by it. Unluckily for him, he had lingered too long. He had passed the west point of Cuba and was working up the back of the island when a hurricane came down on him. The gale lasted four days. The ships' bottoms were foul and they could make no way. Spars were lost and rigging carried away. The *Jesus*, which had not been seaworthy all along, leaked worse than ever and lost her rudder. Hawkins looked for some port in Florida, but found the coast shallow and dangerous, and was at last obliged to run for San Juan de Ulloa, at the bottom of the Gulf of Mexico.

San Juan de Ulloa is a few miles only from Vera Cruz. It was at that time the chief port of Mexico, through which all the traffic passed between the colony and the mother-country, and was thus a place of some consequence. It stands on a small bay facing towards the north. Across the mouth of this bay lies a narrow ridge of sand and shingle, half a mile long, which acts as a natural breakwater and forms the harbour. This ridge, or island as it was called, was uninhabited, but it had been faced on the inner front by a wall. The water was deep alongside, and vessels could thus lie in perfect security, secured by their cables to rings let into the masonry.

The prevailing wind was from the north, bringing in a heavy surf on the back of the island. There was an opening at both ends, but only one available for vessels of large draught. In this the channel was narrow, and a battery at the end of the breakwater would completely command it. The town stood on the opposite side of the bay.

Into a Spanish port thus constructed Hawkins entered with his battered squadron on September 16, 1568. He could not have felt entirely easy; but he probably thought that he had no ill-will to fear from the inhabitants generally, and that the Spanish authorities would not be strong enough to meddle with him. His ill star had brought him there at a time when Alvarez de Baçan, the same officer who had destroyed the English ships at Gibraltar, was daily expected from Spain – sent by Philip, as it proved, specially to look for him. Hawkins, when he appeared outside, had been mistaken for the Spanish admiral, and it was under this impression that he had been allowed to enter. The error was quickly discovered on both sides.

Though still ignorant that he was himself Baçan's particular object, yet Baçan was the last officer whom in his crippled condition he would have cared to encounter. Several Spanish merchantmen were in the port richly loaded: with these of course he did not meddle, though, if reinforced, they might perhaps meddle with him. As his best resource he dispatched a courier on the instant to Mexico to inform the Viceroy of his arrival, to say that he had an English squadron with him; that he had been driven in by stress of weather and need of repairs; that the Queen was an ally of the King of Spain; and as he understood a Spanish fleet was likely soon to arrive, he begged the Viceroy to make arrangements to prevent disputes.

As yet there was no Inquisition in Mexico. It was established there three years later, for the special benefit of the English. But so far there was no ill-will towards the English – rather the contrary. Hawkins had hurt no one, and the trading had been eminently popular. The Viceroy might perhaps have connived at Hawkins's escape, but again by ill-fortune he was himself under orders of recall, and his successor was coming out in this particular fleet with Baçan.

Had he been well disposed and free to act it would still have been too late, for the very next morning, September 17, Baçan was off the harbour mouth with thirteen heavily armed galleons and frigates. The smallest of them carried probably 200 men, and the odds were now tremendous. Hawkins's vessels lay ranged along the inner bank or wall of the island. He instantly occupied the island itself and mounted guns at the point covering the way in. He then sent a boat off to Baçan to say that he was an Englishman, that he was in possession of the port, and must forbid the entrance of the Spanish fleet till he was assured that there was to be no violence. It was a strong measure to shut a Spanish admiral out of a Spanish port in time of peace. Still, the way in was difficult, and could not be easily forced if resolutely defended. The northerly wind was rising; if it blew into a gale the Spaniards would be on a lee shore. Under desperate circumstances, desperate things will be done. Hawkins in his subsequent report thus explains his dilemma:—

'I was in two difficulties. Either I must keep them out of the port, which with God's grace I could easily have done, in which case with a northerly wind rising they would have been wrecked, and I should have been answerable; or I must risk their playing false, which on the whole I preferred to do.'

The northerly gale it appears did not rise, or the English commander might have preferred the first alternative. Three days passed in negotiation. Baçan and Don Enriquez, the new Viceroy, were naturally anxious to get into shelter out of a dangerous position, and were equally desirous not to promise any more than was absolutely necessary. The final agreement was that Baçan and the fleet should enter without opposition. Hawkins might stay till he had repaired his damages, and buy and sell what he wanted; and further, as long as they remained the English were to keep possession of the island. This article, Hawkins says, was long resisted, but was consented to at last. It was absolutely necessary, for with the island in their hands, the Spaniards had only to cut the English cables, and they would have driven ashore across the harbour.

The treaty so drawn was formally signed. Hostages were given on both sides, and Baçan came in. The two fleets were moored as far apart from each other as the size of the port would allow. Courtesies were exchanged, and for two days all went well. It is likely that the viceroy and the admiral did not at first know that it was the very man whom they had been sent out to sink or capture who was lying so close to them. When they did know it they may have looked on him as a pirate, with whom, as with heretics, there was no need to keep faith. Anyway, the rat was in the trap and Baçan did not mean to let him out. The *Jesus* lay farthest in; the *Minion* lay beyond her towards the entrance, moored apparently to a ring on the quay but free to move; and the

Judith, farther out again, moored in the same way. Nothing is said of the two small vessels remaining.

Baçan made his preparations silently, covered by the town. He had men in abundance ready to act where he should direct. On the third day, the 20th of September, at noon, the *Minion's* crew had gone to dinner, when they saw a large hulk of 900 tons slowly towing up alongside of them. Not liking such a neighbour, they had their cable ready to slip and began to set their canvas. On a sudden shots and cries were heard from the town. Parties of English who were on land were set upon; many were killed; the rest were seen flinging themselves into the water and swimming off to the ships. At the same instant the guns of the galleons and of the shore batteries opened fire on the *Jesus* and her consorts, and in the smoke and confusion 300 Spaniards swarmed out of the hulk and sprang on the *Minion's* decks. The *Minion's* men cut them down or drove them overboard, hoisted sail, and forced their way out of the harbour, followed by the *Judith*.

The *Jesus* was left alone, unable to stir. She defended herself desperately. In the many actions which were fought afterwards between the English and the Spaniards, there was never any more gallant. Baçan's own ship was sunk and the vice-admiral's was set on fire. The Spanish, having an enormous advantage in numbers, were able to land a force on the island, seize the English battery there, cut down the gunners, and turn the guns close at hand on the devoted *Jesus*. Still she fought on, defeating every attempt to board, till at length Baçan sent down fire-ships on her, and then the end came. All that Hawkins had by his voyage, money, bullion, the ship herself, had to be left to their fate. Hawkins himself with the survivors of the crew took to their boats, dashed through the enemy, who vainly tried to take them, and struggled out after the *Minion* and the *Judith*. It speaks ill for Baçan that with so large a force at his command, and in such a position, a single Englishman escaped to tell the story.

Even when outside Hawkins's situation was still critical and might well be called desperate. The *Judith* was but fifty tons; the *Minion* not above a hundred. They were now crowded up with men. They had little water on board, and there had been no time to refill their store-chests or fit themselves for sea. Happily the weather was moderate. If the wind had risen, nothing could have saved them. They anchored two miles off to put themselves in some sort of order. The Spanish fleet did not venture to molest further so desperate a foe. On Saturday the 25th they set sail, scarcely knowing whither to turn. To attempt an ocean voyage as they were would be certain destruction, yet they could not trust longer to Baçan's forbearance. There was supposed to be a shelter of some kind somewhere on the east side of the Gulf of Mexico, where it was hoped they might obtain provisions.

They reached the place on October 8, but found nothing. English sailors have never been wanting in resolution. They knew that if they all remained on board every one of them must starve. A hundred volunteered to land and take their chance. The rest on short rations might hope to make their way home. The sacrifice was accepted. The hundred men were put on shore. They wandered for a few days in the woods, feeding on roots and berries, and shot at by the Indians. At last they reached a Spanish station, where they were taken and sent as prisoners to Mexico.

The new Viceroy, though he had been in the fight at San Juan de Ulloa, was not implacable. They were treated at first with humanity; they were fed, clothed, taken care of, and then distributed among the plantations. Some were employed as overseers, some as mechanics. Others, who understood any kind of business, were allowed to settle in towns, make money, and even marry and establish themselves. The quiet time lasted three years; at the end of those years the Inquisitors arrived, and then, as if these poor men had been the special object of that delightful institution, they were hunted up, thrown into dungeons, examined on their faith, tortured, some burnt in an *auto-da fé*, some lashed through the streets of Mexico naked on horseback and returned to their prisons. Those who did not die under this pious treatment were passed over to the Holy Office at Seville and were condemned to the galleys.

Here I leave them for the moment. We shall presently hear of them again in a singular connection. The *Minion* and *Judith* meanwhile pursued their melancholy way. They parted company. The *Judith*, being the better sailer, arrived first, and reached Plymouth in December, torn and tattered. Drake rode off post immediately to carry the bad news to London. The *Minion's* fate was worse. She made her course through the Bahama Channel, her crew dying as if struck with a pestilence, till at last there were hardly men enough left to handle the sails. They fell too far south for England, and at length had to put into Vigo, where their probable fate would be a Spanish prison. Happily they found other English vessels in the Roads there. Fresh hands were put on board, and fresh provisions. With these supplies Hawkins reached Mount's Bay a month later than the *Judith*, in January 1569.

Drake had told the story, and all England was ringing with it. The Spaniards, already in evil odour with the seagoing population, were accused of abominable treachery. The splendid fight which Hawkins had made raised him into a national idol, and though he had suffered financially, his loss was made up in reputation and authority. Every privateer in the West was eager to serve under the leadership of the hero of San Juan de Ulloa. He speedily found himself in command of a large irregular squadron, and even Cecil recognised his consequence. His chief and constant anxiety was for the comrades whom he had left behind, and he talked of a new expedition to recover them, or revenge them if they had been killed; but all things had to wait.

Elizabeth put a brave face on her disappointment. She had Alva's money, and was less than ever inclined to restore it. She had the best of the bargain in the arrest of the Spanish and English ships and cargoes. Alva would not encourage Philip to declare war with England till the Netherlands were completely reduced, and Philip, with his leaden foot (*pié de plomo*), always preferred patience and intrigue. Time and he and the Pope were three powers which in the end would prove irresistible, and indeed it seemed, after Hawkins's return, as if Philip would turn out to be right. The presence of the Queen of Scots in England had set in flame the Catholic nobles. The wages of Alva's troops had been wrung somehow out of the wretched Provinces, and his ability and inexorable resolution were steadily grinding down the revolt. Every port in Holland and Zealand was in Alva's hands. Elizabeth's throne was threatened by the Ridolfi conspiracy. The only Protestant fighting power left on the sea which could be entirely depended on was in the privateer fleet, sailing, most of them, under a commission from the Prince of Orange.

This fleet was the strangest phenomenon in naval history. It was half Dutch, half English, with a flavour of Huguenot, and was commanded by a Flemish noble, Count de la Mark. Its headquarters were in the Downs or Dover Roads, where it could watch the Narrow Seas, and seize every Spanish ship that passed which was not too strong to be meddled with. The cargoes taken were openly sold in Dover market. If Alva sent cruisers from Antwerp to burn them out, they retreated under the guns of Dover Castle. Roving squadrons of them flew down to the Spanish coasts, pillaged churches, carried off church plate, and the captains drank success to piracy at their banquets out of chalices. The Spanish merchants at last estimated the property destroyed at three million ducats, and they said that if their flag could no longer protect them, they must decline to make further contracts for the supply of the Netherlands army.

The Ridolfi plot, an unpromising conspiracy to give her crown to Mary Stuart and to make away with heresy, was all but complete. The Pope and Philip had approved: Alva was to invade; the Duke of Norfolk was to head an insurrection in the Eastern counties. The intention was known, but the particulars of the conspiracy had been kept secret. The privateers at Dover were a sort of protection; they would at least make Alva's crossing more difficult; but the most pressing exigency was the discovery of the details of the treason. Nothing was to be gained by concession; the only salvation was in daring.

At Antwerp there was a certain Doctor Story, maintained by Alva there to keep a watch on English heretics. Story had been a persecutor under Mary, and had defended heretic burning in Elizabeth's first Parliament. He had at first taken the oath of allegiance, but left the country, and had taken to treason. Cecil wanted evidence, and this man could give it. A pretended informer brought Story word that there was an English vessel in the Scheldt which he would find worth examining. Story was tempted on board. The hatches were closed over him. He was delivered two days later at the Tower, when his secrets were wrenched out of him by the rack and he was then hanged.

Something was learnt, but less still than Cecil needed to take measures to protect the Queen. And now once more, and in a new character, we are to meet John Hawkins. Three years had passed since the catastrophe at San Juan de Ulloa. He had learnt to his sorrow that his poor companions had fallen into the hands of the Holy Office at last; had been burnt, lashed, starved in dungeons or worked in chains in the Seville yards; and his heart, not a very tender one, bled at the thoughts of them. The finest feature in the seamen of those days was their devotion to one another. Hawkins determined that, one way or other, these old comrades of his should be rescued. Entreaties were useless; force was impossible. There might still be a chance with cunning. He would risk anything, even the loss of his soul, to save them.

De Silva had left England. The Spanish ambassador was now Don Guerau or Gerald de Espes, and to him had fallen the task of watching and directing the conspiracy. Philip was to give the signal, the Duke of Norfolk and some of the Catholic peers were to rise and proclaim the Queen of Scots. Success would depend on the extent of the disaffection in England itself; the ambassador's business was to welcome and encourage all symptoms of discontent. Hawkins knew generally what was going on, and he saw in it an opportunity of approaching Philip on his weak side. Having been so much in the Canaries, he spoke Spanish. He called on Don Guerau, and with audacious coolness represented that he and many of his friends were dissatisfied with the Queen's service. He said he had found her faithless and ungrateful, and he and they would gladly transfer their allegiance to the King of Spain, if the King of Spain would receive them. For himself, he would undertake to bring over the whole privateer fleet of the West, and in return he asked for nothing but the release of a few poor English seamen who were in prison at Seville.

Don Guerau was full of the belief that the whole nation was ready to rebel. He eagerly swallowed the bait which Hawkins threw to him. He wrote to Alva, he wrote to Philip's secretary, Cayas, expatiating on the importance of securing such an addition to their party. It was true, he admitted, that Hawkins had been a pirate, but piracy was a common fault of the English, and no wonder when the Spaniards submitted to being plundered so meekly; the man who was offering his services was bold, resolute, capable, and had great influence with the English sailors; he strongly advised that such a recruit should be encouraged.

Alva would not listen. Philip, who shied at the name of Hawkins, was incredulous. Don Guerau had to tell Sir John that the King at present declined his offer, but advised him to go himself to Madrid, or to send some confidential friend with assurances and explanations.

Another figure now enters on the scene, a George Fitzwilliam. I do not know who he was, or why Hawkins chose him for his purpose. The Duke of Feria was one of Philip's most trusted ministers. He had married an English lady who had been a maid of honour to Queen Mary. It is possible that Fitzwilliam had some acquaintance with her or with her family. At any rate, he went to the Spanish Court; he addressed himself to the Ferias; he won their confidence, and by their means was admitted to an interview with Philip. He represented Hawkins as a Catholic who was indignant at the progress of heresy in England, who was eager to assist in the overthrow of Elizabeth, and the elevation of the Queen of Scots, and was willing to carry along with him the Western privateer fleet, which had become so dreadful to the Spanish mind.

Philip listened and was interested. It was only natural, he thought, that heretics should be robbers and pirates. If they could be recovered to the church, their bad habits would leave them. The English navy was the most serious obstacle to the intended invasion. Still, Hawkins! He asked Fitzwilliam if his friend was acquainted with the Queen of Scots or the Duke of Norfolk. Fitzwilliam was obliged to say that he was not. The credentials of John Hawkins were his own right hand. He was making the King a magnificent offer: nothing less than a squadron – not perhaps in the best condition, but easily to be put in order again if the King would pay the seamen's wages and advance some money for repairs. The release of a few poor prisoners was a small price to ask for such a service.

The King was still wary, watching the bait like an old pike, but hesitating to seize it; but the duke and duchess were willing to be themselves securities for Fitzwilliam's faith. Philip promised at last that if Hawkins would send him a letter of recommendation from the Queen of Scots herself, he would then see what could be done. The Ferias were dangerously enthusiastic. They talked freely to Fitzwilliam of the Queen of Scots and her prospects. They trusted him with letters and presents to her which would secure his admittance to her confidence. Hawkins had sent him over for the single purpose of cheating Philip into releasing his comrades from the Inquisition, and he had been introduced to secrets of high political moment; like Saul, the son of Kish, he had gone to seek his father's asses and he had found a kingdom. Fitzwilliam hurried home with his letters and his news. Hawkins could act no further on his own responsibility. He consulted Cecil. Cecil consulted the Queen, and it was agreed that the practice, as it was called should be carried further. It might lead to the discovery of the whole secret.

Treacherous, think some good people. Well, there are times when one admires even treachery:

> 'nec lex est justior ulla
> Quam necis artifices arte perire sua.'[1]

King Philip was confessedly preparing to encourage an English subject in treason to his sovereign. Was it so wrong to hoist the engineer with his own petard? Was it wrong of Hamlet to finger the packet of Rosencrantz and Guildenstern and rewrite his uncle's dispatch? Let us have done with cant in these matters. Mary Stuart was at Sheffield Castle in charge of

---

1. Nor is any law more just than that the devisers of death should perish by their own device.

Lord Shrewsbury, and Fitzwilliam could not see her without an order from the Crown. Shrewsbury, though loyal to Elizabeth, was notoriously well inclined to Mary, and therefore could not be taken into confidence. In writing to him, Cecil merely said that friends of Fitzwilliam's were in prison in Spain; that if the Queen of Scots would intercede for them, Philip might be induced to let them go. He might therefore allow Fitzwilliam to have a private audience with that Queen.

Thus armed, Fitzwilliam went down to Sheffield. He was introduced. He began with presenting Mary with the letters and remembrances from the Ferias, which at once opened her heart. It was impossible for her to suspect a friend of the duke and duchess. She was delighted at receiving a visitor from the Court of Spain. She was prudent enough to avoid dangerous confidences, but she said she was always pleased when she could do a service to Englishmen, and with all her heart would intercede for the prisoners. She wrote to Philip, she wrote to the duke and duchess, and gave the letters to Fitzwilliam to deliver. He took them to London, called on Don Gerald, and told him of his success. Don Gerald also wrote to his master, wrote unguardedly, and also trusted Fitzwilliam with the dispatch.

The various packets were taken first to Cecil, and were next shown to the Queen. They were then returned to Fitzwilliam, who once more went off with them to Madrid. If the letters produced the expected effect, Cecil calmly observed that divers commodities would ensue. English sailors would be released from the Inquisition and the galleys. The enemy's intentions would be discovered. If the King of Spain could be induced to do as Fitzwilliam had suggested, and assist in the repairs of the ships at Plymouth, credit would be obtained for a sum of money which could be employed to his own detriment. If Alva attempted the projected invasion, Hawkins might take the ships as if to escort him, and then do some notable exploit in mid-Channel.

You will observe the downright directness of Cecil, Hawkins, and the other parties in the matter. There is no wrapping up their intentions in fine phrases, no parade of justification. They went straight to their point. It was characteristic of Englishmen in those stern, dangerous times. They looked facts in the face, and did what fact required. All happened as I have described it: the story is told in letters and documents of the authenticity of which there is not the smallest doubt.

We will follow Fitzwilliam. He arrived at the Spanish court at the moment when Ridolfi had brought from Rome the Pope's blessing on the conspiracy. The final touches were being added by the Spanish

Council of State. All was hope; all was the credulity of enthusiasm! Mary Stuart's letter satisfied Philip. The prisoners were dismissed, each with ten dollars in his pocket. An agreement was formally drawn and signed in the Escurial in which Philip gave Hawkins a pardon for his misdemeanours in the West Indies, a patent for a Spanish peerage, and a letter of credit for £40,000 to put the privateers in a condition to do service, and the money was actually paid by Philip's London agent. Admitted as he now was to full confidence, Fitzwilliam learnt all the particulars of the great plot. The story reads like a chapter from *Monte Cristo*, and yet it is literally true.

It ends with a letter which I will read to you, from Hawkins to Cecil:

MY VERY GOOD LORD, – It may please your Honour to be advertised that Fitzwilliam is returned from Spain, where his message was acceptably received, both by the King himself, the Duke of Feria, and others of the Privy Council. His dispatch and answer were with great expedition and great countenance and favour of the King. The Articles are sent to the ambassador with orders also for the money to be paid to me by him, for the enterprise to proceed with all diligence. The pretence is that my powers should join with the Duke of Alva's powers, which he doth secretly provide in Flanders, as well as with powers which will come with the Duke of Medina Celi out of Spain, and to invade this realm and set up the Queen of Scots.

'They have practised with us for the burning of Her Majesty's ships. Therefore there should be some good care had of them, but not as it may appear that anything is discovered. The King has sent a ruby of good price to the Queen of Scots, with letters also which in my judgment were good to be delivered. The letters be of no importance, but his message by word is to comfort her, and say that he hath now none other care but to place her in her own. It were good also that Fitzwilliam may have access to the Queen of Scots to render thanks for the delivery of the prisoners who are now at liberty. It will be a very good colour for your lordship to confer with him more largely.

'I have sent your lordship the copy of my pardon from the King of Spain, in the order and manner I have it, with my great titles and honours from the King, from which God deliver me. Their practices be very mischievous, and they be never idle; but God, I hope, will confound them and turn their devices on their own necks.

Your Lordship's most faithfully to my power,

JOHN HAWKINS

A few more words will conclude this curious episode. With the clue obtained by Fitzwilliam, and confessions twisted out of Story and other unwilling witnesses, the Ridolfi conspiracy was unravelled before it broke into act. Norfolk lost his head. The inferior miscreants were hanged. The Queen of Scots had a narrow escape, and the Parliament accentuated the Protestant character of the Church of England by embodying the Thirty-nine Articles in a statute. Alva, who distrusted Ridolfi from the first and disliked encouraging rebellion, refused to interest himself further in Popish plots. Elizabeth and Cecil could now breathe more freely, and read Philip a lesson on the danger of plotting against the lives of sovereigns.

So long as England and Spain were nominally at peace, the presence of De la Mark and his privateers in the Downs was at least indecent. A committee of merchants at Bruges represented that their losses by it amounted to three million ducats. Elizabeth, being now in comparative safety, affected to listen to remonstrances, and orders were sent down to De la Mark that he must prepare to leave. It is likely that both the Queen and he understood each other, and that De la Mark knew where he was to go and what he was to do.

Alva now held every fortress in the Low Countries, whether inland or on the coast. The people were crushed. The duke's great statue stood in the square at Antwerp as a symbol of the annihilation of the ancient liberties of the Provinces. By sea alone the Prince of Orange still continued the unequal struggle; but if he was to maintain himself as a sea power anywhere, he required a harbour of his own in his own country. Dover and the Thames had served for a time as a base of operations, but it could not last, and without a footing in Holland itself eventual success was impossible. All the Protestant world was interested in his fate, and De la Mark, with his miscellaneous gathering of Dutch, English, and Huguenot rovers, was ready for any desperate exploit.

The order was to leave Dover immediately, but it was not construed strictly. He lingered in the Downs for six weeks. At length, one morning at the end of March 1572, a Spanish convoy known to be richly loaded appeared in the Straits. De la Mark lifted anchor, darted out on it, seized two of the largest hulks, rifled them, flung their crews overboard, and chased the rest up Channel. A day or two after he suddenly showed himself off Brille, at the mouth of the Meuse. A boat was sent on shore with a note to the governor, demanding the instant surrender of the town to the admiral of the Prince of Orange. The was sent on shore with a note to the governor, demanding the instant surrender of the town to the admiral of the Prince of Orange. The inhabitants rose in enthusiasm; the garrison was small, and the governor was obliged to comply. De la Mark took possession. A few priests and monks attempted resistance, but were put down without difficulty, and the leaders killed. The churches were cleared of their idols, and the Mass replaced by the Calvinistic service. Cannon and stores, furnished from London, were landed, and Brille was made impregnable before Alva had realised what had happened to him. He is said to have torn his beard in anger. Flushing followed suit. In a week or two all the strongest places on the coast had revolted, and the pirate fleet had laid the foundation of the great Dutch Republic, which at England's side was to strike out of Philip's hand the sceptre of the seas.

We may think as we please of these Beggars of the Ocean, these Norse corsairs come to life again with the flavour of Genevan theology in them; but for daring, for ingenuity, for obstinate determination to be spiritually free or to die for it, the like of the Protestant privateers of the sixteenth century has been rarely met with in this world.

England rang with joy when the news came that Brille was taken. Church bells pealed and bonfires blazed. Exiled familes went back to their homes – which were to be their homes once more – and the Zealanders and Hollanders, entrenched among their ditches, prepared for an amphibious conflict with the greatest power then upon the earth.

Drake's Voyage Round the World

I suppose some persons present have heard the name of Lope de Vega, the Spanish poet of Philip II's time. Very few of you probably know more of him than his name, and yet he ought to have some interest for us, as he was one of the many enthusiastic Spaniards who sailed in the great Armada. He had been disappointed in some love affair. He wanted distraction, and it is needless to say that he found distraction enough in the English Channel to put his love troubles out of his mind. His adventures brought before him with some vividness the character of the nation with which his own country was then in the death-grapple, especially the character of the English seamen to whom the Spaniards universally attributed their defeat.

Lope studied the exploits of Francis Drake from his first appearance to his end, and he celebrated those exploits, as England herself has never yet thought it worthwhile to do, by making him the hero of an epic poem. Lope de Vega's epic is called 'The Dragon-tea.' Drake himself is the dragon, the ancient serpent of the Apocalypse. The English have been contented to allow Drake a certain qualified praise. We admit that he was a bold, dexterous sailor, that he did his country good service at the invasion. We allow that he was a famous navigator, and sailed round the world, which no one else had done before him. But he was a corsair, and the only excuse for him is that he was no worse than most of his contemporaries. To Lope de Vega he was a great deal worse. He was the incarnation of evil, the arch-enemy of the Church of God.

It is worthwhile to look more particularly at the figure of a man who appeared to the Spaniards in such terrible proportions. I, for my part, believe a time will come when we shall see better than we see now what the Reformation was, and what we owe to it. These sea-captains of Elizabeth will then form the subject of a national epic. Meanwhile I shall try in these lectures to draw you a sketch of Drake and his doings as they appear to myself. Today I can but give you a part of the rich and varied story, but if all goes well I hope I may be able to continue it at a future time.

I have not yet done with Sir John Hawkins. We shall hear of him again. He became the manager of Elizabeth's dockyards. He it was who turned out the ships that fought Philip's fleet in the Channel in such condition that not a hull leaked, not a spar was sprung, not a rope parted at an unseasonable moment, and this at a minimum of cost. He served himself in the squadron which he had equipped. He was one of the small group of admirals who met that Sunday afternoon in the cabin of the *Ark Raleigh* and sent the fire-ships down to stir Medina Sidonia out of his anchorage at Calais. He was a child of the sea, and at sea he died. But of this hereafter. I must speak now of his still more illustrious kinsman, Francis Drake.

I told you the other day who Drake was and where he came from; how he went to sea as a boy, found favour with his master, became early an owner of his own ship, sticking steadily to trade. You hear nothing of him in connection with the Channel pirates. It was not till he was five-and-twenty that he was tempted by Hawkins into the slave-trading business, and of this one experiment was enough. He never tried it again.

The best likeness of Drake that I know is an engraving in Sir William Stirling-Maxwell's collection of sixteenth-century notabilities, representing him, as a scroll says at the foot of the plate, at the age of forty-three. The face is round, the forehead broad and full, with the short brown hair curling crisply on either side. The eyebrows are highly arched, the eyes firm, clear, and open. I cannot undertake for the colour, but I should judge they would be dark grey. The nose is short and thick, the mouth and chin hid by a heavy moustache on the upper lip, and close-clipped beard well spread over chin and cheek. The expression is good-humoured, but absolutely inflexible, not a weak line to be seen. He was of middle height, powerfully built, perhaps too powerfully for grace, unless the quilted doublet in which the artist has dressed him exaggerates his breadth.

I have seen another portrait of him, with pretensions to authenticity, in which he appears with a slighter figure, eyes dark, full, thoughful, and stern, a sailor's cord about his neck with a whistle attached to it, and a ring into which a thumb is carelessly thrust, the weight of the arms resting on it, as if in a characteristic attitude.

We left him returned home in the *Judith* from San Juan de Ulloa, a ruined man. He had never injured the Spaniards. He had gone out with his cousin merely to trade, and he had met with a hearty reception from the settlers wherever he had been. A Spanish admiral had treacherously set upon him and his kinsman, destroyed half their vessels, and robbed them of all that they had. They had left a hundred of their comrades behind them, for whose fate they might fear the worst. Drake thenceforth considered Spanish property as fair game till he had made up his own losses. He waited quietly for four years till he had re-established himself, and then prepared to try fortune again in a more daring form.

The ill-luck at San Juan de Ulloa had risen from loose tongues. There had been too much talk about it. Too many parties had been concerned. The Spanish Government had notice and were prepared. Drake determined to act for himself, have no partners, and keep his own secret. He found friends to trust him with money without asking for explanations. The Plymouth sailors were eager to take their chance with him. His force was absurdly small: a sloop or brigantine of a hundred tons, which he called the *Dragon* (perhaps, like Lope de Vega, playing on his own name), and two small pinnaces. With these he left Plymouth in the fall of the summer of 1572. He had ascertained that Philip's gold and silver from the Peruvian mines was landed at Panama, carried across the isthmus on mules' backs on the line of M de Lesseps' canal, and re-shipped at Nombre de Dios, at the mouth of the Chagre River.

He told no one where he was going. He was no more communicative than necessary after his return, and the results, rather than the particulars, of his adventure are all that can be certainly known. Discretion told him to keep his counsel, and he kept it.

The Drake family published an account of this voyage in the middle of the next century, but obviously nowhere to be depended on. It can be made out, however, that he did go to Nombre de Dios, that he found his way into the town, and saw stores of bullion there which he would have liked to carry off but could not. A romantic story of a fight in the town I disbelieve, first because his numbers were so small that to try force would have been absurd, and next because if there had been really anything like a battle an alarm would have been raised in the neighbourhood, and it is evident that no alarm was given. In the woods were parties of runaway slaves, who were called Cimarons. It was to these that Drake addressed himself, and they volunteered to guide him where he could surprise the treasure convoy on the way from Panama. His movements were silent and rapid. One interesting incident is mentioned which is authentic. The Cimarons took him through the forest to the watershed from which the streams flow to both oceans. Nothing could be seen through the jungle of undergrowth; but Drake climbed a tall tree, saw from the top of it the Pacific glittering below him, and made a vow that one day he would himself sail a ship in those waters.

For the present he had immediate work on hand. His guides kept their word. They led him to the track from Panama, and he had not long to wait before the tinkling was heard of the mule bells as they were coming up the pass. There was no suspicion of danger. The mule train had but its ordinary guard, who fled at the first surprise. The immense booty fell all into Drake's hands – gold, jewels, silver bars – and got with much ease, as Prince Hal said at Gadshill. The silver they buried, as too heavy for transport. The gold, pearls, rubies, emeralds, and diamonds they carried down straight to their ship. The voyage home went prosperously. The spoils were shared among the adventurers, and they had no reason to complain. They were wise enough to hold their tongues, and Drake was in a condition to look about him and prepare for bigger enterprises.

Rumours got abroad, in spite of reticence. Imagination was high in flight just then; rash amateurs thought they could make their fortunes in the same way, and tried it, to their sorrow. A sort of inflation can be traced in English sailors' minds as their work expanded. Even Hawkins – the clear practical Hawkins – was infected. This was not in Drake's line. He kept to prose and fact. He studied the globe. He examined all the charts that he could get. He became known to the Privy Council and the Queen, and prepared for an enterprise which would make his name and alarm Philip in earnest.

The ships which the Spaniards used on the Pacific were usually built on the spot. But Magellan was known to have gone by the Horn, and where a Portuguese could go an Englishman could go. Drake proposed to try. There was a party in Elizabeth's Council against these adventures, and in favour of peace with Spain; but Elizabeth herself was always for enterprise of pith and moment. She was willing to help, and others of her Council were willing too, provided their names were not to appear. The responsibility was to be Drake's own. Again the vessels in which he was preparing to tempt fortune seem preposterously small. The *Pelican*, or *Golden Hind*, which belonged to Drake himself, was called but 120 tons, at best no larger than a modern racing yawl, though perhaps no racing yawl ever left White's yard better found for the work which she had to do. The next, the *Elizabeth*, of London, was said to be eighty tons; a small pinnace of twelve tons, in which we should hardly risk a summer cruise round the Land's End, with two sloops or frigates of fifty and thirty tons, made the rest. The *Elizabeth* was commanded by Captain Winter, a Queen's officer, and perhaps a son of the old admiral.

We may credit Drake with knowing what he was about. He and his comrades were carrying their lives in their hands. If they were taken they would be inevitably hanged. Their safety depended on speed of sailing, and specially on the power of working fast to windward, which the heavy square-rigged ships could not do. The crews all told were 160 men and boys. Drake had his brother John with him. Among his officers were the chaplain, Mr Fletcher, another minister of some kind who spoke Spanish, and in one of the sloops a mysterious Mr Doughty. When an expedition of consequence was on hand, the Spanish party in the Council usually attached to it some second in command whose business was to defeat the object. When Drake went to Cadiz in after years to singe King Philip's beard, he had a colleague sent with him whom he had to lock into his cabin before he could get to his work. Mr Doughty had a similar commission. On this occasion secrecy was impossible. It was generally known that Drake was going to the Pacific through Magellan's Straits, to act afterwards on his own judgment. The Spanish ambassador, now Don Bernardino de Mendoza, in informing Philip of what was intended, advised him to send out orders for the instant sinking of every English ship that appeared on either side the isthmus in West Indian waters. The orders were dispatched, but so impossible it seemed than an English pirate could reach the Pacific, that the attention was confined to the Caribbean Sea, and not a hint of alarm was sent across to the other side.

On November 15, 1577, the *Pelican* and her consort sailed out of Plymouth Sound. The elements frowned on their start. On the second day they were caught in a winter gale. The *Pelican* sprung her mainmast, and they put back to refit and repair. But Drake defied auguries. Before the middle of December all was again in order. The weather mended, and with a fair wind and smooth water they made a fast run across the Bay of Biscay and down the coast to the Cape Verde Islands. There taking up the north-east trades, they struck across the Atlantic, crossed the line, and made the South American continent in latitude 33° South. They passed the mouth of the Plate River, finding to their astonishment fresh water at the ship's side, in fifty-four fathoms. All seemed so far going well, when one morning Mr Doughty's sloop was missing, and he along with her. Drake, it seemed, had already reason to distrust Doughty, and guessed the direction in which he had gone. The *Marigold* was sent in pursuit, and he was overtaken and brought back. To prevent a repetition of such a performance, Drake took the sloop's stores out of her, burnt her, distributed the crew through the other vessels, and took Mr Doughty under his own charge. On June 20 they reached Port St Julian, on the coast of Patagonia. They had been long on the way, and the southern winter had come round, and they had to delay further to make more particular inquiry into Doughty's desertion.

An ominous and strange spectacle met their eyes as they entered the harbour. In that utterly desolate spot a skeleton was hanging on a gallows, the bones picked clean by the vultures. It was one of Magellan's crew who had been executed there for mutiny fifty years before. The same fate was to befall the unhappy Englishman who had been guilty of the same fault. Without the strictest discipline it was impossible for the enterprise to succeed, and Doughty had been guilty of worse than disobedience. We are told briefly that his conduct was found tending to contention, and threatening the success of the voyage. Part he was said to have confessed; part was proved against him. A court was formed out of the crew. He was tried, as near as circumstances allowed, according to English usage. He was found guilty, and was sentenced to die. He made no complaint, or none of which a record is preserved. He asked for the sacrament, which was of course allowed, and Drake himself communicated with him. They then kissed each other, and the unlucky Doughty took leave of his comrades, laid his head on the block, and so ended. His offence can be only guessed; but the suspicious curiosity about his fate which was shown afterwards by Mendoza makes it likely that he was in Spanish pay.

'This done,' writes an eye witness, 'the general made divers speeches to the whole company, persuading us to unity, obedience, and regard of our voyage, and for the better confirmation thereof willed every man the Sunday following to prepare himself to receive the communion as Christian brothers and friends ought to do, which was done in very reverend sort; and so with good contentment every man went about his business.'

You must take this last incident into your conception of Drake's character, think of it how you please.

It was now mid-winter, the stormiest season of the year, and they remained for six weeks in Port St Julian. They burnt the twelve-ton pinnace, as too small for the work they had now before them, and there remained only the *Pelican*, the *Elizabeth*, and the *Marigold*. In cold wild weather they weighed at last, and on August 20 made the opening of Magellan's Straits. The passage is seventy miles long, tortuous and dangerous. They had no charts. The ships' boats led, taking soundings as they advanced. Icy mountains overhung them on either side; heavy snow fell below. They brought up occasionally at an island to rest the men, and let them kill a few seals and penguins to give them fresh food. Everything they saw was new, wild, and wonderful.

Having to feel their way, they were three weeks in getting through. They had counted on reaching the Pacific that the worst of their work was over, and that they could run north at once into warmer and calmer latitudes. The peaceful ocean, when they entered it, proved the stormiest they had ever sailed on. A fierce westerly gale drove them 600 miles to the south-east outside the Horn. It had been supposed, hitherto, that Tierra del Fuego was solid land to the South Pole, and that the Straits were the only communication between the Atlantic and the Pacific. They now learnt the true shape and character of the Western Continent.

In the latitude of Cape Horn a westerly gale blows for ever round the globe; the waves the highest anywhere known. The *Marigold* went down in the tremendous encounter. Captain Winter, in the *Elizabeth*, in the Straits lay for three weeks, lighting fires nightly to show Drake where he was, but no Drake appeared. They had agreed, if separated, to meet on the coast in the latitude of Valparaiso; but Winter was chicken-hearted, and sore 'against the mariners' will,' when the three weeks were out, he sailed away for England. He reported that all the ships were lost but the *Pelican*, and that the *Pelican* was probably lost too.

Drake had believed better of Winter, and had not expected to be so deserted. He had himself taken refuge among the islands which form the Cape, waiting for the spring and milder weather. He used the time in making surveys, and observing the habits of the native Patagonians, whom he found a tough race, going naked amidst ice and snow. The days lengthened, and the sea smoothed at last. He then sailed for

Valparaiso, hoping to meet Winter there, as he had arranged. At Valparaiso there was no Winter, but there was in the port instead a galleon just come in from Peru. The galleon's crew took him for a Spaniard, hoisted their colours and beat their drums. The *Pelican* shot alongside. The English sailors in high spirits leapt on board. A Plymouth lad who could speak Spanish knocked down the first man he met with an 'Abajo, perro!' 'Down, you dog, down!' No life was taken; the crew jumped overboard, and swam ashore. The prize was examined. Four hundred pounds' weight of gold was found in her, besides other plunder.

The galleon being disposed of, Drake and his men pulled ashore to look at the town. The people had all fled. In the church they found a chalice, two cruets, and an altar cloth which were made over to the chaplain to improve his communion furniture. A few pipes of wine and a Greek pilot who knew the way to Lima completed the booty.

Still hoping to find Winter in advance of him, Drake went on next to Tarapaca, where silver from the Andes mines was shipped for Panama. At Tarapaca there was the same unconsciousness of danger. The silver bars lay piled on the quay; the muleteers who had brought them were sleeping peacefully in the sunshine at their side. The muleteers were left to their slumbers. The bars were lifted into the English boats. A train of mules or llamas came in at the moment with a second load as rich as the first. This, too, went into the *Pelican's* hold. The bullion taken at Tarapaca was worth near half a million ducats.

Still there was no news of Winter. Drake began to realise that he was now entirely alone, and had only himself and his own crew to depend on. There was nothing to do but to go through with it, danger adding to the interest. Arica was the next point visited. Half a hundred blocks of silver were picked up at Arica. After Arica came Lima, the chief depôt of all, where the grandest haul was looked for. At Lima, alas! they were just too late. Twelve hulks lay anchored there. The sails were unbent, the men were ashore. They contained nothing but some chests of reals and a few bales of silk and linen. But a thirteenth, called the *Cacafuego*, had sailed a few days before for the isthmus, with the whole produce of the Lima mines for the season. Her ballast was silver, her cargo gold and emeralds and rubies.

Drake deliberately cut the cables of the ships in the Roads, that they might drive ashore and be unable to follow him. The *Pelican* spread her wings, every feather of them, and sped away in pursuit. He would know the *Cacafuego*, so he learnt at Lima, by the peculiar cut of her sails. The first man who caught sight of her was promised a gold chain for his reward. A sail was seen on the second day. It was not the chase, but it was worth stopping for. Eighty pounds' weight of gold was found, and a great gold crucifix, set with emeralds said to be as large as pigeon's eggs. They took the kernel. They left the shell. We learn from the Spanish accounts that the Viceroy of Lima, as soon as he recovered from his astonishment, dispatched ships in pursuit. They came up with the last plundered vessel, heard tales of the rovers' strength, and went back for a larger force. The *Pelican* meanwhile went along upon her course for 800 miles. At length, when in the latitude of Quito and close under the shore, the *Cacafuego's* peculiar sails were sighted, and the gold chain was claimed. There she was, going lazily along a few miles ahead. Care was needed in approaching her. If she guessed the *Pelican's* character, she would run in upon the land and they would lose her. It was afternoon. The sun was still above the horizon, and Drake meant to wait till night, when the breeze would be off the shore, as in the tropics it always is.

The *Pelican* sailed two feet to the *Cacafuego's* one. Drake filled his empty wine skins with water and trailed them astern to stop his way. The chase supposed that she was followed by some heavy-loaded trader, and, wishing for company on a lonely voyage, she slackened sail and waited for him to come up. At length the sun went down into the ocean, the rosy light faded from off the snows of the Andes; and when both ships had become invisible from the shore, the skins were hauled in, the night wind rose, and the water began to ripple under the *Pelican's* bows. The *Cacafuego* was swiftly overtaken, and when within a cable's length a voice hailed her to put her head into the wind. The Spanish commander, not undertstanding so strange an order, held on his course. A broadside brought down his mainyard, and a flight of arrows rattled on his deck. He was himself wounded. In a few minutes he was a prisoner, and the *Cacafuego* and her precious freight were in the corsair's power. The wreck was cut away; the ship was cleared; a prize crew was put on board. Both vessels turned their heads to the sea.

At daybreak no land was to be seen, and the examination of the prize began. The full value was never acknowledged. The invoice, if there was one, was destroyed. The accurate figures were known only to Drake and Queen Elizabeth. A published schedule acknowledged to twenty tons of silver bullion, thirteen chests of silver coins, and a hundredweight of gold, but there were gold nuggets besides in indefinite quantity, and 'a great store' of pearls, emeralds, and diamonds. The Spanish government proved a loss of a million and a half ducats, excluding what belonged to private persons.

Drake we are told was greatly satisfied. He thought it prudent to stay in the neighbourhood no longer than necessary. He went north with all sail set, taking his prize with him. The master, San Juan de Anton, was removed on board the *Pelican* to have his wound attended to. He remained as Drake's guest for a week, and sent in a report of what he observed to the Spanish government. One at least of Drake's party spoke excellent Spanish. This person took San Juan over the ship. She showed signs, San Juan said, of rough service, but was still in fine condition, with ample arms, spare rope, mattocks, carpenters' tools of all descriptions. There were eighty-five men on board all told, fifty of them men-of-war, the rest young fellows, ship-boys and the like. Drake himself was treated with great reverence; a sentinel stood always at his cabin door. He dined alone with music.

No mystery was made of the *Pelican's* exploits. The chaplain showed San Juan the crucifix set with emeralds. San Juan asked Drake how he meant to go home. Drake showed him a globe with three courses traced on it. There was the way that he had come, there was the way by China and the Cape of Good Hope, and there was a third way which he did not explain. San Juan asked if Spain and England were at war. Drake said he had a commission from the Queen. His captures were for her, not for himself. He added afterwards that the Viceroy of Mexico had robbed him and his kinsman, and he was making good his losses.

Then, touching the point of the sore, he said, 'I know the Viceroy will send for thee to inform himself of my proceedings. Tell him he shall do well to put no more Englishmen to death, and to spare those he has in his hands. This is how an English gentleman keeps his word.'

After a week's detention San Juan and his men were restored to the empty *Cacafuego*, and allowed to go. On their way back they fell in with two cruisers sent in pursuit from Lima, reinforced by a third from Panama. They were now fully armed; they went in chase, and according to their own account came up with the *Pelican*. But, like Lope de Vega, they seemed to have been terrified at Drake. They confessed that they dared not attack him, and again went back for more assistance. The Viceroy abused them as cowards, arrested the officers, dispatched others again with peremptory orders to seize Drake; but by that time their questionable visitor had flown.

A dispatch went instantly across the Atlantic to Philip. One squadron was sent off from Cadiz to watch the Straits of Magellan, and another to patrol the Caribbean Sea. It was thought that Drake's third way was no seaway at all, that he meant to leave the *Pelican* at Darien, carry his plunder over the mountains, and build a ship at Honduras to take him home. His real idea was that he might hit off the passage to the north of which Frobisher and Davis thought they had found the eastern entrance. He stood on towards California, picking up an occasional straggler in the China trade, with silk, porcelain, gold, and emeralds. Fresh water was a necessity. He put in at Guatulco for it, and his proceedings were humorously prompt. The alcaldes at Guatulco were in session trying a batch of blacks. An English boat's crew appeared in court, tied the alcaldes hand and foot, and carried them off to the *Pelican*, there to remain as hostages till the water-casks were filled.

North again he fell in with a galleon carrying out a new governor to the Philippines. The governor was relieved of his boxes and his jewels, and then, says one of the party, 'Our General, thinking himself in respect of his private injuries received from the Spaniards, as also their contempt and indignities offered to our country and Prince, sufficiently satisfied and revenged, and supposing Her Majesty would rest contented with this service, began to consider the best way home.' The first necessity was a complete overhaul of the ship. Before the days of copper sheathing weeds grew thick under water. Barnacles formed in clusters, stopping the speed, and sea-worms bored through the planking. Twenty thousand miles lay between the *Pelican* and Plymouth Sound, and Drake was not a man to run idle chances. Still holding his north course till be had left the farthest Spanish settlement far to the south, he put into Canoas Bay in California, laid the *Pelican* ashore, set up forge and workshop, and repaired and re-rigged her with a month's labour from stem to stern. With every rope new set up and new canvas on every yard, he started again on April 16th, 1579, and continued up the cost to Oregon.

The air grew cold though it was summer. The men felt it from having been so long in the tropics, and dropped out of health. There was still no sign of a passage. If passage there was, Drake perceived that it must be of enormous length. Magellan's Straits, he guessed, would be watched for him, so he decided on the route by the Cape of Good Hope. In the Philippine ship he had found a chart of the Indian Archipelago. With the help of this and his own skill he hoped to find his way. He went down again to California, landed there, made acquaintance with the local Indians, and took formal possession of the soil in the name of Elizabeth I whose officer he was. Avoiding the course from Mexico to the Philippines, he made a direct course to the

Moluccas, and brought up again at the Island of Celebes. Here the *Pelican* was a second time docked and scraped. The crew had a month's rest among the fireflies and vampires of the tropical forest. Leaving Celebes, they entered on the most perilous part of the whole voyage. They wound their way among coral reefs and low islands scarcely visible above the water-line. In their chart the only outlet marked into the Indian Ocean was by the Straits of Malacca. But Drake guessed rightly that there must be some nearer opening, and felt his way looking for it along the coast of Java.

In spite of all his care, he was once on the edge of destruction. One evening as night was closing in a grating sound was heard under the *Pelican's* keel. In another moment she was hard and fast on a reef. The breeze was light and the water smooth, or the world would have heard no more of Francis Drake. She lay immovable till daybreak. At dawn the position was seen not to be entirely desperate. Drake himself showed all the qualities of a great commander. Cannon were thrown over and cargo that was not needed. In the afternoon, the wind changing, the lightened vessel lifted off the rocks and was saved. The hull was uninjured, thanks to the Californian repairs. All on board had behaved well with the one exception of Mr Fletcher, the chaplain. Mr Fletcher, instead of working like a man, had whined about Divine retribution for the execution of Doughty.

For the moment Drake passed it over. A few days after, they passed out through the Straits of Sunda where they met the great ocean swell, Homer's μέγα κυμα Θαλασσηδ,[1] and they knew then that all was well.

There was now time to call Mr Fletcher to account. It was no business of the chaplain to discourage and dispirit men in a moment of danger, and a court was formed to sit upon him. An English captain on his own deck represents the sovereign, and is head of Church as well as State. Mr Fletcher was brought to the forecastle, where Drake, sitting on a sea-chest with a pair of *pantoufles* in his hand, pronounced him cut off from the Church of God, and left him chained by the leg to a ring-bolt to repent of his cowardice.

In the general good-humour punishment could not be of long duration. The next day the chaplain had his absolution, and returned to his berth and his duty. The *Pelican* met with no more adventures. Sweeping in fine clear weather round the Cape of Good Hope, she

---

1. The mighty billow of the sea.

touched once for water at Sierra Leone, and finally sailed in triumph into Plymouth Harbour, where she had been long given up for lost, having traced the first furrow round the globe. Winter had come home eighteen months before, but could report nothing. The news of the doings on the American coast had reached England through Madrid. The Spanish ambassador had been furious. It was known that Spanish squadrons had been sent in search. Complications would arise if Drake brought his plunder home, and timid politicians hoped that he was at the bottom of the sea. But here he was, actually arrived with a monarch's ransom in his hold.

English sympathy with an extraordinary exploit is irresistible. Shouts of applause rang through the country, and Elizabeth, every bit of her an Englishwoman, felt with her subjects. She sent for Drake to London, made him tell his story over and over again, and was never weary of listening to him. As to injury to Spain, Philip had lighted a fresh insurrection in Ireland, which had cost her dearly in lives and money. For Philip to demand compensation of England on the score of justice was a thing to make the gods laugh.

So thought the Queen. So unfortunately did not think some members of her Council, Lord Burghley among them. Mendoza was determined that Drake should be punished and the spoils disgorged, or else that he would force Elizabeth upon the world as the confessed protectress of piracy. Burghley thought that, as things stood, some satisfaction (or the form of it) would have to be made.

Elizabeth hated paying back as heartily as Falstaff, nor had she the least intention of throwing to the wolves a gallant Englishman, with whose achievements the world was ringing. She was obliged to allow the treasure to be registered by a responsible official, but for all that she meant to keep the bulk of the spoils. She meant, too, that Drake and his brave crew should not go unrewarded. Drake himself should have ten thousand pounds at least.

Her action was eminently characteristic of her. On the score of real justice there was no doubt at all how matters stood between herself and Philip, who had tried to dethrone her.

The *Pelican* lay still at Plymouth with the bullion and jewels untouched. She directed that it should be landed and scheduled. She trusted the business to Edmund Tremayne, of Collacombe, a neighbouring magistrate, on whom she could depend. She told him not to be too inquisitive, and allowed Drake to go back and arrange the cargo before the examination was made. Let me now read you a letter from Tremayne himself to Sir Francis Walsingham:

'To give you some understanding how I have proceeded with Mr Drake: I have at no time entered into the account to know more of the value of the treasure than he made me accquainted with; and to say truth I persuaded him to impart to me no more than need, for so I saw him commanded in Her Majesty's behalf that he should reveal the certainty to no man living. I have only taken notice of so much as he *has* revealed, and the same I have seen to be weighed, registered, and packed. And to observe Her Majesty's commands for the ten thousand pounds, we agreed he should take it out of the portion that was landed secretly, and to remove the same out of the place before my son Henry and I should come to the weighing and registering of what was left; and so it was done, and no creature living by me made privy to it but himself; and myself no privier to it than as you may perceive by this.

'I see nothing to charge Mr Drake further than he is inclined to charge himself, and withal I must say he is inclined to advance the value to be delivered to Her Majesty, and seeking in general to recompense all men that have been in the case dealers with him. As I dare take an oath, he will rather diminish his own portion than leave any of them unsatisfied. And for his mariners and followers I have seen here as eye-witness, and have heard with my ears, such certain signs of goodwill as I cannot yet see that any of them will leave his company. The whole course of his voyage hath shown him to be of great valour; but my hap has been to see some particulars, and namely in this discharge of his company, as doth assure me that he is a man of great government, and that by the rules of God and His book, so as proceeding on such foundation his doings cannot but prosper.'

The result of it all was that deductions were made from the capture equivalent to the property which Drake and Hawkins held themselves to have been treacherously plundered at San Juan de Ulloa, with perhaps other liberal allowances for the cost of recovery. An account on part of what remained was then given to Mendoza. It was not returned to him or to Philip, but was laid up in the Tower till the final settlement of Philip's and the Queen's claims on each other – the cost, for one thing, of the rebellion in Ireland. Commissioners met and argued and sat on ineffectually till the Armada came and the discussion ended, and the talk of restitution was over.

Meanwhile, opinion varied about Drake's own doings as it has varied since. Elizabeth listened spellbound to his adventures, sent for him to London again, and walked with him publicly about the park and gardens. She gave him a second ten thousand pounds. The *Pelican* was sent round to Deptford; a royal banquet was held on board, Elizabeth attended and Drake was knighted. Mendoza clamoured for the treasure in the Tower to be given up to him; Walsingham wished to give it to the Prince of Orange; Leicester and his party in the Council, who had helped to fit Drake out, thought it ought to be divided among themselves. Elizabeth thought it should be kept as a captured pawn in the game, and so in fact it remained after the deductions which we have seen had been made.

Drake was lavish of his presents. He presented the Queen with a diamond cross and a coronet set with splendid emeralds. He gave Bromley, the Lord Chancellor, 800 dollars' worth of silver plate, and as much more to other members of the Council. The Queen wore her coronet on New Year's Day; the Chancellor was content to decorate his sideboard at the cost of the Catholic King. Burghley and Sussex declined the temptation.

Burgley lived to see better into Drake's value. Meanwhile, what now are we, looking back over our history, to say of these things – the Channel privateering; the seizure of Alva's army money; the sharp practice of Hawkins with the Queen of Scots and King Philip; or this amazing performance of Sir Francis Drake in a vessel no larger than a second-rate yacht of a modern noble lord?

Resolution, daring, professional skill, all historians allow to these men; but they regard what they did as piracy. So cried the Catholics who wished Elizabeth's ruin; so cried Lope de Vega and King Philip. In milder language the modern philosopher repeats the unfavourable verdict, rejoices that he lives in an age when such doings are impossible, and apologises for the excesses of an imperfect age. May I remind the philosopher that if he and his friends were liable when they went abroad to be snapped by the familiars of the Inquisition, whipped, burnt alive, or sent to the galleys, he would perhaps think more leniently of any measures by which that institution and its masters might be induced to treat philosophers with greater consideration?

Again, remember Dr Johnson's warning, Beware of cant. In that intensely serious century men were more occupied with the realities than the forms of things. By encouraging rebellion in England and Ireland, by burning so many scores of English seamen and merchants at Seville, the King of Spain had given Elizabeth a hundred occasions for declaring war against him. Situated as she was, she could not *begin* a war on such a quarrel. She had to use such resources as she had, and of these resources the best was a splendid race of men who were not afraid to do for her at their own risk what commissioned officers would and might have justly done had formal war been declared. Men who defeated the national enemy with materials conquered from himself, who were devoted enough to dispense with the personal security which the sovereign's commission would have extended to prisoners of war, and face the certainty of being hanged if they were taken. The common sense of Europe saw through the form to the substance which lay below it, and the instinct of their countrymen gave them a place among the fighting heroes of England, from which I do not think they will be deposed by the eventual verdict of history.

Parties in the State

On December 21, 1585, a remarkable scene took place in the English House of Commons. The Prince of Orange, after many attempts had failed, had been successfully disposed of in the Low Countries. A fresh conspiracy had just been discovered for a Catholic insurrection in England, supported by a foreign invasion; the object of which was to dethrone Elizabeth and to give her crown to Mary Stuart. The Duke of Alva, at the time of the Ridolfi plot, had pointed out as a desirable preliminary, if the invasion was to succeed, the assassination of the Queen of England. The succession being undecided, he had calculated that the confusion would paralyse resistance, and the notorious favour with which Mary Stuart's pretensions were regarded by a considerable English party would ensure her an easy victory were Elizabeth once removed. But this was an indispensible condition. It had become clear at last that so long as Elizabeth was alive Philip would not willingly sanction the landing of a Spanish army on English shores.

Thus, among the more ardent Catholics, especially the refugees at the seminary at Rheims, a crown in heaven was held out to any spiritual knight-errant who would remove the obstacle. The enterprise itself was not a difficult one. Elizabeth was aware of her danger, but she was personally fearless. She refused to distrust the Catholics. She admitted anyone to her presence who desired a private interview. Dr Parry, a Member of Parliament, primed by encouragement from the Cardinal of Como and the Vatican, had undertaken to risk his life to win the glorious prize. He introduced himself into the palace, properly provided with arms. He professed to have information of importance to give. The Queen received him. Once he was with her in the palace garden, he was on the point of killing her, when he was awed, as he said, by the likeness to her father. Parry was discovered and hanged. When there were so many aspirants for the honour of removing Jezebel, and Jezebel was so easy of approach, it was felt that one might at least succeed; and the loyal part of the nation, led by Lord Burghley, formed themselves into an association to protect a life so vital to them.

The subscribers bound themselves to pursue to the death all manner of persons who should attempt or consent to anything to the harm of Her Majesty's person; never to allow or submit to any pretended successor by whom or for whom such detestable act should be attempted or committed; but to pursue such persons to death and act the utmost revenge upon them.

The bond in its first form implied a condition of things in which order would have ceased to exist. The lawyers vehemently objected; yet so passionate was public feeling that it was signed throughout the kingdom, and Parliament was called to pass an Act which would secure the same object. Mary Stuart, at any rate, was not to benefit by the crimes either of herself or her admirers. It was provided that if the realm was invaded, or a rebellion instigated by or for any one pretending a title to the crown after the Queen's death, such a pretender should be disqualified for ever. In the event of the Queen's assassination the government was to devolve on a Committee of Peers and Privy Councillors, who were to examine the particulars of the murder and execute the perpetrators and their accomplices; while, with a significant allusion, all Jesuits and seminary priests were required to leave the country instantly, under pain of death.

The House of Commons was heaving with emotion when the Act was sent up to the Peers. To give expression to their feelings Sir Christopher Hatton proposed that before they separated they should join him in a prayer for the Queen's preservation. The 400 members all rose, and knelt on the floor of the House, repeating Hatton's words after him, sentence by sentence.

Jesuits and seminary priests! Attempts have been made to justify the conspiracies against Elizabeth from what is called the persecution of the innocent enthusiasts who came from Rheims to preach the Catholic faith to the English people. Popular writers and speakers dwell on the executions of Campion and his friends, and these martyred saints have been lately canonised. Their mission, it is said, was purely religious. Was it so? The chief article in the religion which they came to teach was the duty of obedience to the Pope, who had excommunicated the Queen, had absolved her subjects from their allegiance, and, by a relaxation of the Bull, had permitted them to pretend to loyalty *ad illud tempus*, till a Catholic army of deliverance should arrive. A Pope had

85

sent a legate to Ireland, and was at that moment stirring up a bloody insurrection there.

But what these seminary priests were, and what their object was, will best appear from an account of the condition of England, drawn up for the use of the Pope and Philip, by Father Parsons, who was himself head of the mission. The date of it is 1585, almost simultaneous with the scene in Parliament which I have just been describing. The English refugees, from Cardinal Pole downwards, had been the most active and passionate preachers of a Catholic crusade against England. They failed, but they have revenged themselves in history. Pole, Sanders, Allen, and Parsons have coloured what we suppose ourselves to know of Henry VIII and Elizabeth. What I am about to read to you does not differ essentially from what we have already heard from these persons; but it is new, and, being intended for practical guidance, is complete in its way. It comes from the Spanish archives, and it is not therefore open to suspicion. Parsons, as you know, was a Fellow of Balliol before his conversion; Allen was a Fellow of Oriel, and Sanders of New College, Oxford.

Parsons describes his statement as a 'brief note on the present condition of England,' from which may be inferred the ease and opportuneness of the holy enterprise. 'England,' he says, 'contains fifty-two counties, of which forty are well inclined to the Catholic faith. Heretics in these are few, and are hated by all ranks. The remaining twelve are infected more or less, but even in these the Catholics are in the majority. Divide England into three parts; two-thirds at least are Catholic at heart, though many conceal their convictions in fear of the Queen. English Catholics are of two sorts – one which makes an open profession regardless of consequences, the other believing at the bottom, but unwilling to risk life or fortune, and so submitting outwardly to the heretic laws, but as eager as the Catholic confessors for redemption from slavery.

'The Queen and her party,' he goes on, 'more fear these secret Catholics than those who wear their colours openly. The latter they can fine, disarm, and make innocuous. The others, being outwardly compliant, cannot be touched, nor can any precaution be taken against their rising when the day of divine vengeance shall arrive.

'The counties specially Catholic are the most warlike and contain harbours and other conveniences for the landing of an invading army. The north towards the Scotch border has been trained in constant fighting. The Scotch nobles on the other side are Catholic and will lend their help. So will all Wales.

'The inhabitants of the midland and southern provinces, where the taint is deepest, are indolent and cowardly, and do not know what war means. The towns are more corrupt than the Country districts. But the strength of England does not lie, as on the continent, in towns and cities. The town population are merchants and craftsmen, rarely or never nobles or magnates.

'The nobility, who have the real power, reside with their retinues in castles scattered over the land. The wealthy yeomen are strong and honest, all attached to the ancient faith, and may be counted on when an attempt is made for the restoration of it. The knights and gentry are generally well affected also, and will be well to the front. Many of their sons are being now educated in our seminaries. Some are in exile, but all, whether at home or abroad, will be active on our side.

'Of the great peers, marquises, earls, viscounts, and barons, part are with us, part against us. But the latter sort are new creations, whom the Queen has promoted either for heresy or as her personal lovers, and therefore universally abhorred.

'The premier peer of the old stock is the Earl of Arundel, son and heir of the late Duke of Norfolk, whom she has imprisoned because he tried to escape out of the realm. This earl is entirely Catholic, as well as his brothers and kinsmen; and they have powerful vassals who are eager to revenge the injury of their lord. The Earl of Northumberland and his brothers are Catholics. They too have family wrongs to repay, their father having been this year murdered in the Tower, and they have placed themselves at my disposal. The Earl of Worcester and his heir hate heresy, and are devoted to us with all their dependents. The Earls of Cumberland and Southampton and Viscount Montague are faithful, and have a large following. Besides these we have many of the barons – Dacre, Morley, Vaux, Windsor, Wharton, Lovelace, Stourton, and others besides. The Earl of Westmorland, with Lord Paget and Sir Francis Englefield, who reside abroad, have been incredibly earnest in promoting our enterprise. With such support, it is impossible that we can fail. These lords and gentlemen, when they see efficient help coming to them, will certainly rise, and for the following reasons:

'1. Because some of the principals among them have given me their promise.

'2. Because, on hearing that Pope Pius intended to excommunicate and depose the Queen sixteen years ago, many Catholics did rise. They only failed because no support was sent them, and the Pope's sentence had not at that time been actually published. Now, when the Pope has spoken and help is certain, there is not a doubt how they will act.

'3. Because the Catholics are now much more numerous, and have received daily instruction in their religion from our priests. There is now no orthodox Catholic in the whole realm who supposes that he is any longer bound in conscience to obey the Queen. Books for the occasion have been written and published by us, in which we prove that it is not only lawful for Catholics, but their positive duty, to fight against the Queen and heresy when the Pope bids them; and these books are so greedily read among them that when the time comes they are certain to take arms.

'4. The Catholics in these late years have shown their real feeling in the martyrdoms of priests and laymen, and in attempts made by several of them against the person and state of the Queen. Various Catholics have tried to kill her at the risk of their own lives, and are still trying.

'5. We have three hundred priests dispersed among the houses of the nobles and honest gentry. Every day we add to their number; and these priests will direct the consciences and actions of the Catholics at the great crisis.

'6. They have been so harried and so worried that they hate the heretics worse than they hate the Turks.

'Should any of them fear the introduction of a Spanish army as dangerous to their national liberties, there is an easy way to satisfy their scruples. Let it be openly declared that the enterprise is undertaken in the name of the Pope and there will be no more hesitation. We have ourselves prepared a book for their instruction, to be issued at the right moment. If his Holiness desires to see it we will have it translated into Latin for his use.

'Before the enterprise is undertaken the sentence of excommunication and deposition ought to be reissued, with special clauses.

'It must be published in all adjoining Catholic countries; all Catholic kings and princes must be admonished to forbid every description of intercourse with the pretended Queen and her heretic subjects, and themselves especially to make or observe no treaties with her, to send no embassies to her and admit none; to render no help to her of any sort or kind.

'Besides those who will be our friends for religion's sake we shall have others with us – neturals or heretics of milder sort, or atheists, with whom England now abounds, who will join us in the interest of the Queen of Scots. Among them are the Marquis of Winchester, the Earls of Shrewsbury, Derby, Oxford, Rutland, and several other peers. The

Queen of Scots herself will be of infinite assistance to us in securing these. She knows who are her secret friends. She has been able so far, and we trust will always be able, to communicate with them. She will see that they are ready at the right time. She has often written to me to say that she hopes that she will be able to escape when the time comes. In her last letter she urges me to be vehement with his Holiness in pushing on the enterprise, and bids him have no concern for her own safety. She believes that she can take care for herself. If not, she says she will lose her life willingly in a cause so sacred.

'The enemies that we shall have to deal with are the more determined heretics whom we call Puritans, and certain creatures of the Queen, the Earls of Leicester and Huntingdon, and a few others. They will have an advantage in the money in the Treasury, the public arms and stores, and the army and navy, but none of them have ever seen a camp. The leaders have been nuzzled in love-making and Court pleasures, and they will all fly at the first shock of war. They have not a man who can command in the field. In the whole realm there are but two fortresses which could stand a three days' siege. The people are enervated by long peace, and, except a few who have served with the heretics in Flanders, cannot bear their arms. Of those few some are dead and some have deserted to the Prince of Parma, a clear proof of the real disposition to revolt. There is abundance of food and cattle in the country, all of which will be at our service and cannot be kept from us. Everywhere there are safe and roomy harbours, almost all undefended. An invading force can be landed with ease, and there will be no lack of local pilots. Fifteen thousand trained soldiers will be sufficient, aided by the Catholic English, though, of course, the larger the force, particularly if it includes cavalry, the quicker the work will be done and the less the expense. Practically there will be nothing to overcome save an unwarlike and undisciplined mob.

'Sixteen times England has been invaded. Twice only the native race have repelled the attacking force. They have been defeated on every other occasion, and with a cause so holy and just as ours we need not fear to fail. The expenses shall be repaid to his Holiness and the Catholic King out of the property of the heretics and the Protestant clergy. There will be ample in these resources to compensate all who give us their hand. But the work must be done promptly. Delay will be infinitely dangerous. If we put off, as we have done hitherto, the Catholics will be tired out and reduced in numbers and strength. The nobles and priests now in exile, and able to be of such service, will break down in poverty. The Queen of Scots may be executed or die a natural death, or something may happen to the Catholic King or his Holiness. The Queen of England may herself die, a heretic government may be reconstructed under a heretic successor, the young Scotch King or some other, and our case will then be desperate; whereas if we can prevent this and save the Queen of Scots there will be good hope of converting her son and reducing the whole island to the obedience of the faith. Now is the moment. The French government cannot interfere. The Duke of Guise will help us for the sake of the faith and for his kinswoman. The Turks are quiet. The Church was never stronger or more united. Part of Italy is under the Catholic King; the rest is in league with his Holiness. The revolt in the Low Countries is all but crushed. The sea provinces are on the point of surrendering. If they give up the contest their harbours will be at our service for the invasion. If not, the way to conquer them is to conquer England.

'I need not urge how much it imports his Holiness to undertake this glorious work. He, supremely wise as he is, knows that from this Jezebel and her supporters come all the perils which disturb the Christian world. He knows that heretical depravity and all other miseries can only end when this woman is chastised. Reverence for his Holiness and love for my afflicted country force me to speak. I submit to his most holy judgement myself and my advice.'

The most ardent Catholic apologist will hardly maintain, in the face of this document, that the English Jesuits and seminary priests were the innocent missionaries of religion which the modern enemies of Elizabeth's government describe them. Father Parsons, the writer of it, was himself the leader and director of the Jesuit mission, and cannot be supposed to have misrepresented the purpose for which they had been sent over. The point of special interest is the account which he gives of the state of parties and general feeling in the English people. Was there that wide disposition to welcome an invading army in so large a majority of the nation? The question is supposed to have been triumphantly answered three years later, when it is asserted that the difference of creed was forgotten, and Catholics and Protestants fought side by side for the liberties of England.

But, in the first place, the circumstances were changed. The Queen of Scots no longer lived, and the success of the Armada implied a foreign sovereign. But, next, the experiment was not tried. The battle was fought at sea, by a fleet four-fifths of which was composed of

Protestant seamen, fitted out and manned by those zealous people whose fidelity to the Queen Parsons himself admitted. Lord Howard may have been an Anglo-Catholic; Roman Catholic he never was; but he and his brother were the only loyalists in the House of Howard. Arundel and the rest of his kindred were what Parsons claimed for them. It is likely that if the Spanish army had gained a first success, there might have been some who would have behaved as Sir William Stanley did. It is observable that Parsons mentions Leicester and Huntingdon as the only powerful peers on whom the Queen could rely.

The Duke of Alva and his master Philip, both of them distrusted political priests. Political priests, they said, did not understand the facts of things. Theological enthusiasm made them credulous of what they wished. But Father Parsons's estimate was assumed to be true by the letters of Mendoza, the Spanish ambassador in London.

Burghley, Walsingham, Mildmay, Knolles, the elder Bacon, were believing Protestants, and would have had the Queen put herself openly at the head of a Protestant European league. They believed that right and justice were on their side, that their side was God's cause, as they called it, and that God would care for it. Elizabeth had no such complete conviction. She disliked dogmatism, Protestant as well as Catholic. She thought, like Erasmus, that the articles of faith, for which men were so eager to kill one another, were subjects which they knew very little about, and that every man might think what he would on such matters without injury to the commonwealth.

To become 'head of the name' would involve open war with the Catholic powers. War meant war taxes, which more than half her subjects would resent or resist. Religion as she understood it was a development of the law of moral conduct. You could not have two laws in one country, and you could not have two religions; but the outward form mattered comparatively little. The people she ruled over were divided about these forms. They were mainly fools, and if she let them each have chapels and churches of their own, molehills would become mountains, and the congregations would go from arguing into fighting. With Parliament to help her, therefore, she established a liturgy, in which those who wished to find the Mass could hear the Mass, while those who wanted predestination and justification by faith could find it in the Articles. Both could meet under a common roof, and use a common service, if they would only be reasonable.

The system continued for the first eleven years of Elizabeth's reign. No Catholic, she could proudly say, had during that time been molested for his belief. There was a small fine for non-attendance at church, but even this was rarely levied, and by the confession of the Jesuits the Queen's policy was succeeding too well. Sensible men began to see that the differences of religion were not things to quarrel over. The elder generation, who had lived through the Edward and Mary revolutions, were satisfied to be left undisturbed; a new generation was growing up, with new ideas; and so the Church of Rome bestirred itself. Elizabeth was excommunicated.

The cycle began of intrigue and conspiracy, assassination plots, and Jesuit incursions. Punishments had to follow, and in spite of herself Elizabeth was driven into what the Catholics could call religious persecution. Relgious it was not, for the Jesuits were missionaries of treason. But religious it was made to appear. The English gentleman who wished to remain loyal, without forfeiting his faith, was taught to see that a sovereign under the Papal curse had no longer a claim on his allegiance. If he disobeyed the Pope, he had ceased to be a member of the Church of Christ. The Papal party grew in coherence, while, opposed to them as their purpose came in view, the Protestants, who at first had been inclined to Lutheranism, adopted the deeper and sterner creed of Calvin and Geneva. The memories of the Marian cruelties revived again. They saw themselves threatened with a return to stake and fagot. They closed their ranks and resolved to die rather than submit.

A great mistake had been made by Parsons. He could not estimate what he could not understand. He admitted that the inhabitants of the towns were mainly heretic – London, Bristol, Plymouth, and the rest – but he despised them as merchants, craftsmen, mean persons who had no heart to fight in them. Nothing is more remarkable in the history of the sixteenth century than the effect of Calvinism in levelling distinctions of rank and in steeling and ennobling the character of common men. In Scotland, in the Low Countries, in France, there was the same phenomenon. In Scotland, the Kirk was the creation of the preachers and the people, and peasants and workmen dared to stand in the field against belted knights and barons, who had trampled on their fathers for centuries. The artisans of the Low Countries had for twenty years defied the whole power of Spain. The Huguenots were not a fifth part of the French nation, yet defeat could never dishearten them. Again and again they forced Crown and nobles to make terms with them. It was the same in England. The allegiance to their feudal leaders dissolved into a higher obligation to the King of kings, whose elect they believed themselves to be. Election to them was not a theological phantasm, but an enlistment in the army of God. A little flock they might be, but they were a dangerous people to deal with, most of all in the towns on the sea.

The sea was the element of the Reformers. The Popes had no jurisdiction over the winds and waves. Rochelle was the citadel of the Huguenots. The English merchants and mariners had wrongs of their own, perpetually renewed, which fed the bitterness of their indignation. Touch where they would in Spanish ports, the inquisitor's hand was on their ships' crews, and the crews, unless they denied their faith, were handed over to the stake or the galleys. The Calvinists are accused of intolerance. I fancy that even in these humane and enlightened days we should not be very tolerant if the King of Dahomey were to burn every European visitor to his dominions who would not worship Mumbo Jumbo. The Duke of Alva was not very merciful to heretics, but he tried to bridle the zeal of the Holy Office in burning the English seamen. Even Philip himself remonstrated. I am not the least surprised if the English seamen were intolerant. I should be very much surprised if they had not been. The Queen could not protect them. They had to protect themselves as they could, and make Spanish vessels, when they could catch them, pay for the iniquities of their rulers.

With such a temper rising on both sides, Elizabeth's policy had but a poor chance. She still hoped that the better sense of mankind would keep the doctrinal enthusiasts in order. Elizabeth wished her subjects would be content to live together in unity of spirit, if not in unity of theory, in the bond of peace, not hatred, in righteousness of life, not in orthodoxy preached by stake and gibbet. She was content to wait and to persevere. She refused to declare war. She knew that if the Protestants were crushed in Scotland, in France, and in the Low Countries, her own turn would follow. To protect insurgents avowedly would be to justify insurrection against herself. But what she would not do openly she would do secretly. What she would not do herself she let her subjects do.

Thousands of English volunteers fought in Flanders for the States, and in France for the Huguenots. When the English Treasury was shut to the entreaties of Coligny or William of Orange the London citizens untied their purse-strings. Her friends in Scotland fared ill. They were encouraged by promises. They committed themselves for her sake. They fell one after another – Murray, Morton, Gowrie – into bloody graves. Others took their places and struggled on. The Scotch Reformation was saved. Scotland was not allowed to open its arms to an invading army to strike England across the Border. They cared for their cause as well as for the English Queen, and they had their reward. If they saved her they saved their own country. She too did not lie on a bed of roses. To prevent open war she was exposing her own life to the assassin. A pistol shot or a stab with a dagger might add Elizabeth to the list of victims; yet she went on upon her own policy, and faced in her person her own share of the risk. One thing only she did. If she would not defend her friends and her subjects as Queen of England, she left them free to defend themselves. She allowed traitors to be hanged when they were caught at their work. She allowed the merchants to fit out their privateering fleets, to defend at their own cost the shores of England, and to teach the Spaniards to fear their vengeance.

But how long was all this to last? How long were loyal citizens to feel that they were living over a loaded mine? The Queen might be indifferent to her own danger, but on the Queen's life hung the peace of the whole realm. A stroke of a poniard, a touch of a trigger, and swords would be flying from their scabbards; England might become, like France, one wild scene of anarchy and civil war. No successor had been named. The Queen refused to hear a successor declared. Mary Stuart's hand had been in every plot since she crossed the Border. Twice the House of Commons had petitioned for her execution. Elizabeth would neither touch her life nor allow her hopes of the crown to be taken from her. The Bond of Association was but a remedy of despair, and the Act of Parliament would have passed for little in the tempest which would immediately rise. The agony reached a height when the fatal news came from the Netherlands that there at last assassination had done its work. The Prince of Orange, after many failures, had been finished, and a libel was found in the Palace at Westminster exhorting the ladies of the household to provide a Judith among themselves to rid the world of the English Holofernes.

One part of Elizabeth's subjects, at any rate, were not disposed to sit down in patience under the circumstances. From Spain was to come the army of deliverance for which the Jesuits were so passionately longing. To the Spaniards the Pope was looking for the execution of the Bull of Deposition. Father Parsons had left out of his estimate the Protestant adventurers of London and Plymouth, who, besides their creed and their patriotism, had their private wrongs to revenge. Philip might talk of peace, and perhaps in weariness might seriously wish for it; but between the Englishmen whose life was on the ocean and the

Spanish Inquisition, which had burned so many of them, there was no peace possible. To them, Spain was the natural enemy. Among the daring spirits who had sailed with Drake round the globe, who had waylaid the Spanish treasure ships, and startled the world with their exploits, there was but one wish – for an honest open war. The great galleons were to them no objects of terror. The Spanish naval power seemed to them a 'Colossus stuffed with clouts.' They were Protestants all of them, but their theology was rather practical than speculative. Their quarrel was with the pretence of Catholics to force their creed on others with sword and cannon. The spirit which was working in them was the genius of freedom.

The Reformation at its origin was no introduction of novel heresies. It was a revolt of the laity of Europe against the profligacy and avarice of the clergy. The popes and cardinals, when called to account for abuse of their powers, had behaved precisely as mere corrupt human kings and aristocracies behave. They had intrigued; they had excommunicated; they had set nation against nation, sovereigns against their subjects; they had encouraged assassination; they had made themselves infamous by horrid massacres, and had taught one half of Christendom to hate the other.

I found in the Record Office an unsigned letter of some inspired old sea-dog, written in a bold round hand and addressed to Elizabeth. The ships' companies which in summer served in Philip's men-of-war went in winter in thousands to catch cod on the banks of Newfoundland. 'Give me five vessels,' the writer said, 'and I will go out and sink them all, and the galleons shall rot in Cadiz Harbour for want of hands to sail them. But decide, Madam, and decide quickly. Time flies, and will not return. *The wings of man's life are plumed with the feathers of death.*'

The Queen did not decide. But in spite of herself Elizabeth was driven forward by the tendencies of things. The death of the Prince of Orange left the States without a government. The Prince of Parma was pressing them hard. Without a leader they were lost. They offered themselves to Elizabeth, to be incorporated in the English Empire. They said that if she refused they must either submit to Spain or become provinces of France. The Netherlands, whether Spanish or French, would be equally dangerous to England. The Netherlands once brought back under the Pope, England's turn would come next; while to accept the proposal meant war both with France and Spain too – for France would never allow England again to gain a foot on the Continent. She did not accept. Philip, who was as fond of indirect ways as herself, proposed to quicken her resolution.

The harvest had failed in Galicia, and the population were starving. England grew more corn than she wanted, and, under a special promise that the crews should not be molested, a fleet of corn traders had gone with cargoes of grain to Coruña, Bilbao, and Santander. The King of Spain, on hearing that Elizabeth was treating with the States, issued a sudden order to seize the vessels, confiscate the cargoes, and imprison the men. The order was executed. One English ship only was lucky enough to escape by the adroitness of her commander. The *Primrose*, of London, lay in Bilbao Roads with a captain and fifteen hands. The mayor, on receiving the order, came on board to look over the ship. He then went on shore for a sufficient force to carry out the seizure. After he was gone the captain heard of the fate which was intended for him. The mayor returned with two boatloads of soldiers, stepped up the ladder, touched the captain on the shoulder, and told him he was a prisoner. The Englishmen snatched pike and cutlass, pistol and battleaxe, killed seven or eight of the Spanish boarders, threw the rest overboard, and flung stones on them as they scrambled into their boats. The mayor, who had fallen into the sea, caught a rope and was hauled up when the fight was over. The cable was cut, the sails hoisted, and in a few minutes the *Primrose* was under way for England, with the Mayor of Bilbao below the hatches. No second vessel got away.

If Philip had meant to frighten Elizabeth he could not have taken a worse means of doing it, for he had exasperated that particular part of the English propulation which was least afraid of him. He had broken faith besides, and had seized some hundreds of merchants and sailors who had gone merely to relieve Spanish distress. Elizabeth, as usual, would not act herself. She sent no ships from her own navy to demand reparation; but she gave the adventurers a free hand.

The London and Plymouth citizens determined to read Spain a lesson which should make an impression. They had the worst fears for the fate of the prisoners; but if they could not save, they could avenge them. Sir Francis Drake, who wished for nothing better than to be at work again, volunteered his services, and a fleet was collected at Plymouth of twenty-five sail, every one of them fitted out by private enterprise. Of seamen and soldiers there were between two and three thousand. Drake's name was worth an army. The cost was to be recovered out of the expedition; the Spaniards were to be made to pay for it; but how or when was left to Drake's judgment. This time there was no second in command sent by the friends of Spain to hang upon his arm. By universal consent he had the absolute command. His instructions were merely to inquire at Spanish ports into the meaning of the arrest. Beyond that he was left to go where he pleased and do what he pleased on his own responsibility. The Queen said frankly that if it proved convenient she would disown him. Drake had no objection to being disowned, so he could teach the Spaniards to be more careful how they handled Englishmen. What came of it will be the subject of the next lecture.

The Great
Expedition to the
West Indies

Queen Elizabeth and her brother-in-law of Spain were reluctant champions of opposing principles. In themselves they had no wish to quarrel, but each was driven forward by fate and circumstance – Philip by the genius of the Catholic religion, Elizabeth by the enthusiasts for freedom and by the advice of statesmen who saw no safety for her except in daring. Both wished for peace, but both were compelled to yield to their subjects' eagerness. Philip had to threaten England with invasion; Elizabeth had to show Philip that England had a long arm, which Spanish wisdom would do well to fear. It was a singular position. Philip had outraged orthodoxy and dared the anger of Rome by maintaining an ambassador at Elizabeth's Court after her excommunication. He had laboured for a reconciliation with a sincerity which his secret letters make it impossible to doubt. He had condescended even to sue for it, in spite of Drake and the voyage of the *Pelican*; yet he had helped the Pope to set Ireland in a flame. He had encouraged Elizabeth's Catholic subjects in conspiracy after conspiracy. Elizabeth had retaliated, though with half a heart, by letting her soldiers volunteer into the service of the revolted Netherlands, by permitting English privateers to plunder the Spanish colonies, seize the treasure ships, and revenge their own wrongs. Each, perhaps, had wished to show the other what an open war would cost them both, and each drew back when war appeared inevitable.

Events went their way. Holland and Zeeland, driven to extremity, had petitioned for union with England; as a counter-stroke and a warning, Philip had arrested the English corn ships and imprisoned the owners and the crews. The safety of the English shores depended on the spirit of the adventurers, and Elizabeth could not afford to check the anger with which the news was received. To accept the offer of the States was war, and war she would not have; but in her usual way she might let her subjects act for themselves, and plead, as Philip pleaded in excuse for the Inquisition, that she could not restrain them. And thus it was that in September 1585, Sir Francis Drake found himself with a fleet of twenty-five privateers and 2,500 men who had volunteered to serve with him under his own command.

The expedition had been fitted out as a private undertaking. Neither officers nor crews had been engaged for the service of the Crown. They received no wages. They were going on their own account to read the King of Spain a necessary lesson and pay their expenses at the King of Spain's cost. Young Protestant England had taken fire. The name of Drake set every Protestant heart burning, and hundreds of gallant gentlemen had pressed to join. A grandson of Burghley had come, and Edward Winter the Admiral's son, and Francis Knolles the Queen's cousin, and Martin Frobisher, and Christopher Carlile. Philip Sidney had wished to make one also in the glory; but Philip Sidney was needed elsewhere. The Queen's consent had been won from her at a bold interval in her shifting moods. The hot fit might pass away, and Burghley sent Drake a hint to be off before her humour changed.

On the morning of September 14 the signal flag was flying from Drake's maintop to up anchor and away. Drake, as he admitted after, 'was not the most assured of Her Majesty's perseverance to let them go forward.' Past Ushant he would be beyond reach of recall. With light winds and calms they drifted across the Bay. They fell in with a few Frenchmen homeward-bound from the Banks, and let them pass uninjured. A large Spanish ship which they met next day, loaded with excellent fresh salt fish, was counted lawful prize. The fish was new and good, and was distributed through the fleet. Standing leisurely on, they cleared Finisterre and came up with the Isles of Bayona, at the mouth of Vigo Harbour. They dropped anchor there, and 'it was a great matter and a royal sight to see them.' The Spanish governor, Don Pedro Bemandero, sent off with some astonishment to know who and what they were. Drake answered with a question whether England and Spain were at war, and if not why the English merchants had been arrested.

Don Pedro could but say that he knew of no war, and for the merchants an order had come for their release. For reply Drake landed part of his force on the islands, and Don Pedro found it best to propitiate them with cartloads of wine and fruit. The weather, which had been hitherto fine, showed signs of change. The wind rose, and the sea with it. The anchorage was exposed, and Drake sent Christopher Carlile, with one of his ships and a few pinnaces, up the harbour to look out for better shelter.

Their appearance created a panic in the town. The alarmed inhabitants took to their boats, carrying off their property and their Church plate. Carlile who had a Calvinistic objection to idolatry, took the liberty of detaining part of these treasures. From one boat he took a massive silver cross belonging to the High Church at Vigo; from another an image of Our Lady, which the sailors treated with some indignity. Carlile's report being satisfactory, the whole fleet was brought the next day up the harbour moored above the town. The news had by this time spread into the country. The governor of Galicia came down with all the force which he could collect in a hurry. Perhaps he was in time to save Vigo itself. Perhaps Drake, having other aims in view, did not care to be detained over a smaller object. The governor, at any rate, saw that the English were too strong for him to meddle with. The best that he could look for was to persuade them to go away on the easiest terms. Drake and he met in boats for a parley. Drake wanted water and fresh provisions. He was to be allowed to furnish himself undisturbed. He had secured what he most wanted. He had shown the King of Spain that he was not invulnerable in his own home dominion, and he sailed away unmolested.

Madrid was in consternation. That the English could dare insult the first prince in Europe on the sacred soil of the Peninsula itself seemed like a dream. The Council of State sat for three days considering the meaning of it. Drake's name was already familiar in Spanish ears. It was not conceivable that he had come only to inquire after the arrested ships and seamen. But what could the English Queen be about? Did she know the King of Spain's force? Little England, it was said by some of these councillors, could be swallowed by the King of half the world. The old Admiral Santa Cruz was less confident. He observed that England had many teeth, and that instead of boasting of Spanish greatness it would be better to provide against what she might do with them. Till now the corsairs had appeared only in twos and threes. With such a fleet behind him Drake might go where he pleased. He might be going to the South Seas again. He might take Madeira if he liked, or the Canary Islands. Santa Cruz himself thought he would make for the West Indies and Panama, and advised the sending out there instantly every available ship that they had.

The treasure fleet was Drake's real object. He had information that it would be on its way to Spain by the Cape de Verde Islands, and he had learnt the time when it was to be expected. From Vigo he sailed for the Canaries, looked in at Palma, with 'intention to have taken our pleasure there,' but found the landing dangerous and the town itself not worth the risk. He ran on to the Cape de Verde Islands. He had measured his time too narrowly. The treasure fleet had arrived and had gone. He had missed it by twelve hours, 'the reason,' as he said with a sigh, 'best known to God.' The chance of prize-money was lost, but the political purpose of the expedition could still be completed. The Cape de Verde Islands could not sail away, and a beginning could be made with Sant Iago. Sant Iago was a thriving, well populated town, and down in Drake's book as specially needing notice, some Plymouth sailors having been recently murdered there. Christopher Carlile, always handy and trustworthy, was put on shore with a thousand men to attack the place on the undefended side. The Spanish commander, the bishop, and most of the people fled, as at Vigo, into the mountains with their plate and money. Carlile entered without opposition, and flew St George's cross from the castle as a signal to the fleet. Drake came in, landed the rest of his force, and took possession.

It happened to be November 17 – the anniversary of the Queen's accession – and ships and batteries, dressed out with English flags, celebrated the occasion with salvos of cannon. Houses and magazines were then searched and plundered. Wine was found in large quantities, rich merchandise for the Indian trade, and other valuables. Of gold and silver nothing – it had all been removed. Drake waited for a fortnight, hoping that the Spaniards would treat for the ransom of the city. When they made no sign, he marched twelve miles inland to a village where the governor and the bishop were said to have taken refuge. But the village was found deserted. The Spaniards had gone to the mountains, where it was useless to follow them, and were too proud to bargain. Sant Iago was a beautifully built city, and Drake would perhaps have spared it; but a ship-boy who had strayed was found murdered and barbarously mutilated. The order was given to burn. Houses, magazines, churches, public buildings were turned to ashes, and the work being finished Drake went on, as Santa Cruz expected, for the Spanish West Indies.

The Spaniards were magnificent in all that they did and touched. They built their cities in their new possessions on the most splendid models of the Old World. St Domingo and Carthagena had their castles and cathedrals, palaces, squares, and streets, grand and solid as those at Cadiz and Seville, and raised as enduring monuments of the power and greatness of the Castilian monarchs. To these Drake meant to pay a visit. Beyond them was the Isthmus, where he had made his first fame and fortune, with Panama behind, the depôt of the Indian treasure. So far all had gone well with him. He had taken what he wanted out of Vigo; he had destroyed Sant Iago and had not lost a man. Unfortunately he had now a worse enemy to deal with than Spanish galleons or Spanish garrisons. He was in the heat of the tropics. Yellow fever broke out and spread through the fleet. Of those who caught the infection few recovered, or recovered only to be the wrecks of themselves. It was swift in its work. In a few days more than two hundred had died. But the north-east trade blew merrily. The fleet sped on before it. In eighteen days they were in the Roads at Dominica, the island of brooks and rivers and fruit. Limes and lemons and oranges were not as yet. But there were leaves and roots of the natural growth, known to the Caribs as antidotes to the fever, and the Caribs, when they learnt that the English were the Spaniards' enemies, brought them this precious remedy and taught them the use of it. The ships were washed and ventilated, and the water-casks refilled. The infection seemed to have gone as suddenly as it appeared, and again all was well.

Christmas was kept at St Kitts, which was then uninhabited. A council of war was held to consider what should be done next. St Domingo lay nearest to them. It was the finest of all the Spanish colonial cities. It was the capital of the West Indian government, the great centre of West Indian commerce. In the cathedral, before the high altar, lay Columbus and his brother Diego. In natural wealth no island in the world outrivals Española, where the city stood. A large population had collected there, far away from harm, protected, as they supposed, by the majesty of the mother country, the native inhabitants almost exterminated, themselves undreaming that any enemy could approach them from the ocean, and therefore negligent of defence and enjoying themselves in easy security.

Drake was to give them a new experience and a lesson for the future. On their way across from St Kitts the adventurers overhauled a small vessel bound to the same port as they were. From the crew of this vessel they learnt that the harbour at St Domingo was formed, like so many others in the West Indies, by a long sandspit, acting as a natural breakwater. The entrance was a narrow inlet at the extremity of the spit, and batteries had been mounted there to cover it. To land on the outer side of the sandbank was made impossible by the surf. There was one sheltered point only where boats could go on shore, but this was ten miles distant from the town.

Ten miles was but a morning's march. Drake went in himself in a pinnace, surveyed the landing-place, and satisfied himself of its safety. The plan of attack at Sant Iago was to be exactly repeated. On New Year's Eve Christopher Carlile was again landed with half the force in the fleet. Drake remained with the rest, and prepared to force the entrance of the harbour if Carlile succeeded. Their coming had been seen from the city. The alarm had been given, and the women and children, the money in the treasury, the consecrated plate, movable property of all kinds, were sent off inland as a precaution. Of regular troops there seem to have been none, but in so populous a city there was no difficulty in collecting a respectable force to defend it. The noblemen formed a body of cavalry. The people generally were unused to arms, but they were Spaniards and brave men, and did not mean to leave their homes without a fight for it.

Carlile lay still for the night. He marched at eight in the morning on New Year's Day, advanced leisurely, and at noon found himself in front of the wall. So far he had met no resistance, but a considerable body of horse – gentlemen and their servants chiefly – charged down on him out of the bush and out of the town. He formed into a square to receive them. They came on gallantly, but were received with pike and shot, and after a few attempts gave up and retired. Two gates were in front of Carlile, with a road to each leading through a jungle. At each gate were cannon, and the jungle was lined with musketeers. He divided his men and attacked both together. One party he led in person. The cannon opened on him, and an Englishman next to him was killed. He dashed on, leaving the Spaniards no time to reload, carried the gate at a rush, and cut his way through the streets to the great square. The second division had been equally successful, and St Domingo was theirs except the castle, which was still untaken. Carlile's numbers were too small to occupy a large city. He threw up barricades and fortified himself in the square for the night.

Drake brought the fleet in at daybreak, and landed guns, when the castle surrendered. A messenger – a black boy – was sent to the governor to learn the terms which he was prepared to offer to save the city from pillage. The Spanish officers were smarting with the disgrace. One of them struck the lad through the body with a lance. He ran back bleeding to the English lines and died at Drake's feet. Sir Francis was a dangerous man to provoke. Such doings had to be promptly stopped. In the part of the town which he occupied was a monastery with a number of friars in it. The religious orders, he well knew, were the chief instigators of the policy which was provoking the world. He sent two of these friars with the provost-marshal to the spot where the boy had been struck, promptly hanged them, and then dispatched another to tell the governor that he would hang two more every day at the same place till the officer was punished. The Spaniards had long learnt to call Drake the Draque, the serpent, the devil. They feared that the devil might be a man of his word. The offender was surrendered. It was not enough. Drake insisted that they should do justice on him themselves. The governor found it prudent to comply, and the too hasty officer was executed.

The next point was the ransom of the city. The Spaniards still hesitating, 200 men were told off each morning to burn, while the rest searched the private houses, and palaces, and magazines. Government House was the grandest building in the New World. It was approached by broad flights of marble stairs. Great doors opened on a spacious gallery leading into a great hall, and above the portico hung the arms of Spain – a globe representing the world, a horse leaping upon it, and in the horse's mouth a scroll with the haughty motto, 'Non sufficit orbis.' Palace and scutcheon were levelled into dust by axe and gunpowder, and each day for a month the destruction went on, Drake's demands steadily growing and the unhappy governor vainly pleading impossibility.

Vandalism, atrocity unheard of among civilised nations, dishonour to the Protestant cause, Drake deserving to swing at his own yardarm; so indignant liberalism shrieked, and has not ceased shrieking. Let it be remembered that for fifteen years the Spaniards had been burning English seamen whenever they could catch them. The English nation, the loyal part of it, were replying to the wild pretension by the hands of their own admiral.

It was found in the end that the governor's plea of impossibility was more real than was at first believed. The gold and silver had been really carried off. All else that was valuable had been burnt or taken by the English. The destruction of a city so solidly built was tedious and difficult. Nearly half of it was blown up. The cathedral was spared, perhaps as the resting place of Columbus. Drake had other work before him. After staying a month in undisturbed occupation he agreed to accept 25,000 ducats as a ransom for what was left and sailed away.

It was now February. The hot season was coming on, when the climate would be dangerous. There was still much to do and the time was running short. Panama had to be left for another opportunity. Drake's object was to deal blows which would shake the faith of Europe in the Spanish power. Carthagena stood next to St Domingo among the Spanish West Indian fortresses. The situation was strong. In 1740 Carthagena was able to beat off Vernon and a great English fleet. But Drake's crews were in high health and spirits, and he determined to see what he could do with it. Surprise was no longer to be hoped for. The alarm had spread over the Caribbean Sea.

Drake's name carried terror before it. Every non-combatant – old men, women, and children – had been cleared out before he arrived, but the rest prepared for a smart defence. The harbour at Carthagena was formed, as at St Domingo and Port Royal, by a sandspit. The spit was long, narrow, in places not fifty yards wide, and covered with prickly bush, and along this, as before, it was necessary to advance to reach the city. A trench had been cut across at the neck, and a stiff barricade built and armed with heavy guns; behind this were several hundred musketeers, while the bush was full of Indians with poisoned arrows. Pointed stakes had been driven into the ground along the approaches. Two large galleys, full of men, patrolled inside the bank on the harbour edge, and with these preparations the inhabitants hoped to keep Drake from reaching them. Carlile, as before, was to do the land fighting.

He was set on shore three miles down the spit. The tide is slight in those seas, but he waited till it was out, and advanced along the outer shore at low-water mark. He was thus covered by the bank from the harbour galleys, and their shots passed over him. Two squadrons of horse came out, but could do nothing to him on the broken ground. The English pushed on to the wall, scarcely losing a man. They charged, scaled the parapets, and drove the Spanish infantry back at point of pike. Carlile killed their commander with his own hand. The rest fled after a short struggle, and Drake was master of Carthagena. Here for six weeks he remained. The Spaniards withdrew out of the city, and there were again parleys over the ransom money. Courtesies were exchanged among the officers. Drake entertained the governor and his suite. The governor returned the hospitality and received

Drake and the English captains. Drake demanded 100,000 ducats. The Spaniards offered 30,000, and protested that they could pay no more. The dispute might have lasted longer, but it was cut short by the reappearance of the yellow fever in the fleet, this time in a deadlier form. The Spanish offer was accepted, and Carthagena was left to its owners.

It was time to be off, for the heat was telling, and the men began to drop with appalling rapidity. Nombre de Dios and Panama were near and under their lee, and Drake threw longing eyes on what, if all else had been well, might have proved an easy capture. But on a review of their strength it was found that there were but 700 fit for duty who could be spared for the service, and a council of war decided that a march across the Isthmus with so small a force was too dangerous to be ventured. Enough had been done for glory, enough for the political impression to be made in Europe. The King of Spain had been dared in his own dominions. Three fine Spanish cities had been captured by storm and held to ransom.

In other aspects the success had fallen short of expectation. This time they had taken no *Cacafuego* with a year's produce of the mines in her hold. The plate and coin had been carried off, and the spoils had been in a form not easily turned to value. The expedition had been fitted out by private persons to pay its own cost. The result in money was but £60,000. Forty thousand had to be set aside for expenses. There remained but £20,000 to be shared among the ships' companies. Men and officers had entered, high and low, without wages, on the chance of what they might get. The officers and owners gave a significant demonstration of the spirit in which they had gone about their work. They decided to relinquish their own claims on the ransom paid for Carthagena, and bestow the same on the common seamen, 'wishing it were so much again as would be a sufficient reward for their painful endeavour.'

Thus all were well satisfied, conscious all that they had done their duty to their Queen and country. The adventurers' fleet turned homewards at the beginning of April. What men could do they had achieved. They could not fight against the pestilence of the tropics. For many days the yellow fever did its deadly work among them, and only slowly abated. They were delayed by calms and unfavourable winds. Their water ran short. They had to land again at Cape Antonio, the western point of Cuba, and sink wells to supply themselves. Drake himself, it was observed, worked with spade and bucket, like the meanest person in the whole company, always foremost where toil was to be endured or honour won, the wisest in the devising of enterprises, the calmest in danger, the first to set an example of energy in difficulties, and, above all, the firmest in maintaining order and discipline. The fever slackened as they reached the cooler latitudes. They worked their way up the Bahama Channel, going north to avoid the trades. The French Protestants had been attempting to colonise in Florida. The Spaniards had built a fortress on the coast, to observe their settlements and, as occasion offered, cut Huguenot throats. As he passed by, Drake paid this fortress a visit and wiped it out. Farther north again he was in time to save the remnant of an English settlement, rashly planted there by another brilliant servant of Queen Elizabeth.

Of all the famous Elizabethans Sir Walter Raleigh is the most romantically interesting. His splendid and varied gifts, his chequered fortunes, and his cruel end will embalm his memory in English history. But Raleigh's great accomplishments promised more than they performed. His hand was in everything, but of work successfully completed he had less to show than others far his inferiors, to whom fortune had offered fewer opportunities. His life is a record of undertakings begun in enthusiasm, maintained imperfectly, and failures in the end. Among his other adventures he had sent a colony to Virginia. He had hoped that there was an Indian people crying to be admitted within the charmed circle of Gloriana's subjects. His princes and princesses proved things of air, or mere Indian savages; and of Raleigh there remains nothing in Virginia save the name of the city which is called after him. The starving survivors of his settlement on the Roanoke River were taken on board by Drake's returning squadron and carried home to England, where they all arrived safely, to the glory of God, as our pious ancestors said and meant in unconventional sincerity, on July 28, 1586.

The expedition, as I have said, barely paid its cost. In the shape of wages the officers received nothing, and the crews but a few pounds a man, but there was, perhaps, not one of them who was not better pleased with the honour which he had brought back than if he had come home loaded with doubloons.

Startled Catholic Europe meanwhile rubbed its eyes and began to see that the 'enterprise of England,' as the intended invasion was called, might not be the easy thing which the seminary priests described it. I have often asked my Radical friends what is to be done if out of every hundred enlightened voters two-thirds will give their votes one way, but are afraid to fight, and the remaining third will not only vote but will fight too if the poll goes against them? Which has then the right to rule? I can tell them which will rule. The brave and resolute minority will rule. Plato says that if one man was stronger than all the rest of mankind he would rule all the rest of mankind. It must be so, because there is no appeal. The majority must be prepared to assert their Divine right with their right hands, or it will go the way that other Divine rights have gone before. I will not believe the world to have been so ill-constructed that there are rights which cannot be enforced. It appears to me that the true right to rule in any nation lies with those who are best and bravest, whether their numbers are large or small; and three centuries ago the best and bravest part of this English nation had determined that Pope and Spaniard should be no masters of theirs. Imagination goes for much in such excited times. To the imagination of Europe in the sixteenth century the power of Spain appeared irresistible if she chose to exert it. Heretic Dutchmen might rebel in a remote province, English pirates might take liberties with Spanish traders, but the Prince of Parma was making the Dutchmen feel their master at last. The pirates were but so many wasps, with venom in their stings, but powerless to affect the general tendencies of things. Except to the shrewder eyes of such men as Santa Cruz, the strength of the English at sea had been left out of count in the calculations of the resources of Elizabeth's government.

Suddenly a fleet of these same pirates, sent out, unassisted by their sovereign, by the private impulse of a few individuals, had insulted the soil of Spain herself, sailed into Vigo, pillaged the churches, taken anything that they required, and had gone away unmolested. They had attacked, stormed, burnt, or held to ransom three of Spain's proudest colonial cities, and had come home unfought with. The Catholic conspirators had to recognise that they had a worse enemy to deal with than Puritan controversialists or spoilt Court favourites. The Protestant English mariners had to be encountered on an element which did not bow to popes or princes. It was a revelation to all parties. Elizabeth herself had not expected – perhaps had not wished – so signal a success. War was now looked on as inevitable. The Spanish admirals represented that the national honour required revenge for an injury so open and so insolent. The Pope, who had been long goading the lethargic Philip into action, believed that now at last he would be compelled to move; and even Philip himself, enduring as he was, had been roused to perceive that intrigues and conspiracies would serve his turn no longer.

He must put out his strength in earnest, or his own Spaniards might turn upon him as unworthy of the crown of Isabella. Very reluctantly he allowed the truth to be brought home to him. He had never liked the thought of invading England. If he conquered it, he would not be allowed to keep it. Mary Stuart would have to be made Queen, and Mary Stuart was part French, and might be wholly French.

If the thing was to be done, the Pope, it was clear, ought to pay part of the cost, and this was what the Pope did not intend to do if he could help it. The Pope was flattering himself that Drake's performance would compel Spain to go to war with England whether he assisted or did not. In this matter Philip attempted to undeceive his Holiness. He instructed Olivarez, his ambassador at Rome, to tell the Pope that nothing had yet been done to him by the English which he could not overlook, and unless the Pope offered a handsome contribution he would make peace.

To Philip it was painfully certain that if he invaded and conquered England the English Catholics would insist that he must make Mary Stuart queen. He did not like Mary Stuart. He disapproved of her character. He distrusted her promises. In spite of Jesuits and seminary priests, he believed that she was a Frenchwoman at heart. Yet something he must do for the outraged honour of Castile. He concluded, in his slow way, that he would collect a fleet, the largest and best appointed that had ever floated on the sea. He would send or lead it in person to the English Channel. He would command the situation with an overwhelming force, and then would choose some course which would be convenient to himself. On the whole he was inclined to let Elizabeth continue queen. If she remained obstinate his great fleet would cover the passage of the Prince of Parma's army, and he would then dictate his own terms in London.

Attack on Cadiz

I recollect being told when a boy, on sending in a bad translation of Horace, that I ought to remember that Horace was a man of intelligence and did not write nonsense. The same caution should be borne in mind by students of history. They see certain things done by kings and statesmen which they believe they can interpret by assuming such persons to have been knaves or idiots. Once an explanation given from the baser side of human nature, they assume that it is necessarily the right one, and they make their Horace into a fool without a misgiving that the folly may lie elsewhere. Remarkable men and women have usually had some rational motive for their conduct, which may be discovered, if we look for it with our eyes open.

Nobody has suffered more from bad translators than Elizabeth. The circumstances of Queen Elizabeth's birth, the traditions of her father, the interests of England, and the sentiments of the party who had sustained her claim to the succession, obliged her on coming to the throne to renew the separation from the Papacy. The Church of England was re-established on an Anglican basis, which the rival factions might interpret each in their own way. To allow more than one form of public worship would have led in the heated temper of men's minds to quarrels and civil wars. But conscience might be left free under outward conformity, and those whom the liturgy did not suit might use their own ritual in their private houses. Elizabeth and her wise advisers believed that if her subjects could be kept from fighting and killing one another, and were not exasperated by outward displays of difference, they would learn that righteousness of life was more important than orthodoxy, and to estimate at their real value the rival dogmas of theology. Had time permitted the experiment to have a fair trial, it would perhaps have succeeded, but, unhappily for the Queen and for England, the fire of controversy was still too hot under the ashes.

Protestants and Catholics had been taught to look on one another as enemies of God, and were still reluctant to take each other's hands at the bidding of an Act of Parliament. The more moderate of the Catholic laity saw no difference so great between the English Service and the Mass as to force them to desert the churches where their fathers had worshipped for centuries. They petitioned the Council of Trent for permission to use the English Prayer Book; and had the Council consented, religious dissension would have dissolved at last into an innocent difference of opinion. But the Council and the Pope had determined that there should be no compromise with heresy, and the request was refused, though it was backed by Philip's ambassador in London. The action of the Papacy obliged the Queen to leave the administration in the hands of Protestants, on whose loyalty she could rely. As the struggle with the Reformation spread and deepened she was compelled to assist indirectly the Protestant party in France and Scotland. But she still adhered to her own principle; she refused to put herself at the head of a Protestant League. She took no step without keeping open a line of retreat on a contrary policy. She had Catholics in her Privy Council who were pensioners of Spain. Her household contained Catholics. Her constant effort was to disarm the antagonism of the adherents of the old belief, by admitting them to her confidence, and showing them that one part of her subjects was as dear to her as another.

For ten years she went on struggling. For ten years she was proudly able to say that during all that time no Catholic had suffered for his belief either in purse or person. The advanced section of Catholic clergy was in despair. They saw the consciences of their flocks benumbed and their faith growing lukewarm. They stirred up the rebellion of the North. They persuaded Pius V to force them to a sense of their duties by declaring Elizabeth excommunicated. They sent their missionaries through the English counties to recover sheep that were straying under the sin of submission to a sovereign whom the Pope had deposed. Then had followed the Ridolfi plot, deliberately encouraged by the Pope and Spain, which had compelled the government to tighten the reins. One conspiracy had followed another. Any means were held legitimate to rid the world of an enemy of God. The Queen's character was murdered by the foulest slanders, and daggers were sharpened to murder her person.

The King of Spain had not advised the excommunication, because he knew that he would be expected to execute it, and he had other things to do. When called on to act, he and Alva said that if the English Catholics wanted Spanish help they must do something for themselves. To do the priests justice, they were brave enough. What they did, and how far they had succeeded in making the country disaffected, Father Parsons has told you in the paper which I read to you in a former lecture. Elizabeth refused to take care of herself. She would show no distrust. She would not dismiss the Catholic ladies and gentlemen from the household. She would allow penal laws not to be enforced against Catholics as such. Repeated conspiracies to assassinate her were detected and exposed, but she would have no bodyguard. The utmost that she would do was to allow the Jesuits and seminary priests, who, by Parsons' own acknowledgement, were sowing rebellion, to be banished from the realm, and if they persisted in remaining afterwards, to be treated as traitors. When executions are treated as martydoms, candidates will never be wanting for the crown of glory, and the flame only burnt the hotter. Tyburn and the quartering knife was a horrid business, and Elizabeth sickened over it. She hated the severity which she was compelled to exercise. Her name was defiled with the grossest calumnies. She knew that she might be murdered. For herself she was proudly indifferent; but her death would and must be followed by a furious civil war. She told the Privy Council one day after some stormy scene, that she would come back afterwards and amuse herself with seeing the Queen of Scots making their heads fly.

Philip was weary of it too. He had enough to do in ruling his own dominions without quarrelling for ever with his sister-in-law. He had seen that she had subjects, few or many, who, if he struck, would strike back again. English money and English volunteers were keeping alive the war in the Netherlands. English privateers had plundered his ships, damaged his commerce, and burnt his West Indian cities. The Duke of Alva, while he was alive, and the Prince of Parma, who commanded in the Netherlands in Alva's place, advised peace if peace could be had on reasonable terms. If Elizabeth would consent to withdraw her help from the Netherlands, and would allow the English Catholics the tacit toleration with which her reign had begun, they were of opinion, and Philip was of opinion too, that it would be better to forgive Drake and St Domingo, abandon Mary Stuart and the seminary priests, and meddle no more with English internal politics.

Tired with a condition which was neither war nor peace, tired with hanging traitors and the endless problem of her sister of Scotland, Elizabeth saw no reason for refusing offers which would leave her in

112

peace for the rest of her own life. Philip, it was said, would restore the Mass in the churches in Holland. She might stipulate for such liberty of conscience to the Holland Protestants as she was herself willing to allow the English Catholics. She saw no reason why she should insist on a liberty of public worship which she had herself forbidden at home. She did not see why the Hollanders should be so precise about hearing Mass. She said she would rather hear a thousand Masses herself than have on her conscience the crimes committed for the Mass or against it. She would not have her realm in perpetual torment for Cecil's brothers in Christ.

This was Elizabeth's personal feeling. It could not be openly avowed. The States might then surrender to Philip in despair, and obtain better securities for their political liberties than she was ready to ask for them. They might then join the Spaniards and become her mortal enemies. But she had a high opinion of her own statecraft. Her Catholic friends assured her that, once at peace with Philip, she would be safe from all the world. At this moment accident revealed suddenly another chasm which was opening unsuspected at her feet.

Both Philip and she were really wishing for peace. A treaty of peace between the Catholic King and an excommunicated princess would end the dream of a Catholic revolution in England. If the English peers and gentry saw the censures of the Church set aside so lightly by the most orthodox prince in Europe, Parsons and his friends would preach in vain to them the obligation of rebellion. If this deadly negotiation was to be broken off, a blow must be struck, and struck at once. There was not a moment to be lost.

The enchanted prisoner at Tutbury was the sleeping and waking dream of Catholic chivalry. The brave knight who would slay the dragon, deliver Mary Stuart, and place her on the usurper's throne, would outdo Orlando or St George, and be sung of for ever as the noblest hero who had ever wielded brand or spear. Many a young British heart had thrilled with hope that for him the enterprise was reserved. One of these was a certain Anthony Babington, a gentleman of some fortune in Derbyshire. A seminary priest named Ballard, excited, like the rest, by the need of action, and anxious to prevent the peace, fell in with this Babington, and thought he had found the man for his work. Elizabeth dead and Mary Stuart free, there would be no more talk of peace. A plot was easily formed. Half a dozen gentlemen, five of them belonging to or connected with Elizabeth's own household, were to shoot or stab her and escape in the confusion; Babington was to make a dash on Mary Stuart's prison house and carry her off to some safe place; while Ballard undertook to raise the Catholic peers and have her proclaimed queen. Elizabeth once removed, it was supposed that they would not hesitate. Parma would bring over the Spanish army from Dunkirk. The Protestants would be paralysed. All would be begun and ended in a few weeks or even days. The Catholic religion would be re-established and the hated heresy would be trampled out for ever. Mary Stuart had been consulted and had enthusiastically agreed.

This interesting lady had been lately profuse in her protestations of a desire for reconciliation with her dearest sister. Elizabeth had almost believed her sincere. Sick of the endless trouble with Mary Stuart and her pretensions and schemings, she had intended that the Scotch Queen should be included in the treaty with Philip, with an implied recognition of her right to succeed to the English throne after Elizabeth's death. It had been necessary, however, to ascertain in some way whether her protestations were sincere. A secret watch had been kept over her correspondence, and Babington's letters and her own answers had fallen into Walsingham's hands. There it was all in her own cipher, the key to which had been betrayed by the carelessness of a confederate. The six gentlemen who were to have rewarded Elizabeth's confidence by killing her were easily recognised. They were seized, with Babington and Ballard, when they imagined themselves on the eve of their triumph. Babington flinched and confessed, and they were all hanged. Mary Stuart herself had outworn compassion. Twice already on the discovery of her earlier plots the House of Commons had petitioned for her execution.

For this last piece of treachery she was tried at Fotheringay before a commission of Peers and Privy Councillors. She denied her letters, but her complicity was proved beyond a doubt. Parliament was called, and a third time insisted that the long drama should now be ended and loyal England be allowed to breathe in peace. Elizabeth signed the warrant. France, Spain, any other power in the world would have long since made an end of a competitor so desperate and so incurable. Torn by many feelings – natural pity, dread of the world's opinion – Elizabeth paused before ordering the warrant to be executed. If nothing had been at stake but her own life, she would have left the lady to weave fresh plots and at last, perhaps, to succeed. If the nation's safety required an end to be made with her, she felt it hard that the duty should be thrown on herself. Where were all those eager champions who had signed the Association Bond, who had talked so loudly? Could none of them be found to recollect their oaths and take the law into their own hands?

Her Council, Burghley, and the rest, knowing her disposition and feeling that it was life or death to English security, took the responsibility on themselves. They sent the warrant down to Fotheringay at their own risk, leaving their mistress to deny, if she pleased, that she had meant it to be executed; and the wild career of Mary Stuart ended on the scaffold.

They knew what they were doing immediately. They knew that if treason had a meaning Mary Stuart had brought her fate upon herself. They did not, perhaps, realise the full effects that were to follow, or that with Mary Stuart had vanished the last serious danger of a Catholic insurrection in England; or perhaps they did realise it, and this was what decided them to act.

I cannot dwell on this here. As long as there was a Catholic princess of English blood to succeed to the throne, the allegiance of the Catholics to Elizabeth might have been easily shaken. If she was spared now, many of them would look on her as their future sovereign. To overthrow Elizabeth might mean the loss of national independence. The Queen of Scots gone, they were paralysed by divided counsels, and love of country proved stronger than their creed.

What concerns us specially at present is the effect on the King of Spain. The reluctance of Philip to undertake the English enterprise (the 'empresa,' as it was generally called) had arisen from a fear that when it was accomplished he would lose the fruit of his labours. He could never assure himself that if he placed Mary Stuart on the throne she would not become eventually French. He now learnt that she had bequeathed to himself her claims on the English succession. He had once been titular King of England. He had pretensions of his own, as in the descent from Edward III. The Jesuits, the Catholic enthusiasts throughout Europe, assured him that if he would now take up the cause in earnest, he might make England a province of Spain. There were still difficulties. He might hope that the English Catholic laity would accept him, but he could not be sure of it. He could not be sure that he would have the support of the Pope. He continued, as the Conde de Feria said scornfully of him, 'meando en vado,' a phrase which I cannot translate; it meant hesitating when he ought to act. But he saw, or thought he saw, that he could now take a stronger attitude towards Elizabeth as a claimant to her throne. If the treaty of peace was to go forward, he could raise his terms. He could insist on the restoration of the Catholic religion in England. The States of the Low Countries had made over five of their strongest towns to Elizabeth as the price of her assistance. He could insist on her restoring them, not to the States, but to himself. Could she be brought to consent to such an act of perfidy, Parma and he both felt that the power would then be gone from her, as effectually as Samson's when his locks were clipped by the harlot, and they could leave her then, if it suited them, on a throne which would have become a pillory – for the finger of scorn to point at.

With such a view before him it was more than ever necessary for Philip to hurry forward the preparations which he had already commenced. The more formidable he could make himself, the better able he would be to frighten Elizabeth into submission.

Every dockyard in Spain was set to work, building galleons and collecting stores. Santa Cruz would command. Philip was himself more inclined than before to accompany the expedition in person and dictate from the English Channel the conditions of the pacification of Europe.

Secrecy was no longer attempted – indeed, was no longer possible. All Latin Christendom was palpitating with expectation. At Lisbon, at Cadiz, at Barcelona, at Naples, the shipwrights were busy night and day. The sea was alive with vessels freighted with arms and provisions streaming to the mouth of the Tagus. Catholic volunteers from all nations flocked into the Peninsula, to take a share in the mighty movement which was to decide the fate of the world, and bishops, priests, and monks were set praying through the whole Latin communion that Heaven would protect its own cause.

Meanwhile the negotiations for peace continued, and Elizabeth, strange to say, persisted in listening. The execution of the Queen of Scots lay on her spirit and threw her back into the obstinate humour which had made Walsingham so often despair of her safety. For two months after that scene at Fotheringay she had refused to see Burghley, and would consult no one but Sir James Crofts and her Spanish-tempered ladies. She knew that Spain now intended that she should betray the towns in the Low Countries. She named commissioners, with Sir James Crofts at their head to go to Ostend and treat with Parma, and if she had not resolved on an act of treachery she at least played with the temptation, and persuaded herself that if she chose to make over the towns to Philip, she would be only restoring them to their lawful owner.

Burghley and Walsingham, you can see from their letters, feared that Elizabeth would ruin herself. Happily her moods were variable as the weather. She was forced to see the condition of affairs in the Low Countries by the appearance of a number of starving wretches who had deserted from the garrisons there and had come across to clamour for their pay at her own palace gates. If she had no troops in the field but a mutinous and starving rabble, she might get no terms at all. It might be well to show Philip that on one element at least she could still be dangerous. She had lost nothing by the bold actions of Drake and the privateers. With half a heart she allowed Drake to fit them out again, take the *Buonaventura*, a ship of her own, to carry his flag, and go down to the coast of Spain and see what was going on. He was not to do too much. She sent a vice-admiral with him, in the *Lion*, to be a check on over-audacity. Drake knew how to deal with embarrassing vice-admirals. His own adventurers would sail, if he ordered, to the Mountains of the Moon. Once under way and on the blue water he would go his own course and run his own risks.

Cadiz Harbour was thronged with transports, provision ships, powder vessels – a hundred sail of them – some of a thousand tons and over, loading with stores for the Armada. There were thirty sail of adventurers, the smartest ships afloat on the ocean, and sailed by the smartest seamen that ever handled rope or tiller. Something might be done at Cadiz if he did not say too much about it. The leave had been given to him to go, but he knew by experience, and Burghley again warned him, that it might, and probably would, be revoked if he waited too long. The moment was his own, and he used it. He was but just in time. Before his sails were under the horizon a courier galloped into Plymouth with orders that under no condition was he to enter port or haven of the King of Spain, or injure Spanish subjects. What else was he going out for? He had guessed how it would be. Comedy or earnest he could not tell. If earnest, some such order would be sent after him, and he had not an instant to lose.

He sailed on the morning of April 12. Off Ushant he fell in with a north-west gale, and he flew on, spreading every stitch of canvas which his spars would bear. In five days he was at Cape St Vincent. On the 18th he had the white houses of Cadiz right in front of him, and could see for himself the forests of masts from the ships and transports with which the harbour was choked. Here was a chance for a piece of service if there was courage for the venture. He signalled for his officers to come on board the *Buonaventura*. There before their eyes was, if not the Armada itself, the materials which were to fit the Armada for the seas. Did they dare to go in with him and destroy them? There were batteries at the harbour mouth, but Drake's mariners had faced Spanish batteries at St Domingo and Carthagena and had not found them very formidable. Go in? Of course they would. Where Drake would lead the corsairs of Plymouth were never afraid to follow. The vice-admiral pleaded danger to her Majesty's ships. It was not the business of an English fleet to be particular about danger. Straight in they went with a fair wind and a flood tide, ran past the batteries and under a storm of shot, to which they did not trouble themselves to wait to reply. The poor vice-admiral followed reluctantly in the *Lion*. A single shot hit the *Lion*, and he edged away out of range, anchored, and drifted to sea again with the ebb. But Drake and all the rest dashed on, sank the guardship – a large galleon – and sent flying a fleet of galleys which ventured too near them and were not seen again.

Further resistance there was none – absolutely none. The crews of the store ships escaped in their boats to land. The governor of Cadiz, the same Duke of Medina Sidonia who the next year was to gain a disastrous immortality, fled 'like a tall gentleman' to raise troops and prevent Drake from landing. Drake had no intention of landing. At his leisure he took possession of the Spanish shipping, searched every vessel, and carried off everything that he could use. He detained as prisoners the few men that he found on board, and then, after doing his work deliberately and completely, he set the hulls on fire, cut the cables, and left them to drive on the rising tide under the walls of the town – a confused mass of blazing ruin. On April 12 he had sailed from Plymouth; on the 19th he entered Cadiz Harbour; on May 1 he passed out again without the loss of a boat or a man.

He said in jest that he had singed the King of Spain's beard for him. In sober prose he had done the King of Spain an amount of damage which a million ducats and a year's labour would imperfectly replace. The daring rapidity of the enterprise astonished Spain, and astonished Europe more than the storm of the West Indian towns. The English had long teeth, as Santa Cruz had told Philip's council. The Spaniards were a gallant race, and a dashing exploit, though at their own expense, could be admired by the countrymen of Cervantes. 'So praised,' we read, 'was Drake for his valour among them, that they said that if he was not a Lutheran there would not be the like of him in the world.' A Court lady was invited by the King to join a party on a lake near Madrid. The lady replied that she dared not trust herself on the water with His Majesty lest Sir Francis Drake should have her.

Drake might well be praised. But Drake would have been the first to divide the honour with the comrades who were his arm and hand. Great admirals and generals do not win their battles single-handed like the heroes of romance. Orders avail only when there are men to execute them. Not a captain, not an officer who served under Drake, ever flinched or blundered. Never was such a school for seamen as that twenty years' privateering war between the servants of the Pope and the West-country Protestant adventurers. Those too must be remembered who built and rigged the ships in which they sailed and fought their battles. We may depend upon it that there was no dishonesty in contractors, no scamping of the work in the yards where the Plymouth rovers were fitted out for sea. Their hearts were in it; they were soldiers of a common cause.

Three weeks had sufficed for Cadiz. No order for recall had yet arrived. Drake had other plans before him, and the men were in high spirits and ready for anything. A fleet of Spanish men-of-war was expected round from the Mediterranean. He proposed to stay for a week or two in the neighbourhood of the Straits, in the hope of falling in with them. He wanted fresh water, too, and had to find it somewhere.

Before leaving Cadiz Roads he had to decide what to do with his prisoners. Many English were known to be in the hands of the Holy Office working in irons as galley slaves. He sent a pinnace to propose an exchange, and had to wait some days for an answer. At length, after a reference to Lisbon, the Spanish authorities replied that they had no English prisoners. If this was true, those they had must have died of barbarous usage; and after a consultation with his officers Sir Francis sent in word that for the future such prisoners as they might take would be sold to the Moors, and the money applied to the redemption of English captives in other parts of the world.

Water was the next point. There were springs at Faro, with a Spanish force stationed there to guard them. Force or no force, water was to be had. The boats were sent on shore. The boats' crews stormed the forts and filled the casks. The vice-admiral again lifted up his voice. The Queen had ordered that there was to be no landing on Spanish soil. At Cadiz the order had been observed. There had been no need to land. Here at Faro there had been direct defiance of Her Majesty's command. He became so loud in his clamours that Drake found it necessary to lock him up in his own cabin, and at length to send him home with his ship to complain. For himself, as the expected fleet from the Straits did not appear, and as he had shaken off his troublesome second in command, he proceeded leisurely up the coast, intending to look in at Lisbon and see for himself how things were going on there.

119

All along as he went he fell in with traders loaded with supplies for the use of the Armada. All these he destroyed as he advanced, and at length found himself under the purple hills of Cintra and looking up into the Tagus.

There lay gathered together the strength of the fighting naval force of Spain – fifty galleons, already arrived, the largest warships which then floated on the ocean. Santa Cruz, the best officer in the Spanish navy, was himself in the town and in command. To venture a repetition of the Cadiz exploit in the face of such odds seemed too desperate even for Drake, but it was one of those occcasions when the genius of a great commander sees more than ordinary eyes. He calculated, and, as was proved afterwards, calculated rightly, that the galleons would be half manned, or not manned at all, and crowded with landsmen bringing on board the stores. Their sides as they lay would be choked with hulks and lighters. They would be unable to get their anchors up, set their canvas, or stir from their moorings. Daring as Drake was known to be, no one would expect him to go with so small a force into the enemy's stronghold, and there would be no preparations to meet him. He could count upon the tides. The winds at that season of the year were fresh and steady, and could be counted on also to take him in or out; there was sea room in the river for such vessels as the adventurers' to manoeuvre and to retreat if overmatched.

Rash as such an enterprise might seem to an unprofessional eye, Drake certainly thought of it, perhaps had meant to try it in some form or other and so make an end of the Spanish invasion of England. He could not venture without asking first for his mistress's permission. He knew her nature. He knew that his service at Cadiz would outweigh his disregard of her orders, and that so far he had nothing to fear; but he knew also that she was still hankering after peace, and that without her leave he must do nothing to make peace impossible. There is a letter from him to the Queen, written when he was lying off Lisbon, very characteristic of the time and the man.

Nelson or Lord St Vincent did not talk much of expecting supernatural assistance. If they had, we should suspect them of using language conventionally which they would have done better to leave alone. Sir Francis Drake, like his other contemporaries, believed that he was engaged in a holy cause, and was not afraid or ashamed to say so. His object was to protest against a recall in the flow of victory. The Spaniards, he said, were but mortal men. They were enemies of the Truth, upholders of Dagon's image, which had fallen in other days before the Ark, and would fall again if boldly defied. So long as he had ships that would float, and there was food on board them for the men to eat, he entreated the Queen to let him stay and strike whenever a chance was offered him. The continuing to the end yielded the true glory. When men were serving religion and their country, a merciful God, it was likely, would give them victory, and Satan and his angels should not prevail.

All in good time. Another year and Drake would have the chance he wanted. Elizabeth's answer came. It was warm and generous. She did not, could not, blame him for what he had done so far, but she desired him to provoke the King of Spain no further. The negotiations for peace had opened, and must not be interfered with.

This prohibition from the Queen prevented, perhaps, what would have been a most remarkable exploit in English naval history. As matters stood it would have been perfectly possible for Drake to have gone into the Tagus, and if he could not have burnt the galleons he could certainly have come away unhurt. He had guessed their condition with entire correctness. The ships were there, but the ships' companies were not on board them. Santa Cruz himself admitted that if Drake had gone in he could have himself done nothing *por falta de gente* (for want of men). And Drake undoubtedly would have gone, and would have done something with which all the world would have rung, but for the positive command of his mistress.

He lingered in the Roads at Cintra, hoping that Santa Cruz would come out and meet him. All Spain was clamouring at Santa Cruz's inaction. Philip wrote to stir the old admiral to energy. He must not allow himself to be defied by a squadron of insolent rovers. He must chase them off the coast or destroy them. Santa Cruz needed no stirring. Santa Cruz, the hero of many fights, was chafing at his own impotence; but he was obliged to tell his master that if he wished to have service out of his galleons he must provide crews to handle them. He told him, moreover, that it was time for him to exert himself in earnest. If he waited much longer, England would have grown too strong for him to deal with.

In strict obedience Drake ought now to have gone home, but the campaign had brought so far more glory than prize-money. His comrades required some consolation for their disappointment at Lisbon. The theory of these armaments of the adventurers was that the cost should be paid somehow by the enemy, and he could be assured that if he brought back a prize or two in which she could claim a share the Queen would not call him to strict account. Homeward-bound galleons or merchantmen were to be met with occasionally at the Azores. On leaving Lisbon Drake headed away to St Michael's and his lucky star was still in the ascendant.

As if sent on purpose for him, the *San Philip*, a magnificent caraque from the Indies, fell straight into his hands, 'so richly loaded,' it was said, 'that every man in the fleet counted his fortune made.' There was no need to wait for more. It was but two months since Drake had sailed from Plymouth. He had struck the King of Spain in his own stronghold. He had disabled the intended Armada for one season at least. He had picked up a prize by the way, worth half a million, to pay his expenses, so that he had cost nothing to his mistress, and had brought back a handsome present for her. I doubt if such a naval estimate was ever presented to an English House of Commons. Above all, he had taught the self-confident Spaniard to be afraid of him.

Our West-country annals still tell how the country people streamed down in their best clothes to see the great *San Philip* towed into Dartmouth Harbour. English Protestantism was no bad cable for the nation to ride by in those stormy times, and deserves to be honourably remembered in a School of History at an English University.

Sailing of the Armada

Peace or war between Spain and England, that was now the question, with a prospect for Philip II of securing the English succession for himself or one of his daughters. With the whole Spanish nation smarting under the indignity of the burning of the ships at Cadiz, Philip's warlike ardour had warmed into something like fire. He had resolved at any rate, if he was to forgive his sister-in-law at all, to insist on more than toleration for the Catholics in England. He did not contemplate as probable that the English privateers, however bold or dexterous, could resist such an armament as he was preparing to lead to the Channel. The Royal Navy, he knew very well, did not exceed twenty-five ships of all sorts and sizes. The adventurers might be equal to sudden daring actions, but would and must be defeated by such a fleet as was being fitted out at Lisbon. He therefore, for himself, meant to demand that the Catholic religion should be restored to its former superiority, and certain towns in England were to be made over to be garrisoned by Spanish troops as securities for Elizabeth's good behaviour. As often happens with irresolute men when they have once been forced to a decision they were too hasty as before they had been too slow.

After Drake had retired from Lisbon the King of Spain sent orders to the Prince of Parma not to wait for the arrival of the Armada, but to cross the Channel immediately with the Flanders army, and bring Elizabeth to her knees. Parma had more sense than that. He represented that he could not cross without a fleet to cover his passage. His transport barges would only float in smooth water, and whether the water was smooth or rough they could be sent to the bottom by half a

123

dozen English cruisers from the Thames. Supposing him to have landed, either in Thanet or other spot, he reminded Philip that he could not have at most more than 25,000 men with him. The English militia were in training. He might have to fight more than one battle. He would have to leave detachments as he advanced to London, to cover his communications, and a reverse would be fatal. He would obey if His Majesty persisted, but he recommended Philip to continue to amuse the English with the treaty till the Armada was ready, and, in evident consciousness that the enterprise would be harder than Philip imagined, he even gave it as his own opinion still (notwithstanding Cadiz), that if Elizabeth would surrender the cautionary towns in Flanders to Spain, and would grant the English Catholics a fair degree of liberty, it would be Philip's interest to make peace at once without stipulating for further terms. He could make a new war if he wished at a future time, when circumstances might be more convenient and the Netherlands revolt subdued.

To such conditions as these it seemed that Elizabeth was inclining to consent. The towns had been trusted to her keeping by the Nether-landers. To give them up to the enemy to make better conditions for herself would be an infamy so great as to have disgraced Elizabeth. She said the towns belonged to Philip and she would only be restoring his own to him. Burghley bade her, if she wanted peace, send back Drake to the Azores and frighten Philip for his gold ships. She was in one of her ungovernable moods. Instead of sending out Drake again she ordered her own fleet to be dismantled and laid up at Chatham, and she condescen-ded to apologise to Parma for burning of the transports at Cadiz as done against her orders.

This was in December 1587, only five months before the Armada sailed from Lisbon. Meanwhile, with enormous effort the destruction at Cadiz had been repaired. The great fleet was pushed on, and in February Santa Cruz reported himself almost ready. Santa Cruz and Philip, however, were not in agreement as to what should be done. Santa Cruz was a fighting admiral, Philip was not a fighting king. He changed his mind as often as Elizabeth. Hot fits varied with cold. His last news from England led him to hope that fighting would not be wanted. The Commissioners were sitting at Ostend. On one side there were the formal negotiations, in which the surrender of the towns was not yet treated as an open question. Had the States been aware that Elizabeth was even in thought entertaining it, they might have made terms on their own account. Besides this, there was a second negotiation underneath, carried on by private agents, in which the surrender was to be the special condition. These complicated schemings Parma purposely protracted, to keep Elizabeth in false security. She had not deliberately intended to give up the towns. At the last moment she would have probably refused, unless the States themselves consented to it as part of a general settlement. The States, she thought, were too obstinate. Peace would be good for them, and she said she might do them good if she pleased, whether they liked it or not.

Parma was content that she should amuse herself with words. By the end of February Santa Cruz was ready. A northerly wind blows strong down the coast of Portugal in the spring months, and he meant to be off before it set in, before the end of March at latest. Unfortunately for Spain, Santa Cruz fell ill at the last moment – ill, it was said, with anxiety. Santa Cruz knew well enough that the expedition would be no holiday parade. He had reason enough to be anxious if Philip was to accompany him and tie his hands and embarrass him. Anyway, Santa Cruz died after a few days' illness. The sailing had to be suspended till a new commander could be decided on, and in the choice which Philip made he gave a curious proof of what he intended the expedition to do. He did not really expect or wish for any serious fighting. He wanted to be sovereign of England again, with the assent of the English Catholics. He did not mean, if he could help it, to irritate the national pride by force and conquest. While Santa Cruz lived, Spanish public opinion would not allow him to be passed over. Santa Cruz must command, and Philip had resolved to go with him, to prevent too violent proceedings. Santa Cruz dead, he could find someone who would do what he was told, and his own presence would no longer be necessary.

The Duke of Medina Sidonia, named El Bueno, or the Good, was a grandee of highest rank. He was enormously rich, fond of hunting and shooting, a tolerable rider, for the rest a harmless creature getting on to forty, conscious of his defects, but not aware that so great a prince had any need to mend them; without vanity, without ambition, and most happy in his orange gardens at San Lucar. Of active service he had seen none. He was Captain-General of Andalusia, and had moved away from Cadiz when Drake came into the harbour; but that was all. To his astonishment and to his dismay he learnt that it was on him that the choice had fallen to be the Lord High Admiral of Spain and commander of the so-much-talked-of expedition to England. He protested his unfitness. He said that he was no seaman; that he knew nothing of fighting by sea or land; that if he ventured out in a boat he was always sick; that he had never seen the English Channel; and that, as to politics, he neither knew nor cared about them. In short, he had not the qualifications which such a post required.

Philip liked his modesty; but in fact the Duke's defects were his recommendations. He would obey his instructions, would not fight unless it was necessary, and would go into no rash adventures. All that Philip wanted him to do was to find the Prince of Parma, and act as Parma should bid him. As to seamanship, he would have the best officers in the navy under him; and for a second in command he should have Don Diego de Valdez, a cautious, silent, sullen sailor, a man after Philip's own heart.

Doubting, hesitating, the Duke repaired to Lisbon. There he was put in better heart by a nun, who said Our Lady had sent her to promise him success. Every part of the service was new to him. He was a fussy, anxious man; set himself to inquire into everything, to meddle with things which he could not understand and had better have left alone. He ought to have left details to the responsible heads of departments. He fancied that in a week of two he could look himself into everything. There were 130 ships, 8,000 seamen, 12,000 Spanish infantry with gentlemen volunteers, officers, priests, surgeons, galley slaves – at least 3,000 more – provisioned for six months. Then there were the ships' stores, arms small and great, powder, spars, cordage, canvas, and such other million necessities as ships on service need. The whole of this the Duke took on himself to examine into. Everyone's mind was, in fact, so much absorbed by the spiritual side of the thing that they could not attend to vulgar commonplaces. Don Quixote, when he set out on his expedition, and forgot money and a change of linen, was not in a state of wilder exaltation than Catholic Europe at the sailing of the Armada. Every noble family in Spain had sent one or other of its sons to fight for Christ and Our Lady.

For three years the stream of prayer had been ascending from church, cathedral, or oratory. The King had emptied his treasury. The noblemen and the tradesmen had offered their contributions. The crusade against the Crescent itself had not kindled a more intense or more sacred enthusiasm. All pains were taken to make the expedition spiritually worthy of its purpose. Swearing, quarrelling, gambling, were prohibited under penalties. The galleons were named after the apostles and saints to whose charge they were committed, and every seaman and soldier confessed and communicated on going on board. The ship-boys at sunrise were to sing their Buenos Dias at the foot of the mainmast, and their Ave Maria as the sun sank into the ocean. On the Imperial banner were embroidered the figures of Christ and His Mother, and as a motto the haughty 'Plus Ultra' of Charles V was replaced with the more pious aspiration, 'Exsurge, Deus, et vindica causam tuam.'[1]

Nothing could be better if the more vulgar necessities had been looked to equally well. Unluckily, Medina Sidonia was unable to correct the information which any rascal chose to give him.

At length, at the end of April, he reported himself satisfied. The banner was blessed in the cathedral, men and stores all on board, and the Invincible Armada prepared to go upon its way. No wonder Philip was confident. A hundred and thirty galleons, from 1,300 to 700 tons, 23,000 fighting men, besides slaves and servants, made up a force which the world might well think invincible. The guns were the weakest part. There were as many as the English, but they were for the most part nine and six pounders, and with but fifty rounds to each. The Spaniards had done their sea fighting hitherto at close range, grappling and trusting to musketry. They were to receive a lesson about this before the summer was over. But Philip himself meanwhile expected evidently that he would meet with no opposition. Of priests he had provided 180; of surgeons and surgeons' assistants eighty-five only for the whole fleet.

In the middle of May he sent down his last orders. The Duke was not to seek a battle. If he fell in with Drake he was to take no notice of him, but thank God, as Dogberry said to the watchman, that he was rid of a knave. He was to go straight to the North Foreland, there anchor and communicate with Parma. The experienced admirals who had learnt their trade under Santa Cruz – Martinez de Recalde, Pedro de Valdez, Miguel de Oquendo – strongly urged the securing Plymouth or the Isle of Wight on their way up the Channel. This had evidently been Santa Cruz's own design, and the rational one to have followed. Philip did not believe it would prove necessary; but as to this and as to fighting he left them, as he knew he must do, a certain discretion.

The Duke then, flying the sacred banner on the *San Martin*, dropped down the Tagus on the 14th of May, followed by the whole fleet. The *San Martin* had been double-timbered with oak, to keep the shot out. He liked his business no better. In vain he repeated to himself that it was God's cause. God would see they came to no harm. He was no sooner in the open sea than he found no cause, however holy, saved

1. Arise O God, and avenge The cause.

men from consequences of their own blunders. They were late out, and met the north trade wind, as Santa Cruz had foretold.

They drifted to leeward day by day till they had dropped down to Cape St Vincent. Infinite pains had been taken with the spiritual state of everyone on board. The carelessness or roguery of contractors and purveyors had not been prevented. The water had been taken in three months before. It was found foul and stinking. The salt beef, the salt pork, and fish were putrid, the bread full of maggots and cockroaches. Cask was opened after cask. It was the same story everywhere. They had to be thrown overboard. The men went down in hundreds with dysentery. The Duke bewailed his fate as innocently as Sancho Panza. He hoped God would help. He had left his home and his family to please the King, and he trusted the King would remember it. He wrote piteously for fresh stores, if the King would not have them all perish. The admirals said they could go no farther without fresh water. All was dismay and confusion. The wind at last fell round south, and they made Finisterre. It then came on to blow, and they were scattered. The Duke with half the fleet crawled into Corunna, the crews scarce able to man the yards and trying to desert in shoals.

The missing ships dropped in one by one, but a week passed and a third of them were still absent. Another despairing letter went off from the Duke to his master. He said that he concluded from their misfortunes that God disapproved of the expedition, and that it had better be abandoned. Diego Florez was of the same opinion. The stores were worthless, he said. The men were sick and out of heart. Nothing could be done that season.

It was not by flinching at the first sight of difficulty that the Spaniards had become masters of half the world. The old comrades of Santa Cruz saw nothing in what had befallen them beyond a common accident of sea life. To abandon at the first check an enterprise undertaken with so much pretence, they said, would be cowardly and dishonourable. Ships were not lost because they were out of sight. Fresh meat and bread could be taken on board from Corunna. They could set up a shore hospital for the sick. The sickness was not dangerous. There had been no deaths. A little energy and all would be well again. Pedro de Valdez dispatched a courier to Philip to entreat him not to listen to the Duke's croakings. Philip returned a speedy answer telling the Duke not to be frightened at shadows.

There was nothing, in fact, really to be alarmed at. Fresh water took away the dysentery. Fresh food was brought in from the country.

Galician seamen filled the gaps made by the deserters. The ships were laid on shore and scraped and tallowed. Tents were pitched on an island in the harbour, with altars and priests, and everyone confessed again and received the sacrament. 'This,' wrote the Duke, 'is great riches and a precious jewel, and all now are well content and cheerful.' The scattered flock had reassembled. Damages were all repaired, and the only harm had been loss of time. Once more, on July 23, the Armada in full numbers was under way for England, and streaming across the Bay of Biscay with a fair wind for the mouth of the Channel.

Leaving the Duke for the moment, we must now glance at the preparations made in England to receive him. The winter months had been wild and changeable. In December the fleet had been paid off at Chatham. The danger of leaving the country without regular defence was pressed vehemently to allow part of the ships to be recommissioned. The *Revenge* was given to Drake. He and Howard, the Lord Admiral, were to have gone with a mixed squadron from the Royal Navy and the adventurers down to the Spanish coast. In every loyal subject there had long been but one opinion, that open war was the only road to an honourable peace.

With the news of Santa Cruz's death came a report that the Armada was dissolving and was not coming at all. Sir James Crofts sang the usual song that Drake and Howard wanted war, because war was their trade. The Queen recalled her orders. She said that she was assured of peace in six weeks, and that beyond that time the services of the fleet would not be required. Half the men engaged were to be dismissed at once to save their pay. Drake and Lord Henry Seymour should cruise with four or five of the Queen's ships between Plymouth and the Solent. Lord Howard was to remain in the Thames with the rest. I know not whether swearing was interdicted in the English navy as well as in the Spanish, but I will answer for it that Howard did not spare his language when this missive reached him. 'Never,' he said, 'since England was England was such a stratagem made to deceive us as this treaty. We have not hands left to carry the ships back to Chatham. We are like bears tied to a stake; the Spaniards may come to worry us like dogs, and we cannot hurt them.'

March went by, and sure intelligence came that the Armada was not dissolving. Again Drake prayed the Queen to let him take the *Revenge* and the Western adventurers down to Lisbon; but the commissioners wrote full of hope from Ostend, and Elizabeth was afraid 'the King of Spain might take it ill.' She found fault with Drake's expenses. She charged him with wasting ammunition in target practice. She kept a sharp hand on the victualling houses. April went, and her four finest ships – the *Triumph*, the *Victory*, the *Elizabeth Jonas*, and the *Bear* – were still with sails unbent, 'keeping Chatham church.' She hoped they would not be wanted and it would be waste of money to refit them. Again she was forced to yield at last, and the four ships were got to sea in time, the workmen in the yards making up for the delay; but she had few enough when her whole fleet was out upon the Channel, and but for the privateers there would have been an ill reckoning when the trial came. The Armada was coming now. There was no longer a doubt of it. Lord Henry Seymour was left with five Queen's ships and thirty London adventurers to watch Parma and the Narrow Seas. Howard, carrying his own flag in the *Ark Raleigh*, joined Drake at Plymouth with seventeen others.

Food and supplies had been issued to the middle of June, and no more was to be allowed. The weather was desperate – wildest summer ever known. The south-west gales brought the Atlantic rollers into the Sound. Drake lay inside, perhaps behind the island which bears his name. Howard rode out the gales under Mount Edgecumbe, the days going by and the provisions wasting. The rations were cut down to make the stores last longer. Owing to the many changes the crews had been hastily raised. They were ill-clothed, ill-provided every way, but they complained of nothing, caught fish to mend their mess dinners, and prayed only for the speedy coming of the enemy. Even Howard's heart failed him now. English sailors would do what could be done by man, but they could not fight with famine. 'Awake, Madam,' he wrote to the Queen, 'awake for the love of Christ, and see the villainous treasons round about you.' He goaded her into ordering supplies for one more month, but this was to be positively the last. The victuallers inquired if they should make further preparations.

The contractors were to blame for the beer which had been furnished for the fleet turned sour, and those who drank it sickened. The officers, on their own responsibility, ordered wine and arrowroot for the sick out of Plymouth. Again the rations were reduced. Four weeks' allowance was stretched to serve for six, and still the Spaniards did not come. The preparations on land were better. The militia had been called out. A hundred thousand men had given their names, and the stations had been arranged where they were to assemble if the enemy attempted a landing. For a general the Queen had chosen the Earl of Leicester, who might have the merit of fidelity to herself, but otherwise was less well fitted; and the Prince of Parma was coming, if he came at all, at the head of the best provided and best disciplined troops in Europe. The hope of England at that moment was in her patient sailors at Plymouth. Each morning they looked out passionately for the Spanish sails. Time was a worse enemy than the galleons. The six weeks would be soon gone, and the Queen's ships must then leave the seas if the crews were not to starve. Drake had certain news that the Armada had sailed. Where was it? Once he dashed out as far as Ushant, but turned back, lest it should pass him in the night and find Plymouth undefended.

The last week of July had now come. There were half-rations for one week more, and powder for few days' fighting. On Friday, the 23rd, the Armada had started for the second time, the numbers undiminished; religious fervour burning again, and heart and hope high as ever. Saturday, Sunday, and Monday they sailed on with a smooth sea and soft south winds, and on Monday night the Duke found himself at the Channel mouth with all his flock about him. Tuesday morning the wind shifted to the north, then backed to the west, and blew hard. The sea got up, broke into the stern galleries of the galleons, and sent the galleys looking for shelter in French harbours. The fleet hove to for a couple of days, till the weather mended. On Friday afternoon they sighted the Lizard and formed into fighting order: the Duke in the centre, Alonzo de Leyva leading in a vessel of his own called the *Rata Coronada*, Don Martinez de Recalde covering the rear. The entire line stretched to about seven miles.

The sacred banner was run up to the masthead of the *San Martin*. Each ship saluted with all her guns, and every man – officer, noble, seaman, or slave – knelt on the decks at a given signal to commend themselves to Mary and her son. We shall miss the meaning of this high epic story if we do not realise that both sides had the conviction that they were fighting the battle of the Almighty. Two principles, freedom and authority, were contending for the guidance of mankind. In the evening the Duke sent off two fast flyboats to Parma to announce his arrival in the Channel, with another reporting progress to Philip, and saying that till he heard from the Prince he meant to stop at the Isle of Wight. It is commonly said that his officers advised him to go in and take Plymouth. There is no evidence for this. The island would have been a far more useful position for them.

At dark that Friday night the beacons were seen blazing all up the coast and inland on the tops of the hills. They crept on slowly through Saturday, with reduced canvas, feeling their way – not a sail to be seen.

At midnight a pinnace brought in a fishing-boat, from which they learnt that on the sight of the signal fires the English had come out that morning from Plymouth. Presently, when the moon rose, they saw sails passing between them and the land. With daybreak the whole scene became visible, and the curtain lifted on the first act of the drama. The Armada was between Rame Head and the Eddystone, or a little to the west of it. Plymouth Sound was right open to their left. The breeze, which had dropped in the night, was freshening from the south-west, and right ahead of them, outside the Mew Stone, were eleven ships manoeuvring to recover the wind. Towards the land were some forty others, of various sizes, and this formed, as far as they could see, the whole English force. In numbers the Spaniards were nearly three to one.

With this advantage the Duke decided to engage, and a signal was made to hold the wind and keep the enemy apart. The eleven ships ahead were Howard's squadron; those inside were Drake and the adventurers. With some surprise the Spanish officers saw Howard reach easily to windward out of range and join Drake. The whole English fleet then passed out close-hauled in line behind them and swept along their rear, using guns more powerful than theirs and pouring in broadsides from safe distance with deadly effect. Recalde, with Alonzo de Leyva and Oquendo, who came to his help, tried desperately to close; but they could make nothing of it. They were out-sailed and out-cannoned. The English fired five shots to one of theirs, and the effect was the more destructive because, as with Rodney's action at Dominica, the galleons were crowded with troops, and shot and splinters told terribly among them.

The experience was new and not agreeable. Recalde's division was badly cut up, and a Spaniard present observed that certain officers showed cowardice – a hit at the Duke, who was out of fire. The action lasted till four in the afternoon. The wind was then freshening fast and the sea rising. Both fleets had by this time passed the Sound, and the Duke, seeing that nothing could be done, signalled to bear away up Channel, the English following two miles astern. Recalde's own ship had been an especial sufferer. She was observed to be leaking badly, to drop behind, and to be in danger of capture. Pedro de Valdez wore round to help him in the *Capitana*, of the Andalusian squadron, fouled the *Santa Catalina* in turning, broke his bowsprit and foretopmast, and became unmanageable. The Andalusian *Capitana* was one of the finest ships in the Spanish fleet, and Don Pedro one of the ablest and most popular commanders. She had 500 men on board, a large sum of money, and, among other treasurers, a box of jewel-hilted swords, which Philip was sending over to the English Catholic peers. But it was growing dark. Sea and sky looked ugly. The Duke was flurried, and signalled to go on and leave Don Pedro to his fate. Alonzo de Leyva and Oquendo rushed on board the *San Martin* to protest. It was no use. Diego Florez said he couuld not risk the safety of the fleet for a single officer. The deserted *Capitana* made a brave defence, but could not save herself, and fell, with the jewelled swords, 50,000 ducats, and a welcome supply of powder, into Drake's hands.

Off the Start there was a fresh disaster. Everyone was in ill-humour. A quarrel broke out between the soldiers and seamen in Oquendo's galleon. He was himself still absent. Some one or other flung a torch into the powder magazine. The deck was blown off, and 200 men along with it.

Two such accidents following an unsuccessful engagement did not tend to reconcile the Spaniards to the Duke's command. Pedro de Valdez was loved and honoured, and his desertion in the face of an enemy not superior in numbers was regarded as scandalous. Monday morning broke heavily. The wind was gone, but there was still a considerable swell. The English were hull down behind. The day was spent in repairing damages and nailing lead over the shot-holes. Recalde was moved to the front, to be out of harm's way, and De Leyva took his post in the rear.

At sunset they were outside Portland. The English had come up within a league; but it was now dead calm, and they drifted apart in the tide. The Duke thought of nothing, but at midnight the Spanish officers stirred him out of his sleep to urge him to set his great galleasses to work; now was their chance. The dawn brought a chance still better, for it brought an east wind, and the Spaniards had now the weather-gage. Could they once close and grapple with the English ships, their numbers would then assure them a victory, and Howard, being to leeward and inshore, would have to pass through the middle of the Spanish line to recover his advantage. However, it was the same story. The Spaniards could not use an opportunity when they had one. New-modelled for superiority of sailing, the English ships had the same advantage over the galleons as the steam-cruisers would have over the old three-deckers. While the breeze held they went where they pleased. The Spaniards were out-sailed, outmatched, damaged by guns of longer range than theirs. Their own shot flew high over the low English hulls, while many shots found their way through their own towering sides. This time the *San Martin* was in the thick of it. Her double timbers were ripped and torn; the holy standard was cut in two; the water poured through the shot-holes. The men lost nerve.

At the end of that day's fighting the English powder gave out. Howard had pressed for a more liberal supply at the last moment, and a small addition had been despatched to Weymouth or Poole, and no more could be done till it arrived. The Duke, meanwhile, was left to smooth his ruffled plumes and drift on upon his way. But by this time England was awake. Fresh privateers, with powder, meat, bread, anything that they could bring, were pouring out from the Dorsetshire harbours. Sir George Carey had come from the Needles in time to share the honours of the last battle, 'round shot,' as he said, 'flying thick as musket balls in a skirmish on land.'

The Duke had observed uneasily from the *San Martin's* deck that his pursuers were growing numerous. He had made up his mind to go for the Isle of Wight, shelter his fleet in the Solent, land 10,000 men in the island, and stand on his defence till he heard from Parma. He must fight another battle; but, cut up as he had been, he had as yet lost but two ships, and those by accident. He might fairly hope to force his way in with help from above, for which he had special reason to look in the next engagement. Wednesday was a breathless calm. The English were taking in their supplies. The Armada lay still, repairing damages. Thursday would be St Dominic's Day. St Dominic belonged to the Duke's own family, and was his patron saint. St Dominic, he felt sure, would now stand by his kinsman.

The morning broke with a light air. The English would be less able to move, and with the help of the galleasses he might hope to come to close quarters at last. Howard seemed inclined to give him his wish. With just wind enough to move, the Lord Admiral led in the *Ark Raleigh* straight down on the Spanish centre. The *Ark* outsailed her consorts and found herself alone with the galleons all round her. At that moment the wind dropped. The Spanish boarding-parties were at their posts. The tops were manned with musketeers, the grappling irons all prepared to fling into the *Ark's* rigging. In imagination the English admiral was at risk. But each day's experience was to teach them a new lesson. Eleven boats dropped from the *Ark's* sides and took her in tow. The breeze rose again as she began to move. Her sails filled, and she slipped away through the water, leaving the Spaniards as if they were at anchor, staring in helpless amazement.

The wind brought up Drake and the rest, and then began again the cannonade from which the Armada had already suffered. It seemed that morning as if the English were using guns of heavier metal than on either of the preceding days. The Duke had other causes for uneasiness. His own magazines were also giving out under the unexpected demands upon them. One battle was the utmost which he had looked for. He had fought three, and the end was no nearer than before. With resolution he might perhaps have made his way into St Helen's Roads, for the English were evidently afraid to close with him. But when St Dominic, too, failed him he lost heart, and losing heart he lost all. In the Solent he might have been comparatively safe, and he might have taken the Isle of Wight; but his one thought now was to find safety under Parma's gaberdine and made for Calais or Dunkirk. He supposed Parma to have already embarked, on hearing of his coming, with a second armed fleet, and in condition for immediate action. He sent on another pinnace, pressing for help, pressing for ammunition, and flyboats to protect the galleons; while Parma was himself looking to be supplied from the Armada, with no second fleet at all, only a flotilla of river barges which would need a week's work to be prepared for the crossing.

Philip had provided a splendid fleet, a splendid army, and the finest sailors in the world except the English. He had failed to realise that the grandest preparations are useless without command. The Duke was less to blame than his master. An office had been thrust upon him for which he knew that he had not a single qualification. His one anxiety was to find Parma, lay the weight on Parma's shoulders, and so have done with it.

On Friday he was left alone to make his way up Channel towards the French shore. The English still followed, but he counted that in Calais Roads he would be in French waters, where they would not dare to meddle with him. As he dropped anchor in the dusk outside Calais on Saturday evening he saw, to his disgust, that the *endemoniada gente*[1] – the infernal devils – as he called them, had brought up at the same moment with himself, half a league astern of him. His one trust was in the Prince of Parma, and Parma at any rate was now within touch.

---

1. Men possessed with devils.

Defeat of the Armada

In the gallery at Madrid there is a picture, painted by Titian, representing the Genius of Spain coming to the delivery of the afflicted Bride of Christ. Titian was dead, but the temper of the age survived, and in the study of that great picture you will see the spirit in which the Spanish nation had set out for the conquest of England. The scene is the seashore. The Church a naked Andromeda, with dishevelled hair, fastened to the trunk of an ancient disbranched tree. The cross lies at her feet, the cup overturned, the serpents of heresy biting at her from behind with uplifted crests. Coming on before a leading breeze is the sea monster, the Moslem fleet, eager for their prey; while in front is Perseus, the Genius of Spain, banner in hand, with the legions of the faithful laying not raiment before him, but shield and helmet, the apparel of war for the Lady of Nations to clothe herself with strength and smite her foes.

In the Armada the crusading enthusiasm had reached its point and focus. England was the stake to which the Virgin, the daughter of Sion, was bound in captivity. Perseus had come at last in the person of the Duke of Medina Sidonia, and with him all that was best and brightest in the countrymen of Cervantes, to break her bonds and replace her on her throne. They had sailed into the Channel in pious hope, with the blessed banner waving over their heads.

To be the executor of the decrees of Providence is a lofty ambition, but men in a state of high emotion overlook the precautions which are not to be dispensed with even on the sublimest of errands. Don Quixote, when he set out to redress the wrongs of humanity, forgot that a change of linen might be necessary, and that he must take money with him to pay his hotel bills. Philip II, in sending the Armada to England, and confident in supernatural protection, hoped for a triumphal procession. He forgot that contractors might be rascals, that water four months in the casks in a hot climate turned putrid, and that putrid water would poison his ships' companies, though his crews were companies of angels. He forgot that the servants of the evil one might fight for their mistress after all, and that he must send adequate supplies of powder, and, worst forgetfulness of all, that a great naval expedition required a leader who understood his business. Perseus, in the shape of the Duke of Medina Sidonia, after a week of disastrous battles, found himself at the end of it in an exposed roadstead, where he ought never to have been, nine-tenths of his provisions thrown overboard as unfit for food, his ammunition exhausted by the unforeseen demands upon it, the seamen and soldiers harassed and dispirited, officers the whole week without sleep, and the enemy, who had hunted him from Plymouth to Calais, anchored within half a league of him.

Still, after all his misadventures, he had brought the fleet, if not to the North Foreland, yet within a few miles of it, and to outward appearance not materially injured. Two of the galleons had been taken; a third, the *Santa Aña*, had strayed; and his galleys had left him, being found too weak for the Channel sea; but the great armament had reached its destination substantially uninjured so far as English eyes could see. Hundreds of men had been killed and hundreds more wounded, and the spirit of the rest had been shaken. But the loss of life could only be conjectured on board the English fleet. The English admiral could only see that the Duke was now in touch with Parma. Parma, they knew, had an army at Dunkirk with him, which was to cross to England. He had been collecting men, barges, and transports all the winter and spring, and the backward state of Parma's preparations could not be anticipated, still less relied upon. The Calais anchorage was unsafe; but at that season of the year, especially after a wet summer, the weather usually settled, and to attack the Spaniards in a French port might be dangerous for many reasons. It was uncertain after the Day of the Barricades whether the Duke of Guise or Henry of Valois was master of France, and a violation of the neutrality laws might easily at that moment bring Guise and France into the field on the Spaniards' side.

It was, no doubt, with some such expectation that the Duke and his advisers had chosen Calais as the point at which to bring up. It was now Saturday, the 7th of August. The governor of the town came off in the evening to the *San Martin*. He expressed surprise to see the Spanish fleet in so exposed a position, but he was profuse in his offers of service. Anything which the Duke required should be provided, especially every facility for communicating with Dunkirk and Parma. The Duke thanked him, said that he supposed Parma to be already embarked with his troops, ready for the passage, and that his own stay in the Roads would be but brief. On Monday morning at latest he expected that the attempt to cross would be made. The Governor took his leave, and the Duke was left to a peaceful night. He was disturbed on the Sunday morning by an express from Parma informing him that, so far from being embarked, the army could not be ready for a fortnight. The barges were not in condition for sea. The troops were in camp. The arms and stores were on the quays at Dunkirk. As for the flyboats and ammunition which the Duke had asked for, he had none to spare. He had himself looked to be supplied from the Armada. He promised to use his best expedition, but the Duke, meanwhile, must see to the safety of the fleet.

Unwelcome news to a harassed landsman thrust into the position of an admiral and eager to be rid of his responsibilities. If by evil fortune the north-wester should come down upon him, with the shoals and sandbanks close under his lee, he would be in a bad way. Nor was the view behind him calculated for comfort. There lay the enemy almost within gunshot, who had hunted him like a pack of bloodhounds, and, worse than all, in double strength; for the Thames squadron – three Queen's ships and thirty London adventurers – under Lord H. Seymour and Sir John Hawkins, had crossed in the night. There they were between him and Cape Grisnez, and the reinforcement meant plainly enough that mischief was in the wind.

After a week so trying the Spanish crews would have been glad of a Sunday's rest if they could have had it; but the rough handling which they had gone through had thrown everything into disorder. The sick and wounded had to be cared for, torn rigging looked to, splintered timbers mended, decks scoured, and guns and arms cleaned up and put to rights. And so it was that no rest could be allowed; so much had to be done, and so busy was everyone, that the usual rations were not served out and the Sunday was kept as a fast. In the afternoon the stewards went ashore for fresh meat and vegetables. They came back with their boats loaded, and the prospect seemed a little less gloomy. Suddenly, as the Duke and a group of officers were watching the English fleet from the *San Martin's* poop deck, a small smart pinnace, carrying a gun in her bow, shot out from Howard's lines, bore down on the *San Martin*, sailed round her, sending in a shot or two as she passed, and went off unhurt. The Spanish officers could not help admiring such airy impertinence. Hugo de Monçada sent a ball after the pinnace, which went through her mainsail, but did no damage, and the pinnace again disappeared behind the English ships.

So a Spanish officer describes the scene. The English story says nothing of the pinnace; but she doubtless came and went as the Spaniard says, and for sufficient purpose. The English, too, were in straits, though the Duke did not dream of it. You will remember that the last supplies which were allowed to the fleet had been issued in the middle of June. They were to serve for a month, and the contractors were forbidden to prepare more. The Queen had clung to her hope that her differences with Philip were to be settled by the Commission at Ostend; and if Drake and Howard were too well furnished they would venture some fresh rash stroke on the coast of Spain, which might mar the negotiations. Their month's provisions had been stretched to serve for six weeks, and when the Armada appeared but two full days' rations remained. On these they had fought their way up Channel. Something had been brought out by private exertion on the Dorsetshire coast, and Seymour had, perhaps, brought a little more. The adventurers were in better state, having been equipped by private owners. But the Queen's ships in a day or two more must either go home or their crews would be starving. They had been on reduced rations for near two months. The Queen had changed her mind so often, now ordering the fleet to prepare for sea, then recalling her instructions and paying off the men, that those whom Howard had with him had been enlisted in haste. The fighting and the sight of the flying Spaniards were meat and drink, and clothing too, and had made them careless of all else. There was no fear of mutiny; but there was a limit to the toughest endurance. If the Armada was left undisturbed a long struggle might be still before them. The enemy would recover from its flurry, and Parma would come out from Dunkirk. To attack them directly in French waters might lead to perilous complications, while delay meant famine. The Spanish fleet had to be started from the Roads in some way. Done it must be, and done immediately.

Then, on that same Sunday afternoon, a memorable council of war was held in the *Ark's* main cabin. Howard, Drake, Seymour, Hawkins, Martin Frobisher, and two or three others met to consult, knowing that on them at that moment the liberties of England were depending.

Their resolution was taken promptly. After nightfall a strong flood tide would be setting up along shore to the Spanish anchorage. They would try what could be done with fire-ships, and the excursion of the pinnace, which was taken for bravado, was probably for a survey of the Armada's exact position. Meantime eight useless vessels were coated with pitch – hulls, spars, and rigging. Pitch was poured on the decks and over the sides, and parties were told off to steer them to their destination and then fire and leave them.

The hours stole on, and twilight passed into dark. The night was without a moon. The Duke paced his deck late with uneasy sense of danger. He observed lights moving up and down the English lines, and imagining that the *endemoniada gente* – the infernal devils – might be up to mischief, ordered a sharp look-out. A faint westerly air was curling the water, and towards midnight the watchers on board the galleons made out dimly several ships which seemed to be drifting down upon them. Their experience since the action off Plymouth had been so strange and unlooked for that anything unintelligible which the English did was alarming.

The phantom forms drew nearer, and were almost among them when they broke into a blaze from water-line to truck, and the two fleets were seen by the lurid light of the conflagration; the anchorage, the walls and windows of Calais, and the sea shining red as far as the eye could see, as if the ocean itself was burning. Among the dangers which they might have to encounter, English fireworks had been especially dreaded by the Spaniards. Fire-ships had worked havoc among the Spanish troops, when the bridge was blown up at Antwerp. They imagined that similar infernal machines were approaching the Armada. A capable commander would have sent a few launches to grapple the burning hulks, which of course were now deserted, and tow them out of harm's way. Spanish sailors were not cowards, and would not have flinched from duty because it might be dangerous; but the Duke and Diego Florez lost their heads again. A signal gun from the *San Martin* ordered the whole fleet to slip their cables and stand out to sea.

Orders given in panic are doubly unwise, for they spread the terror in which they originate. The danger from the fire-ships was chiefly from the effect on the imagination, for they appear to have drifted by and done no real injury. And it speaks well for the seamanship and courage of the Spaniards that they were able, crowded together as they were, at midnight and in sudden alarm to set their canvas and clear out without running into one another. They buoyed their cables, expecting to return for them at daylight, and with only a single accident, to be mentioned directly, they executed successfully a really difficult manoeuvre.

The Duke was delighted. The fire-ships burnt harmlessly out. He brought up a league outside the harbour, and supposed that the whole Armada had done the same. Unluckily for himself, he found it at daylight divided into two bodies. The *San Martin* with forty of the best appointed of the galleons were riding together at their anchors. The rest, two-thirds of the whole, having no second anchors ready, and inexperienced in Channel tides and currents, had been lying to. The west wind was blowing up. Without seeing where they were going they had drifted to leeward, and were two leagues off, towards Gravelines, dangerously near the shore. The Duke was too inexpert to realise the full peril of his situation. He signalled to them to return and rejoin him. As the wind and tide stood it was impossible. He proposed to follow them. The pilots told him that if he did the whole fleet might be lost on the banks. Towards the land the look of things was not more encouraging.

One accident only had happened the night before. The *Capitana* galleass, with Don Hugo de Monçada and eight hundred men on board, had fouled her helm in a cable in getting under way and had become unmanageable. The galleass had gone on the sands, and as the tide ebbed had fallen over on her side. Howard, seeing her condition, had followed her in the *Ark* with four or five other of the Queen's ships, and was furiously attacking her with his boats, careless of neutrality laws. Howard's aim was, as he said, to pluck the feathers one by one from the Spaniard's wing, and here was a feather worth picking up. The galleass was the most splendid vessel of her kind afloat, Don Hugo one of the greatest of Spanish grandees.

Howard was making a double mistake. He took the galleass at last, after three hours' fighting. Don Hugo was killed by a musket ball. The vessel was plundered, and Howard's men took possession, meaning to carry her away when the tide rose. The French authorities ordered him off, threatening to fire upon him; and after wasting the forenoon, he was obliged at last to leave her where she lay. Worse than this, he had lost three precious hours, and had lost along with them, in the opinion of the Prince of Parma, the honours of the great day.

Drake and Hawkins thought better than to waste time plucking single feathers. The fire-ships had been more effective than they could have dared to hope. The enemy was broken up. The Duke was shorn of

141

half his strength, and the Lord had delivered him into their hand. He had got under way, still signalling, and uncertain in which direction to turn. His uncertainties were ended for him by seeing Drake bearing down upon him with the English fleet, save those which were loitering about the galleass. The English had now the advantage of numbers. The superiority of their guns he knew already, and their greater speed allowed him no hope to escape a battle. Forty ships alone were left to him to defend the banner of the crusade and the honour of Castile; but those forty were the largest and the most powerfully armed and manned that he had, and on board them were Oquendo, De Leyva, Recalde, and Bretandona, the best officers in the Spanish navy next to the lost Don Pedro.

The scene of the action which was to decide the future of England was between Calais and Dunkirk, a few miles off shore, and within sight of Parma's camp. There was no more manoeuvring for the weather-gage, no more fighting at long range. Drake dashed straight upon his prey as the falcon stoops upon its quarry. A chance had fallen to him which might never return; not for the vain distinction of carrying prizes into English ports, not for the ray of honour which would fall on him if he could carry off the sacred banner itself and hang it in the Abbey at Westminster, but a chance so to handle the Armada that it should never be seen again in English waters, and deal such a blow on Philip that the Spanish Empire should reel with it. The English ships had the same superiority over the galleons which steamers have now over sailing vessels. They had twice the speed; they could lie two points nearer to the wind. Sweeping round them at cable's length, crowding them in one upon the other, yet never once giving them a chance to grapple, they hurled in their showers of round shot. Short as was the powder supply, there was no sparing it that morning. The hours went on, and still the battle raged, if battle it could be called where the blows were all dealt on one side and the suffering was all on the other. Never on sea or land did the Spaniards show themselves worthier of their great name than on that day. But from the first they could do nothing.

It was said afterwards in Spain that the Duke showed the white feather, that he charged his pilot to keep him out of harm's way, that he shut himself up in his cabin, buried in wool-packs, and so on. The Duke had faults enough, but poltroonery was not one of them. He, who till he entered the English Channel had never been in action on sea or land, found himself, as he said, in the midst of the most furious engagement recorded in the history of the time. As to being out of harm's way, the standard at his masthead drew the hottest of the fire upon him. The *San Martin's* timbers were of oak and doubly thick, but the shot, he said, went through them enough to shatter a rock. Her deck was a slaughter-house; half his company were killed or wounded, and no more would have been heard or seen of the *San Martin* or her commander had not Oquendo and De Leyva pushed in to the rescue and enabled him to creep away under their cover. He himself saw nothing more of the action after this. The smoke, he said, was so thick that he could make out nothing, even from his masthead. But all round it was but a repetition of the same scene. The Spanish shot flew high, as before, above the low English hulls, and they were themselves helpless butts to the English guns. And it is noticeable and supremely creditable to them that not a single galleon struck her colours. One of them, after a long duel with an Englishman, was on the point of sinking. An English officer, admiring the courage which the Spaniards had shown, ran out upon his bowsprit, told them that they had done all which became men, and urged them to surrender and save their lives. For answer they cursed the English as cowards and chickens because they refused to close. The officer was shot. His fall brought a last broadside on them, which finished the work. They went down, and the water closed over them.

The deadly hail rained on. In some ships blood was seen streaming out of the scupper-holes. Yet there was no yielding; all ranks showed equal heroism. The priests went up and down in the midst of the carnage, holding the crucifix before the eyes of the dying. At midday Howard came up to claim a second share in a victory which was no longer doubtful. Towards the afternoon the Spanish fire slackened. Their powder was gone, and they could make no return to the cannonade which was overwhelming them. They admitted freely afterwards that if the attack had been continued but two hours more they must all have struck or gone ashore. But the English magazines were empty also; the last cartridge was shot away, and the battle ended from mere inability to keep it up. It had been fought on both sides with peculiar determination. In the English there was the accumulated resentment of thirty years of menace to their country and their creed, with the enemy in tangible shape at last to be caught and grappled with; in the Spanish, the sense that if their cause had not brought them the help they looked for from above, the honour and faith of Castile should not suffer in their hands.

It was over. The English drew off, regretting that their thrifty mistress had limited their means of fighting for her, and so obliged them to leave their work half done. When the cannon ceased the wind rose, the smoke rolled away, and in the level light of the sunset they could see the results of the action.

A galleon in Recalde's squadron was sinking with all hands. The *San Philip* and the *San Matteo* were drifting dismasted towards the Dutch coast, where they were afterwards wrecked. Those which were left with canvas still showing were crawling slowly after their comrades who had not been engaged, the spars and rigging so cut up that they could scarce bear their sails. The loss of life could only be conjectured, but it had been obviously terrible. The nor'-wester was blowing up and was pressing the wounded ships upon the shoals, from which, if it held, it seemed impossible in their crippled state they would be able to work off.

In this condition Howard left them for the night, not to rest, but from any quarter to collect, if he could, more food and powder. The snake had been scotched, but not killed. More than half the great fleet were far away, untouched by shot, perhaps able to fight a second battle if they recovered heart. To follow, to drive them on the banks if the wind held, or into the North Sea, anywhere so that he left them no chance of joining hands with Parma again, and to use the time before they had rallied from his blows, that was the present necessity. There was but one thought in the whole of them, to be again in chase of the flying foe. Howard was resolute as Drake. All that was possible was swiftly done. Seymour and the Thames squadron were to stay in the Straits and watch Parma. From every attainable source food and powder were collected for the rest – far short in both ways of what ought to have been, but, as Drake said, 'we were resolved to put on a brag and go on as if we needed nothing.' Before dawn the admiral and he were again off on the chase.

The brag was unneeded. What man could do had been done, and the rest was left to the elements. The Invisible Powers in whom they had been taught to trust had deserted them. Their confidence was gone and their spirit broken. Drearily the morning broke on the Duke and his consorts the day after the battle. The Armada had collected in the night. The nor'-wester had freshened to a gale, and they were labouring heavily along, making fatal leeway towards the shoals.

It was St Lawrence's Day, Philip's patron saint, whose shoulder-bone he had lately added to the treasures of the Escurial; but St Lawrence was as heedless as St Dominic. The *San Martin* had but six fathoms under her. Those nearer to the land signalled five, and right before them they could see the brown foam of the breakers curling over the sands, while on their weather-beam, a mile distant and clinging to them like the shadow of death, were the English ships which had pursued them from Plymouth like the dogs of the Furies. The Spanish sailors and soldiers had been without food since the evening when they anchored at Calais. All Sunday they had been at work, no rest allowed them to eat. On the Sunday night they had been stirred out of their sleep by fire-ships. Monday they had been fighting, and Monday night committing their dead to the sea. Now they seemed advancing directly upon inevitable destruction. As the wind stood there was still room for them to wear and thus escape the banks, but they would then have to face the enemy, who seemed only refraining from attacking them because while they continued on their present course the winds and waves would finish the work without help from man. Recalde, De Leyva, Oquendo, and other officers were sent for to the *San Martin* to consult. Oquendo came last. 'Ah, Señor Oquendo,' said the Duke, as the heroic Biscayan stepped on board, 'que haremos?' (what shall we do?). 'Let your Excellency bid load the guns again,' was Oquendo's gallant answer.

It could not be. De Leyva himself said that the men would not fight the English again. Florez advised surrender. The Duke wavered. It was said that a boat was actually lowered to go off to Howard and make terms, and that Oquendo swore that if the boat left the *San Martin* on such an errand he would fling Florez into the sea. Oquendo's advice would have, perhaps, been the safest if the Duke could have taken it. There were still seventy ships in the Armada little hurt. The English were 'bragging,' as Drake said, and in no condition themselves for another serious engagement. But the temper of the entire fleet made a courageous course impossible. There was but one Oquendo. Discipline was gone. The soldiers in their desperation had taken the command out of the hands of the seamen. Officers and men alike abandoned hope, and, with no human prospect of salvation left to them, they flung themselves on their knees upon the decks and prayed the Almighty to have pity on them. But two weeks were gone since they had knelt on those same decks on the first sight of the English shore to thank Him for having brought them so far on an enterprise so glorious. Two weeks; and what weeks! Wrecked, torn by cannon shot, thousands of them dead or dying, the survivors could now but pray to be delivered from a miserable death by the elements. In cyclones the wind often changes suddenly back from north-west to west, from west to south. At that moment, as if in answer to their petition, one of these sudden shifts of wind saved them from the immediate peril. The gale backed round to S.S.W., and ceased to press them on the shoals. They could ease their sheets, draw off into open water, and steer a course up the middle of the North Sea.

So only that they went north, Drake was content to leave them unmolested. Once away into the high latitudes they might go where they would. Neither Howard nor he, in the low state of their own magazines, desired any unnecessary fighting. If the Armada turned back they must close with it. If it held its present course they must follow it till they could be assured it would communicate no more for that summer with the Prince of Parma. Drake thought they would perhaps make for the Baltic or some port in Norway. They would meet no hospitable reception from either Swedes or Danes, but they would probably try. One only imminent danger remained to be provided against. If they turned into the Forth, it was still possible for the Spaniards to redeem their defeat, and even yet shake Elizabeth's throne. Among the many plans which had been formed for the invasion of England, a landing in Scotland had long been a favourite. Guise had always preferred Scotland when it was intended that Guise should be the leader. Santa Cruz had been in close correspondence with Guise on this very subject, and many officers in the Armada must have been acquainted with Santa Cruz's views. Had the Armada anchored in Leith Roads with ten thousand men, half a million ducats, and a Santa Cruz at its head, it might had kindled a blaze at that moment from John o' Groat's Land to the Border.

But no such purpose occurred to the Duke of Medina Sidonia. He probably knew nothing at all of Scotland or its parties. Among the many deficiencies which he had pleaded to Philip as unfitting him for the command, he had said that Santa Cruz had acquaintances among the English and Scotch peers. He had himself none. His chief merit was that he was conscious of his incapacity; and his only anxiety was to carry home the still considerable fleet which had been trusted to him without further loss. Beyond Scotland and the Scotch Isles there was the open ocean, and in the open ocean there were no sandbanks and no English guns. Thus, with all sail set he went on before the wind. Drake and Howard attended him till they had seen him past the Forth, and knew then that there was no more to fear. It was time to see to the wants of their own poor fellows, who had endured so patiently and fought so magnificently. On August 13 they saw the last of the Armada, turned back, and made their way to the Thames.

But the story has yet to be told of the final fate of the great 'enterprise of England' (the 'empresa de Inglaterra'), the object of so many prayers, on which the hopes of the Catholic world had been so long and passionately fixed. It had been ostentatiously a religious crusade. The preparations had been attended with peculiar solemnities. In the eyes of the faithful it was to be execution of Divine justice on a wicked princess and a wicked people. In the eyes of millions whose convictions were less decided it was an appeal to God's judgement to decide between the Reformation and the Pope. There was an appropriateness, therefore, if due to accident, that the other causes besides the action of man should have combined in its overthrow.

The Spaniards were experienced sailors; a voyage round the Orkneys and round Ireland to Spain might be tedious, but at that season of the year need not have seemed either dangerous or difficult. On inquiry, however, it was found that the condition of the fleet was seriously alarming. The provisions placed on board at Lisbon had been found unfit for food, and much had been thrown into the sea. The fresh stores taken in at Corunna had been consumed, and it was found that at the present rate there would be nothing left in a fortnight. Worse than all, the water-casks refilled there had been carelessly stowed. They had been shot through in the fighting and were empty; while of clothing or other comforts for the cold regions which they were entering no thought had been taken. The mules and horses had been flung overboard, and Scotch smacks, which had followed the retreating fleet, reported floating carcases.

The rations were reduced for each man to a daily half-pound of biscuit, a pint of water, and a pint of wine. Thus, sick and hungry, the wounded left to the care of a medical officer, who went from ship to ship, the subjects of so many prayers were left to encounter the climate of the North Atlantic. The Duke blamed all but himself; he hanged one poor captain for neglect of orders, and would have hanged another had he dared; but his authority was gone. They passed the Orkneys in a single body. They then parted, it was said, in a fog; but each commander had to look out for himself and his men. In many ships water must be had somewhere, or they would die. The *San Martin*, with sixty consorts, went north to the sixtieth parallel. From that height the pilots promised to take them down clear of the coast. The wind still clung to the west, each day blowing harder than the last. When they braced round to it their wounded spars gave way, their rigging parted. With the greatest difficulty they made at last sufficient offing, and rolled down somehow out of sight of land, dipping their yards in the enormous seas.

Of the rest, one or two went down among the Western Isles and became wrecks there, their crews, or part of them, making their way through Scotland to Flanders. Others went north to Shetland or the Faroe Islands. Between thirty and forty were tempted on the Irish coasts. There were Irishmen in the fleet, who must have told them that they would find the water there for which they were perishing, safe harbours, and a friendly Catholic people; and they found either harbours which they could not reach or sea-washed sands and reefs. They were wrecked at various places between Donegal and the Blaskets. Some thousands of half-drowned wretches struggled on shore alive. Many were gentlemen, richly dressed, with velvet coats, gold chains, and rings. The common sailors and soldiers had been paid their wages before they started, and each had a bag of ducats lashed to his waist when he landed through the surf. The wild Irish of the coast, tempted by the booty, knocked unknown numbers of them on the head with their battleaxes, or stripped them naked and left them to die of the cold. On one long sand strip in Sligo an English officer estimated eleven hundred bodies, and he heard that there were as many more a few miles distant.

The better educated of the Ulster chiefs, the O'Rourke and O'Donnell, hurried down to stop the butchery and spare Ireland the shame of murdering helpless Catholic friends. Many – how many cannot be said – found protection in their castles. But even so, it seemed as if some inexorable fate pursued all who had sailed in that doomed expedition. Alonzo de Leyva, with half a hundred young Spanish nobles of rank who were under his special charge, made his way in a galleass into Killibeg. He was himself disabled in landing. O'Donnell received and took care of him and his companions. After remaining in O'Donnell's castle for a month he recovered. The weather appeared to mend. The galleass was patched up, and De Leyva ventured an attempt to make his way in her to Scotland. He had passed the worst danger, and Scotland was almost in sight; but fate would have its victims. The galleass struck a rock off Dunluce and went to pieces, and Don Alonzo and the gallant youths who had sailed with him were washed ashore all dead, to find an unmarked grave in Antrim.

Most pitiful of all was the fate of those who fell into the hands of the

English garrisons in Galway and Mayo. Galleons had found their way into Galway Bay – one of them had reached Galway itself – the crews half dead with famine and offering a cask of wine for a cask of water. The Galway townsmen were human, and tried to feed and care for them. Most were too far gone to be revived, and died of exhaustion. Some might have recovered, but recovered they would be a danger to the state. The English in the West of Ireland were but a handful in the midst of a sullen, half-conquered population. The ashes of the Desmond rebellion were still smoking, and Dr Sanders and his legatine commission were fresh in immediate memory. The defeat of the Armada in the Channel could only have been vaguely heard of. All that English officers could have accurately known must have been that an enormous expedition had been sent to England by Philip to restore the Pope; and Spaniards, they found, were landing in thousands in the midst of them with arms and money; distressed for the moment, but sure, if allowed time to get their strength again, to set Connaught in a blaze. They had no fortresses to hold so many prisoners, no means of feeding them, no men to spare to escort them to Dublin. They were responsible to the Queen's government for the safety of the country. The Spaniards had not come on any errand of mercy to her or hers. The stern order went out to kill them all wherever they might be found, and two thousand or more were shot, hanged, or put to the sword. Dreadful! Yes, but war itself is dreadful and has its own necessities.

The sixty ships which had followed the *San Martin* succeeded at last in getting round Cape Clear, but in a condition scarcely less miserable than that of their companions who had perished in Ireland. Half their companies died – died of untended wounds, hunger, thirst, and famine fever. The survivors were moving skeletons, more shadows and ghosts than living men, with scarce strength left them to draw a rope or handle a tiller. In some ships there was no water for fourteen days. The weather in the lower latitudes lost part of its violence, or not one of them would have seen Spain again. As it was, they drifted on outside Scilly and into the Bay of Biscay, and in the second week in September they dropped in one by one. Recalde, with better success than the rest, made Corunna. The Duke, not knowing where he was, found himself in sight of Corunna also. The crew of the *San Martin* were prostrate, and could not work her in. They signalled for help, but none came, and they dropped away to leeward to Bilbao. Oquendo had fallen off still farther to Santander, and the rest of the sixty arrived in the following days at one or other of the Biscay ports. On board them, of the more than twenty thousand who had left those shores but two months before in high hope and passionate enthusiasm, nine thousand only came back alive – if alive they could be called. It is touching to read a letter from Bilbao of their joy at warm Spanish sun, the sight of the grapes on the white walls, and the taste of fresh home bread and water again. But it came too late to save them, and those whose bodies might have rallied died of broken hearts and disappointed dreams. Santa Cruz's old companions could not survive the ruin of the Spanish navy. Recalde died two days after he landed at Bilbao. Santander was Oquendo's home. He had a wife and children there, but he refused to see them, turned his face to the wall, and died too. The common seamen and soldiers were too weak to help themselves. They had to be left on board the diseased ships till hospitals could be prepared to take them in. The authorities of Church and State did all that men could do; but the case was past help, and before September was out all but a few hundred needed no further care.

Philip, it must be said for him, spared nothing to relieve the misery. The widows and orphans were pensioned by the state. The stroke which had fallen was received with a dignified submission to the inscrutable purposes of Heaven. Diego Florez escaped with a brief punishment at Burgos. No-one else else was punished for faults which lay chiefly in the King's own presumption in imagining himself the instrument of Providence.

The Duke thought himself more sinned against than sinning. He did not die, like Recalde or Oquendo, seeing no occasion for it. He flung down his command and retired to his palace at San Lucar; and so far was Philip from resenting the loss of the Armada on its commander, that he continued him in his governorship of Cadiz, where Essex found him seven years later, and where he was as unlucky with Essex as he had been with Howard Drake.

The Spaniards made no attempt to conceal the greatness of their defeat. Unwilling to allow that the Upper Powers had been against them, they set it frankly down to the superior fighting powers of the English.

The English themselves, the Prince of Parma said, were modest in their victory. They thought little of their own gallantry. To them the defeat and destruction of the Spanish fleet was a declaration of the Almighty in the cause of their country and the Protestant faith. Both sides had appealed to Heaven, and Heaven had spoken.

It was the turn of the tide. The wave of reconquest of the

Netherlands ebbed from that moment. Parma took no more towns from the Hollanders. The Catholic peers and gentlemen of England, who had held aloof from the Established Church, waiting *ad illud tempus* for a religious reaction, accepted the verdict of Providence. They discovered that in Anglicanism they could keep the faith of their fathers, yet remain in communion with their Protestant fellow countrymen, use the same liturgy, and pray in the same temples. For the first time since Elizabeth's father broke the bonds of Rome the English became a united nation, joined in loyal enthusiasm for the Queen, and were satisfied that thenceforward no Italian priest should tithe or toll in her dominions.

But all that, and all that went with it, the passing from Spain to England of the sceptre of the seas, must be left to other lectures, or other lecturers who have more years before them than I. My own theme has been the Protestant adventurers who fought through that perilous week in the English Channel and saved their country and their country's liberty.

Part II

Preface

After completing my History of England from the fall of Wolsey to the defeat of the Spanish Armada, I had intended to pursue the story of the sixteenth century, and to write the lives of Charles the Fifth and Philip the Second. To them had fallen the task of confronting the storm which had broken over the rest of Europe. The opening of the Archives of Spain, Paris, and Vienna had for the first time made it possible to see the position in which they found themselves, to understand their characters and to weigh impartially their conduct in a situation so extraordinary. My own partial researches had already shown me that the prevailing opinions about these two princes required wide correction, and I thought that I could not better employ the remainder of my life than on an enquiry so profoundly interesting. To regard the Emperor, to regard Philip merely as reactionary bigots, is as unjust as it is uninstructive. They had to deal with a world in arms, with a condition in which society was disintegrated by a universal spiritual revolt, of which the outcome was still uncertain, and at such a crisis the wisest statesmen must have necessarily been divided on the conduct which duty required of them.

The labour of investigation would have been very great, and the years which I could have devoted to it would at most have been none too many for so ambitious an enterprise. I was obliged by circumstances to lay my purpose aside until it was too late to begin; and it will fall to others, perhaps better qualified than myself, to execute what, if successfully performed, will be the best service that can now be rendered to modern history. Of my own attempts nothing has come, or now can come, save a few separate studies, such as the story of Queen Catherine's Divorce as related by Charles the Fifth's ambassadors, with the essays in this present volume. The Divorce of Catherine has been brought out in a separate form as a supplement to my History of England. The essays I reproduce because they were carefully written, and I hope may have some interest to historical students. The 'Relacion' of Antonio Pérez has, for three centuries, been the chief authority for the private character of Philip the Second. Philip was once titular King of England, and I have thought it worth while to examine the character of his accuser. The defeat of the Armada transferred leadership at sea from Spain to England, and the Spanish account of it cannot be read without curiosity and even sympathy.

Antonio Pérez: Philip II's Secretary and Opponent

One day early in the spring of the year 1590, while Spain was still bleeding from the destruction of the great Armada, Mass was being sung in the church of the Dominican convent at Madrid. The candles were burning, the organ was pealing, the acolytes were swinging the censers, and the King's confessor was before the altar in his robes, when a woman, meanly dressed, rushed forward amidst the fumes of the incense. Turning to the priest, she said: 'Justice! I demand justice; I demand that you hear me! Are you deaf, that I come so often to you and you will not listen? Then I appeal to One who will listen; I appeal to Thee my God who art here present; I call on God to be my witness and my judge; He knows the wrongs which I suffer. Let Him punish yonder man who is my oppressor.'

The confessor stood speechless for a few moments. He then beckoned to the attendants. 'Bid the lady prioress come hither,' he said, 'and the sisterhood, and this woman's sister, who is one of them. Say I require their presence.'

The lady mother came fluttering with her flock behind her. They gathered to the grating which divided the chancel from the convent precincts.

'Holy mother,' the confessor said, 'this lady here present charges me on my soul and conscience. She calls on God to judge her cause, and she clamours for redress. I do not wonder; I should wonder rather if she held her peace. But what can I do that I have left undone? I have told the King that it is his duty to despatch the business of the lady's husband and restore him to his family; what would she have from me more?'

157

'I would have this much more, señor,' the lady replied. 'If the King will not do what you command him, refuse him absolution and withdraw to your cell. You will be nearer heaven there, than where you now stand. As the King's confessor you are his judge. The King is the offender; I am the injured woman of St. Luke's Gospel. The King may wear the crown on his head; but you are higher than he.'

The confessor could not answer her.

The scene shifts to the reception hall of Rodrigo Vasquez, the president of the High Court of Justice. The president was a grave, dignified man, seventy years old. Before him stood a family of children, the eldest a girl of sixteen, the little ones holding her hands or clinging to her dress.

The girl did not seem daunted by the presence in which she stood. 'Your lordship,' she said, 'has promised us this, that, and the other; you tell us one day that something shall be done on the morrow, and then the next, and the next, as if a last 'morrow' there would never be. You have brought our home to desolation. You have deceived a girl like me, and you think it a grand victory, a glorious distinction. You thirst, it seems, for our blood; well, then, you shall have it. Old men, it is said, go again to the breast for milk to keep the life in them. You require blood, fresh from the veins of its owners. We had rather not be swallowed piecemeal, so we are come all to you together. You perhaps would prefer to linger over us, but we cannot wait. Let your lordship make an end with us. Here we are.'

Don Rodrigo started out of his chair. He marched up the hall, and down, and then to the four corners. He twisted his fingers, he crossed his arms. He appealed to an old aunt and uncle who had brought the children.

'Señora, señor,' he said, 'I beseech you make that young woman hold her peace, and say no more.'

The young woman would not hold her peace.

'Pray sit down, your lordship,' she said; 'pray be calm. We are young; some of us were born, so to say, but yesterday. But you have made our lives a burden to us. Finish the work; take our blood, and let our souls depart from this miserable prison.'

These two incidents, if the children's father wrote the truth, happened precisely as I have described them, and are as literal facts as usually pass for history. Perhaps they are not exaggerated. The priest in the Dominican convent was Diego de Chaves, spiritual adviser to Philip the Second. The woman before the altar was Juana de Coello, wife of Antonio Pérez, his Majesty's Secretary of State and confidential minister. The girl in the Court of Justice was his daughter Doña Gregoria, and the little ones were her brothers and sisters.

What strange cause could have wrought a mother and child into a state of passion so unnatural?

For three centuries after the Reformation, Philip the Second was the evil demon of Protestant tradition. Every action which could be traced to him was ascribed to the darkest motives. He was like some ogre or black enchanter sitting in his den in the Escurial, weaving plots in close communion and correspondence with the Antichrist of Rome. He was the sworn enemy of the light which was rising in Europe; he was a tyrant at home, and even in his own household; he was believed universally to have murdered his own son. The Inquisition was his favourite instrument.

All this violence of censure was perfectly natural. Men engaged in a deadly struggle for what they regard as a sacred cause are seldom charitable to their adversaries. It was the Spanish power dominantly which stemmed the Reformation, and more than once was near extinguishing it. The conflict was desperate and at last savage, and deeds were done which have left a stain on all who were concerned in them.

But as time has gone on, and as it has appeared that neither Lutheranism nor Calvinism nor Anglicanism can be regarded as a final revelation, we have been able to review the history of the sixteenth century in a calmer temper. For a thousand years the doctrines of the Catholic Church had been guarded by the civil power as the most precious of human possessions. New ideas on such subjects, shaking as they do the foundations of human society, may be legitimately resisted on their first appearance from better motives than hatred of truth; and although, in a strife so protracted and so deadly, evil passions dressed themselves in sacred colours, yet it has been recognised that right-thinking men might naturally have taken opposite sides, and that Catholics as well as Protestants might have been acting on conscientious convictions. The dust has settled a little, the spiritual atmosphere has cleared itself, and among the consequences the cloud which hung over Philip the Second has partially lifted. The countrymen of Cervantes were not a nation of mere bigots; yet it is clear that the whole Spanish people went with the King enthusiastically in defence of the Church, and complained only when his *pié de plomo,* his foot of lead that he was so proud of, would not move fast enough. The romance of

Don Carlos has gone into the air of which it was made. Don Carlos is known now to have been a lunatic, whom it was necessary to cage; the exact manner of his death is unknown; but his father acted throughout by the advice of the Council of State, and it was by their advice also that so distressing a secret was concealed from public curiosity. As we look at Philip with more impartial attention, the figure comes out before us of a painstaking, laborious man, prejudiced, narrow-minded, superstitious, with a conceit of his own abilities not uncommon in crowned heads, and frequently with less justification, but conscientious from his own point of view, and not without the feelings of a gentleman.

I purpose to reconstruct on these more tolerant lines the story of the relations between Philip the Second and Antonio Pérez which have so long perplexed historical inquirers – on the surface a mere palace intrigue, but developing from its peculiar features into a nine days' wonder throughout Europe, and occasioning, if not causing, the overthrow of the constitutional liberties of Aragon.

Students of the history of the sixteenth century must be familiar with the name of Gonzalo Pérez. He was State Secretary to Charles the Fifth, and his signature stands at the bottom of the page on scores of Charles's despatches which are now extant. When the Emperor abdicated, Gonzalo remained in office with Philip, and had been forty years in the public service when he died. Antonio Pérez passed as Gonzalo's natural son. He was born in 1542, and was legitimatised immediately by an Imperial diploma. There were those who said, and spoke of it as notorious, that Antonio was not Gonzalo's son at all, but the sun of Ruy Gomez, Prince of Eboli and Duke of Pastraña, Philip's favourite minister. Ruy Gomez, at any rate, took charge of the boy, removed him from school, brought him up in his own family, and introduced him into a public department. Being quick and brilliant, he was rapidly promoted; and when Ruy Gomez died in 1567 he left Antonio, at the age of twenty-five, chief secretary to the Council of State with a salary of four thousand ducats a year, in addition to which, as a sinecure, he was Protonotary of Sicily with two thousand ducats a year. A rise so swift implied extraordinary private influence, or extraordinary personal qualities; and this was but the beginning of his fortunes. On losing Ruy Gomez, Philip took Pérez as his own confidential secretary; and along with him another youth, Juan de Escovedo, who had also been a pupil of Ruy Gomez, and had been brought up at Pérez's side. The two young men had been, and still continued, intimate personal friends.

The Spanish administration was divided into separate councils, the secretaries of which were each in close relation with the King, who insisted on knowing all that was going on. Besides these there were the secretaries who deciphered despatches, who were thus admitted into state mysteries and were necessarily treated with confidence. But of the whole number Antonio Pérez and Escovedo were nearest to the King, and Pérez the closer of the two. He alone was admitted into the interior labyrinths of Philip's mind.

He was thus a person of extraordinary consequence. He was courted by great men in Church and State. The Italian princes sent him presents to advance their interests. He was the dispenser of royal favours. He treated dukes as his equals, and the splendour in which he lived was envied and criticised; but his legitimate income was considerable; in all countries in that age influential statesmen accepted homage in the shape of offerings; and, considering the opportunities the favoured secretary had, he does not seem to have exceptionally abused them.

Pérez being thus upon the stage, we introduce a more considerable figure, Don John of Austria, the King's brother, illegitimate son of Charles the Fifth. An illegitimate prince is always in a delicate position, especially when his father happens to have brought him up as a real one. He is of royal blood, but without the rights belonging to it. He is uncertain of his rank, and may generally be presumed to be discontented. But Philip had shown no suspicion of his brother. He had trusted him, employed him, refused him no opportunities which he could have desired had he come more regularly into the world. Don John was chivalrous, ardent, ambitious. He had every quality which promised distinction, if in his youth he had been wisely guided. Ruy Gomez had furnished him with a secretary supposed to be prudence itself, Juan de Soto, who had been trained in the War Office.

Thus accompanied, when the Moors broke into insurrection, Don John was sent to Granada to reduce them. He did his work well; he became a popular favourite, and went next to command the allied Catholic fleet in the Mediterranean. De Soto only had given imperfect satisfaction. Don John had high-flying views for himself, and De Soto, it was feared, had not sufficiently discouraged them. Pérez and Escovedo were instructed to give him an admonition, which they did, and with this friendly warning Don John and his secretary went their way into Italy.

The battle of Lepanto followed, and the young irregular Spanish prince blazed out into a hero of romance. Philip was a faithful son of

161

the Church, and of the Pope in his spiritual capacity; but he was King of Naples and Sicily, with interests in the Peninsula not always identical with the interests of the court of Rome. Pius the Fifth, who had just then absolved England from its allegiance to Queen Elizabeth, and believed it his mission to sweep away heresy, found in Don John a child much nearer to his heart. Don John was to be the Church's knight, the chosen soldier of the Lord, and immediately after Lepanto Pius had formed views for constituting him an independent sovereign.

Tunis was to be the first scene of his greatness. The Emperor Charles had won immortal glory in his African campaign. De Soto had studied history and dreamt of the possibility of reviving the Carthaginian empire. Don John, set on by the Pope, re-fortified the Goleta, and transported on his own authority, out of Italy, the best part of the Spanish troops there, while the Papal Nuncio at Madrid requested Philip in Pope Pius's name to allow his brother to take the title of King of Tunis. The Spanish council knew better than his Holiness the value of the Emperor's African conquests. They had been a drain upon the treasury and the grave of thousands of their bravest men. Instead of indulging Don John they sent orders that the fortresses should be demolished and the troops withdrawn.

But the order came too late. The Goleta was assulted by the Turks in overwhelming numbers, and the garrison was cut off to a man. Philip had good reason to be displeased. The independent action of a commander cannot expect to be regarded, when unsuccessful, with especial leniency, nor were matters mended by the signs which his brother was manifesting of a restless ambition. He replied politely to the Pope, however, that the establishment of a kingdom in Tunis was not at the time expedient. He found no fault with Don John, but laid the blame on bad advisers. He gently removed De Soto, leaving him as commissary-general of the army; and secretary Escovedo, who had been especially eloquent in the cabinet on De Soto's rashness, was sent to take his place as a safer companion to the prince.

Philip, however, was again unfortunate. The mischance at the Goleta had not been sufficient to dim the glories of Lepanto, or cool the hopes which so brilliant a victory had inspired. Don John was still persuaded that there were great things in store for him. It seemed as if he had an especial power of turning the heads of the secretaries, and Escovedo himself was soon embarked with him in a yet wilder scheme, to which the Pope and the Fates were beckoning the way.

After a struggle of ten years with his revolted subjects in the Low

Countries, experience was beginning to teach Philip that it might be expedient to try milder ways with them. The Duke of Alva with his blood and iron had succeeded only in enlisting the whole of the seventeen provinces in a common rebellion, and if the war continued, the not unlikely end of it would be that Spain would finally lose them all. Holland and Zealand might become English, Belgium be absorbed into France, and the rest drift away into Germany. Philip determined on an effort to make up the quarrel. The provinces were to be left with their constitutional rights, securities being given for the safety of religion. The Spanish army was to be withdrawn, and by abandoning attempts at coercion he hoped that it might not be too late to recover the hearts of the people.

To carry out this purpose he had pitched upon his brother Don John. The Emperor's memory was still honoured in the Low Countries. Charles had always been more a Fleming than a Spaniard. Don John with his high rank and chivalrous reputation, was likely to be welcome there, or at least more welcome than any other person who could be selected; and an opportunity was thrown in his way, if he could use it, of winning laurels for himself more enduring than those which grow on battle-fields.

The opportunity, however, was one which a wise man only could appreciate. Young soldiers, especially soldiers who have been distinguished in arms, are seldom in love with constitutions. To be governor at Brussels, with a council of successful rebels to tie his hands, was a situation which would have had no attraction for the victor of Lepanto, had there not been attached to it a more interesting possibility, the *empresa de Inglaterra,* the invasion and conquest of England. Philip himself had for a few years been called King of England. His name remains in our Statute Book. It was asserted by the Jesuits that the English Catholics were waiting only for the help of a few thousand Spaniards to hurl from the throne the excommunicated usurper. The Queen of Scots, the Lady of Romance, was lying a prisoner in Sheffield Castle. To carry over the army when it left the Netherlands, to land in Yorkshire, to deliver the enchanted princess, and reign at her side with the Pope's blessing over an England restored to the faith – this was a glorious enterprise, fit to fire the blood of a Christian knight who was also the countryman of Don Quixote.

Don John was still in Italy when the offer of the appointment was made. If it was accepted, the King's order to him was to proceed with his secretary directly to Brussels without returning to Spain. Not the pacification of Flanders, but the *empresa de Inglaterra* was the thought which rushed into the minds of Don John and Escovedo. Instead of setting out as they were enjoined, they went to Rome to consult Pope Pius's successor, to ask for his sanction, to ask for men, to ask for the title which had been borne by his brother, and all this without so much as going through the form of consulting his brother on the subject.

The Pope was of course delighted. If the attempt was made, God would not allow it to fail. The Jesuits had all along insisted that Philip's dilatoriness had alone allowed heresy to take root in England. Philip himself, who knew something of the country, was under no such illusion. Five years before he had consented unwillingly to the Ridolfi conspiracy. Elizabeth was then to have been dethroned; Spanish troops were to have landed, and the Queen of Scots was to have had the crown. The end of this fine project had been the execution of the Duke of Norfolk, the near escape from execution of Mary Stuart, a plague of pirates and privateers on the shores of Spanish America, and increased severities against the English Catholics. Of the Queen of Scots Philip had the worst opinion. To strike a blow at that moment at Elizabeth could not fail to re-exasperate the Low Countries. English soldiers would land in Holland, English corsairs would swarm in the Atlantic and seize his treasure-ships.

None of these considerations occurred to Don John or his fiery adviser. Escovedo was even hotter than his master, and audacious even to insolence. From Rome, in spite of his orders, he went to Madrid; and Don John soon after followed him thither, leaving their purposes to reach Philip indirectly from another quarter. This was in the summer of 1576, and we now approach the critical part of the story. Shortly after Escovedo arrived at the court, the Nuncio sent one morning for Antonio Pérez and inquired who a certain Escoda was. He had been all night, he said, deciphering a despatch from his Holiness. It referred to the 'enterprise of England' which was to be undertaken, if the King would allow it, by Don John. Escoda would inform him of the particulars.

'Escoda' could be no one but Escovedo. Pérez carried his information to the King, who was again extremely dissatisfied; the more so perhaps that Don John's popularity, and the general favour with which Spanish sentiment was likely to take up the adventure, obliged him to keep his displeasure to himself. Escovedo evidently thought himself secure. He addressed Philip in so rude a letter that Philip complained of it to Pérez. 'If he had spoken to me as he has written,' the King said, 'I believe I could not have contained myself.' Words still more rash had fallen from Escovedo's lips. 'Don John, when master of England, was afterwards to take charge of Spain.'

Philip shrank from meeting difficulties openly. He took no notice of Escovedo's impertinence, and he was afraid or unwilling to quarrel with his brother. He allowed the Nuncio to give him the Pope's message, and put him off with a vague answer. Don John ventured on ground still more delicate by asking for the 'chair and canopy,' the insignia of a legitimate prince of the blood royal. Even this Philip did not refuse. He required only that Don John should repair first to his government, compose the provinces, and withdraw the army. When this was done it would be time to think of 'English enterprises'.

Don John went, and it seemed as if all was smooth again. Escovedo was left at Madrid professedly to complete some defective arrangements for his master. Perhaps Philip was uncertain whether he would trust so doubtful an adviser at his brother's side any more.

I am not writing the history of the wars in the Netherlands; it is enough to say that any hopes which had been built on the popularity of Don John were disappointed. The Estates refused to admit him as governor while the Spanish troops were in the fortresses; the troops were sullen, and would not move till they were paid their wages. Don John wished to remove them by sea, meaning, when they were in the Channel, to fly at England permitted or unpermitted; but Elizabeth and the Prince of Orange had their eyes open; the Estates insisted that the army should retire by land, and declined to advance a dollar till they were on the march. Don John, being without a friend whom he could trust, begged that Escovedo might rejoin him; and Escovedo, not without emphatic warnings and reiterated instructions, was allowed to go. The demands of the Estates were to be complied with to the letter. The army, at whatever sacrifice of bolder purposes, was to retire as the Estates desired. Philip required peace, and was prepared for the price that was to be paid for it.

The humiliation was too deep for Don John. For the knight-errant of the Church to retreat before a burgher council was ignominy. Something, he knew not what, must be done to repair it, and his thoughts went everywhere except where they ought to have been. Escovedo had no sooner arrived than a secret correspondence began again with the Pope. The religious war was raging in France. Don John might join the Duke of Guise and the Catholic league, and they might manage England between them. Then again he thought how he might satisfy his ambition at home. On February 3, 1577, Escovedo wrote to Pérez to revive the request for the chair and canopy. It would give Don John a seat in the Council of State. He and Pérez and their friends the Archbishop of Toledo and the Marques de los Velez could rule the country as they pleased, and relieve his brother of the cares of government. On reflection he perhaps remembered that Philip might not be so anxious to be relieved; for some days after the purpose was changed; Don John was to take his army into France as an adventurer, and help the Duke of Guise to destroy the Huguenots. Victorious there, he could hold the Estates in check, the shame of the retreat would be covered, and the 'great design' on England could go forward. Royal princes are excused their follies at the expense of their servants. These feverish dreams were set down at the Escurial to Escovedo's account, and probably with excellent reason.

Meanwhile, Philip's orders were being obeyed. He had agreed to all which the Estates demanded. On February 12 the arrangement known as the 'Perpetual Edict' was provisionally accepted, and was forwarded to Madrid for ratification. Don John was distracted. He believed that he might write to Pérez confidentially; for Pérez, by Philip's order, had encouraged him to suppose so; and much eloquence has been expended on the assumed treachery. But kings may be judged too harshly in such matters, when they have reason to fear that persons whom they have trusted are playing tricks with them. If Don John was acting loyally, he had nothing to fear. After the edict was sent off, Don John wrote again to Pérez that he must resign. Sooner than remain to govern Flanders on such conditions, he would turn hermit. If the King insisted on keeping him there he would become desperate, fling up the reins and go home, though he lost his life for it. He implored that he might not be driven to choose between disobedience and infamy.

Pérez showed Philip all these letters; and they were considered in the cabinet. The blame was laid on Escovedo, who was held to have betrayed his trust. Don John was informed kindly, but peremptorily, that his return at such a time would be prejudicial to the public service. No one could be so fit as the King's brother to recover the loyalty of the Estates. The King said that he understood his feelings, and could sympathise with him; but he must try to be patient; least of all must he rush off into France, where the Government had not asked for his assistance. The English project and his other wishes should be considered when the time for them was come; but his present duty was to reconcile Flanders, and there he must remain. Escovedo had spoken of returning himself to speak to the King. Pérez told him that if he came back without permission, it would be taken as a serious offence, and was not to be thought of.

Don John acquiesced, or seemed to acquiesce. The Perpetual Edict was ratified. The troops began the evacuation, and on May 2 Don John was received at Brussels, and installed as governor. Had he been sincere, the storm would have blown over; but the next news which arrived about him at Madrid was that he had actually made a private treaty with the Court of Rome. The Pope had promised him 6,000 men and 150,000 ducats for the English expedition, while before the Brussels settlement had lasted a fortnight he was again in correspondence with the Duke of Guise, and was threatening open hostilities against Holland and Zealand, which were making difficulties about liberty of worship. The difficulty need not have been insuperable; and the Estates refused to sanction immediate violence. Don John snatched at the excuse to break with them on his own authority; with such regiments as had not yet gone, he seized Namur; and Escovedo, in spite of his positive orders, rushed home after all, to press Philip to allow the army to return. The war should then be carried on in earnest. The Spanish forces could live in the rebel provinces as in an enemy's country, and lay them waste with fire and sword.

Information more unwelcome never reached Philip. He longed for peace; he had been acting in good faith; he refused to counter-order the troops; he blamed the seizure of Namur, and abhorred the mention of fire and sword. Still at the eleventh hour he clung to the hope of reconciliation. The Estates declared Don John a public enemy, and invited the Archduke Matthias to take his place. Even so, Philip persevered. He sent a commission to offer a complete amnesty, with the instant and perpetual removal of the army. The Estates might choose their own governor, either the Archduke Matthias, or the Archduke Ferdinand, or the Prince of Parma.

But it was too late; the day for peace was gone. Confidence was irrecoverably lost, and the quarrel had to be fought out to the end. The army went back – there was no help for it – with the Prince of Parma at its head; while it was said and believed that Don John was treating with the Duke of Guise for an open alliance, without regard to their respective sovereigns – a very strange and questionable performance. Both Guise and Philip were no doubt defending the Catholic religion. But respect for forms and secular interests were not to pass for nothing. Spain and France were the rivals for Continental supremacy. They had been at war off and on for three-quarters of a century, and, if the religious question was settled, might at any time be at war again. Philip had not forgotten that it was a Duke of Guise who had defended Metz against his father; and for his brother to take on himself to settle points of international policy with the subject of another sovereign, was something not very far removed from treason.

But we must now return to the scapegoat who was to bear the blame for all these things, the unlucky Escovedo. Flying home, as we saw him, in the teeth of a positive command, he landed at Santander on July 21. The worst had not yet happened; for it was not till the January following that the commission went with the last overtures for peace, nor was the treating with Guise as yet more than an unpleasant rumour. But Philip was legitimately incensed with Escovedo, and, if we can believe M. Mignet, had prepared a peculiar reception for him; nay, was expecting that Escovedo was coming with murderous intentions against himself. Pérez having informed the King in a note of Escovedo's approach, Philip, according to his habit, and in his well-known abominable hand, scrawled on the margin, 'Menester será prevenir nos bien de todo y dar nos mucha priesa á despacharle antes que nos maté.' The verb 'despachar,' like its English correspondent 'despatch,' has two meanings, and 'matar' has two meanings. M. Mignet supposes the words to mean, 'We must be quick to assassinate him before he kills us.' He makes Philip suspect Escovedo of intended treason, and resolve to be beforehand with him. But no one would have thought of so intepreting the passage if Escovedo had not in fact been assassinated at a later period. The natural translation would be, 'We must despatch him quickly (i.e. send him about his business) before he worries us to death;' and as Escovedo remained, for some months after his arrival, not only unmolested, but transacting business with the King, I cannot infer, with M. Mignet, that Philip had already formed so sanguinary a purpose against him.

Unquestionably, however, no good will was felt towards a man who has responded so ill to the confidence which had been placed in him. If Philip could have conveniently punished him without irritating his brother, he would gladly have read him a sharp lesson, and the irritation was likely to be increased as the consequences of his misdoings developed themselves. The especial uneasiness was on the side of France. In the autumn (1577), three months after Escovedo's arrival, Philip sent a new ambassador there, Juan de Vargas Mexia, to inquire particularly into what was passing between his brother and the

Duke of Guise. Mexia ascertained that the correspondence was real and that secret agents were going to and fro between them, though to what purpose he could not tell. The suspicious feature was the complete silence on the subject both of Don John and his secretary. Escovedo's manners were abrupt and arbitrary. In January Philip received a letter from him, which he described happily as *descosido*, loose, unstitched, visionary. He handed it to Pérez, that he might see how 'sanguinary' it was.

Don John, at the reopening of the war, had begun with a success. He had defeated the Prince of Orange at Gemblours. He wrote passionately for reinforcements. The victory had to be followed up, and all would be won. He demanded money – money and Escovedo. Philip, unhappily, had won victories before in the Low Countries, and knew better what to expect from them. His own more temperate policy had been thwarted and ruined, and it was but too natural that he should hold his brother's wild adviser as responsible. If he sent him back, it would be only to throw fuel on the fire. Don John, and the Pope, and the Guises would set all Europe in confusion. Escovedo was no fool. He could not be kept waiting at Madrid with dilatory excuses. To imprison him, or bring him to trial, might drive Don John at once into some dangerous course. It would lead to investigations and the publication of state secrets which ought not to be revealed.

There was a theory much in favour at the Spanish Court, that criminals who had forfeited their lives, or persons whose lives were for any reason inconsistent with public safety, might, when the facts were certain, and when an open prosecution would be inconvenient, be removed privately by orders of the Council of State. So Don Carlos had been disposed of; so the Flemish envoy at Simancas. Spain was not the only country where in extreme cases such proceedings were held permissible. Elizabeth would have been grateful to Sir Amyas Paulet if he would have relieved her of the Queen of Scots. In Italy, in France, in Scotland, a stab with a dagger was an expedient adopted in emergencies, with no great care to ascertain that it was deserved. Spain and England were rather in advance of other nations than behind them; and in Spain, heartily loyal as it was, the public had begun to doubt whether these secret executions ought to be continued.

A zealous court preacher had maintained, in a sermon at which Philip was present, that kings had absolute power over the lives and fortunes of their subjects. The Inquisition, of all courts in the world, took up the question. The preacher was obliged to retract his proposition in the same pulpit, and to confess that kings had no more power over their subjects than divine and human law allowed them. The old view, however, held its ground in spite of the Holy Office, and was professed in its extreme form by no less a person than the King's spiritual adviser, the same Diego de Chaves who was mentioned at the opening of our story. Don Diego's opinion was this: 'So far as I understand the law,' he said, 'a secular prince who for sufficient cause can take his subjects' lives from them by course of law can also do it without course of law when the evidence of the guilt is clear. Form and order are not essentials in such sense that they cannot be dispensed with; and if the prince has sufficient reasons for proceeding irregularly, the vassal who by his command puts to death another vassal is doing no more than his duty. He is bound to assume the cause to be adequate. The presumption in all cases is that the prince has reason for what he does.'

This doctrine was still held by Philip; and the difficulty with Escovedo was precisely of the kind where the application of it was convenient. Escovedo's guilt might be assumed. He was a confidential minister who had disobeyed his orders, and had caused a great public calamity, involving the renewal of a civil war. If allowed to live, he would still be dangerous. To bring him to an account openly would be dangerous also. Philip directed Antonio Pérez to consult the Marques de los Velez. The opinion of the marquis was decided, that Escovedo should be killed; yet that the King must not appear to have directed his execution, lest Don John should be exasperated. Some scheme should be contrived by which it could appear that he had been sacrificed to private revenge. A Government must have been singularly helpless which could have recourse to such expedients. But so it was. For the act itself los Velez had so little hesitation that, 'with the sacrament in his mouth,' he was ready to assert the necessity of it. The best method, he thought, would be to give Escovedo 'something to eat' from which he should not recover.

There was nothing in such a proposal to disturb Philip's conscientiousness. He sincerely believed that by consenting he was discharging a public duty, and with no more personal resentment than if he had been signing a warrant for an ordinary execution. It has never been suggested that Philip had any private malice against Escovedo, or had any motive beyond what was afterwards alleged. Why Antonio Pérez should have encouraged him, why he should himself have so readily undertaken a treacherous office, is another question on which speculation has been busy. He had been Escovedo's personal friend. They had grown up as boys together in the family of Ruy Gomez. They had been transferred together to the King's service. They had never differed politically until Escovedo had become Don John's secretary, and they had corresponded afterwards on terms of the closest intimacy. It is true that Pérez had been the strongest advocate for a policy of peace, and Escovedo for war; but an antagonism of opinion scarcely explains the readiness with which one Secretary of State undertook to murder another. And it has been assumed as a matter of course that Pérez must have had some private motives of his own.

Before entering into these dark regions I will describe briefly what actually happened. The 'something to eat' was administered as los Velez recommended. Pérez took into his confidence his own master of the household, Diego Martinez: he told him that the King and council considered Escovedo's life to be dangerous to the peace of Europe, and that Escovedo must be secretly made away with. To satisfy Martinez's scruples he showed him a letter in the King's hand. Enriquez, a page, was also admitted into the mystery. An apothecary was found far away in Aragon who could mix a potion, and Escovedo was invited to dinner. Two or three experiments were tried with imperfect success. The unlucky wretch became very ill after swallowing a dish of cream with some white powder in it; but he had not taken enough. He suspected foul play, and afterwards dined alone in his apartments in the palace. A page in the palace kitchen was bribed to put a larger dose into a plate which was sent up to him. Escovedo discovered the poison, and an innocent slave-girl who had dressed the dish was strangled in the Plaza at Madrid.

The fate of this poor creature, so piteous because so utterly undeserved, passed as a mere incident; Pérez scarcely gave a second thought to it, and the King's conscience could not descend to a kitchen wench. But poison, it was clear, could not be depended on; and steel was a surer method. Escovedo's habits were watched. He was out much after dark, and returned late to his apartments. Bravoes were brought up by the exertions of Diego Martinez from remote parts of the Peninsula. Easter had come, and Pérez, to be out of the way, went for the Holy Week to Alcala de Henares. On the night of Easter Monday, March 31, 1578, Don John's secretary was run through the body in a public street, and was killed on the spot.

Madrid was an orderly city, and open assassinations were unusual. A person, himself of so much consequence, and the notorious favourite of a prince who was the idol of the people, could not be found lying dead without a considerable stir being caused by it. The police were out like hornets. The gates were guarded, and no one was allowed to pass. The hotels and lodging-houses were called on for a list of their guests. The assassins were out of reach, for they were secreted in Pérez's own house, and no clue could be found; yet suspicion at once and instinctively pointed to Pérez as the instigator, and his absence at Alcala was not enough to clear him. His wife, Juana de Coello, called to condole with Escovedo's widow. The widow had not forgotten the dinners and the illness which followed, and the detected attempts at poison. She said significantly she feared the blow had been aimed by a friend's hand.

Pérez hurried back to the capital, pretending to be horrified. He saw Escovedo's son. He told the alcalde of the court that Escovedo had many enemies; there were rumours of a love affair in Flanders; Escovedo, he knew, had lately received a message, bidding him beware of some jealous Fleming. Perhaps he overacted his part. The alcalde and the alcalde's son, Garcia de Arce, cross-questioned him unpleasantly. The King was out at the Escurial, where, of course, reports reached him from the magistrates; but he was anxious for particulars. On April 3, three days after the murder, Pérez wrote to him, and a copy of the letter survives, with Philip's marginal remarks upon it. Pérez told him what had passed with the alcalde, and mentioned what he had said about the love affair. Philip noted, 'This was very right.' Garcia de Arce had asked Pérez whether there had been a quarrel between him and Escovedo, implying that he had heard something to that effect from Escovedo's wife. Philip observed, 'There will be danger from that woman.' 'The alcalde,' Pérez said, 'had discovered that strange things had been going on during the winter in Escovedo's house; mysterious visitors, night expeditions none knew where, and secret boxes of papers, and keys of other people's houses.'

Philip, who evidently looked on himself as a careful, well-intentioned prince, who had disposed of a public enemy in a skilful manner, thought more of Escovedo's plots than of awkward consequences from his murder. He remarked that these keys and visits had a bad complexion; the alcalde must look more closely into that matter, and search it to the bottom. Pérez was uncomfortable about his bravoes, whom he knew not how to dispose of. He had thought of sending them away with despatches as government couriers; but it seemed too dangerous. He recommended Philip to put the inquiry into the alcalde's hands exclusively, and to forbid any other person to meddle with it. Philip prudently observed that to interfere with the investigation would provoke suspicion. He would communicate with the alcalde, and would do what he could. The bravoes must be kept for the present where they were, and Pérez meanwhile might come out to the Escurial to see him. Finally, to quiet Pérez's evident alarm, he said: 'If Escovedo's widow desires to speak with me, I cannot refuse to see her; but do not fear that you will be unsupported. I am with you, and will not fail you in anything that may be expedient or necessary. Assure yourself of this. You know it well.'

There is no doubt at all that in the last extremity, and if Pérez's life was in danger, Philip intended honestly to tell the truth.

Strong, however, as suspicion was, suspicion was not proof; and proof against Pérez there was none. He had been many miles from Madrid when the murder was committed. His servants, Diego Martinez and Enriquez, knew that they had been acting by the King's authority. They had everything to gain by keeping counsel, and might be in serious danger if they betrayed their secret. The bravoes slipped away after a week or two, when the vigilance had relaxed. Each of them had a bag of doubloons with a commission as *alferez* (ensign in the army, unattached). They dispersed to Italy, to Central Europe, to all the winds. Every trace was thus swept out which could connect Pérez with the murder. The excitement died gradually away, and the affair seemed to be forgotten.

But poisoned wounds will not heal, though they be skinned over. The sore was to break out again, and the story to assume a form which has given it a place among the *causes célèbres* of the world.

Brilliant writers of history are subject to one general temptation – they desire to give their narrative dramatic completeness. The drama, if it is to have flavour, must revolve upon personal motives, and history must follow on the same lines. Sovereigns and statesmen who have been charged with the fortunes of nations, are assumed, where their actions require explanation, to have been influenced by no other passions than those which govern private individuals in their own more limited spheres. When a woman's name appears as connected with such high persons, the connection is always assumed to have been of one peculiar kind. To ask for evidence or look for other explanations is taken as a sign of simplicity or of ignorance of human nature.

The legend now stereotyped in European tradition is that the wife of Ruy Gomez, the Princess of Eboli, was the mistress of Philip the Second, and that the Princess of Eboli preferred Antonio Pérez to the

King. Escovedo, it is said, discovered the intrigue and threatened to reveal it. Pérez, in consequence, calumniated Escovedo to Philip. Philip allowed him to be murdered, but discovered afterwards that he had been the dupe of a treacherous minister and a bad woman, and regarded Pérez thenceforward with implacable hatred.

Now, before going further, I have to observe that the eleven years during which Philip is assumed to have been occupied with these emotions and the effort to give effect to them, were the busiest in the whole of his long, laborious reign. They were the years in which he annexed Portugal. They were the years of Parma's administration of the Netherlands. They were the years of preparation for the Armada. There was the civil war in France to be watched and guided. There were Naples and Sicily to be ruled, and the Turks to be held in check in the Mediterranean. There were the ambassadors' despatches from foreign courts. There was a close, constant, and elaborate correspondence to be maintained with the Pope. There were the reports of the Inquisition to be received and studied. There were English, Scotch, and Irish Catholic conspiracies to be kept in hand. There was the great new empire across the Atlantic, and Drake and Hawkins, and the English corsairs. There were the various Councils of State for the internal administration at home, and in every one of these departments Philip not only interfered but exercised the most unrelaxing supervision.

Whether he did his work well or ill is not to the purpose; mind and body were incessantly engaged upon it. Minutes of council, thousands of ciphered despatches with rough drafts of as many ciphered answers to them, survive to witness to the industry of a sovereign who permitted nothing to be done without his knowledge in all his enormous dominions. There is scarcely one of these documents which is not annotated in his hand, and often elaborately; and students who, like myself, have toiled through these mountains of papers, have cursed the writing, the worst perhaps that ever was seen, but have had to confess, when the meaning was arrived at, that the meaning was a real and often a wise one. The King did patiently endeavour to understand the subjects before him, and to resolve upon them with the best efforts of his ability; while if the working hours of every day had been doubled, and thus doubled had been devoted all to duty, they would still seem insufficient for the business which he demonstrably got through.

That a mind so occupied should have had leisure to trouble itself with 'jealousies' and 'mistresses,' or indeed to give more than a passing thought to the Escovedo affair at all after the public dangers from him had ceased, is to me not easily conceivable, for the simple reason that there was no time for it. The King was occupied all but exculsively with other matters. The murder was an angry spot which would not heal; he had fallen into a scrape, and his behaviour was singular; but it can be more easily explained by clumsy efforts to extricate himself than by a romance of which nine-tenths is conjecture, and the tenth remaining inconsistent with admitted facts.

It is, however, true that the Princess of Eboli was soon supposed to have been connected in some way with Escovedo's assassination. The widow of Escovedo knew that high words had passed between her husband and Antonio Pérez in which the name of the Princess had been mentioned. Pérez had been more successful in life than his companion officials, and had borne himself in his prosperity with less moderation than prudence would have recommended. One of these, a priest named Matteo Vasquez, and himself one of Philip's secretaries, disliked Pérez, and was also employed in some law-suit against the Princess. He sought out Escovedo's family and learnt what they had to tell. He was busy all the summer and the winter following pushing his inquiries, and thought at last that he had made a notable discovery.

In December, nine months after the murder, he wrote and circulated an anonymous *pasquil*, full of scandalous reflections on Pérez and the lady, while simultaneously Escovedo's widow and her son directly charged Pérez with the crime, adding that it had been committed to gratify the Princess of Eboli. Pérez carried the *pasquil* to Philip – a daring act on his part if he knew himself to be the King's successful rival. Philip again assured him, both by word and writing, that he need not be uneasy, that no harm should befall him; but Pérez knew his master well; he knew his unwillingness that his own share in the matter should be made public, and he observed that Philip seemed not displeased that Vasquez and the Escovedos should be running on a false statement.

It is time, therefore, to say a few words about this famous lady; to tell who she was, and how she came to be concerned in a matter which appeared to be wholly political.

Doña Aña, widow of Ruy Gomez, Prince of Eboli, was the only child of Don Diego Hurtado, chief of the great house of Mendoza. There were many Mendozas in the Spanish peerage. Don Diego's was the eldest branch. On her father's death a part, but not all, of the inheritance descended to the daughter. She was Princess of Eboli as her husband's widow. Her eldest son, a youth of twenty or thereabouts, was Duke of Pastraña and Prince of Melito. She had five younger children. One of them, a daughter, was married to Alonzo the Good, Duke of Medina Sidonia, known to history as the admiral of the Armada. Family disputes seem to have arisen about Don Diego's succession. Some suit was pending between her and other members of the family. The Princess was detaining money, jewels, and other possessions, to which her relatives laid claim; and the quarrel was further complicated by the political leanings of the young Prince of Melito, who had deserted the old party of his father, Ruy Gomez, and had gone over to the Duke of Alva.

The Princess herself was now thirty-eight years old. She had lost one eye, and was otherwise not beautiful; but she was energetic, imperious, with considerable talents, and able, if she pleased, to be fascinating. That she had been Philip's mistress was an Italian scandal; nothing had then been heard of it in Spain; but Pérez gave mysterious hints that the King would have been more intimate with her if she had encouraged him. Any way, she had lost Philip's favour. Visitors at the Eboli palace were frowned upon at the Escurial; the world said that the King was irritated at the rejection of his advances,[1] and that 'wishes unsatisfied were more exasperating than a thousand offences.'

This was perhaps but court gossip; but, whether fact or legend, it is certain on the other hand that the relations between the Princess and Antonio Pérez were intimate and even affectionate. He had been her husband's adopted son. The Princess professed to believe that Ruy Gomez was his real father, and to her Pérez's devotion was unconcealed and unbounded. He describes in an enigmatic letter the position in which he stood towards her. M. Mignet says that there can be no doubt of his meaning, and rushes to a preconceived conclusion. The letter is intentionally obscure; the press is uncorrected; and the text in parts is hopeless. But he alludes to the suggestion that he was the Princess's lover only to fling it from him with disgust. His love was for his own wife, whose attachment to him is the finest feature in the whole of this distracted story. The Princess of Eboli he worshipped as a being beyond his sphere. He spoke of her as 'a jewel enamelled in the rarest graces of nature and fortune.' To her husband he owed all that he had become, and he repaid his debt by helping his widow in her difficulties. He made her large advances of money, he collected her rents from Italy; she in turn made

---

1. 'Por vivir el Rey offendido de la antigua y continua duracion de la entereza de la Princesa de Eboli haciendole menosprecio.' – *Relacion de Antonio Pérez.*

him handsome presents; but that either with the King or with Pérez the Princess had any personal intrigue is a romantic imagination like the legend of Don Carlos and his step-mother.[1]

It was but natural, under the circumstances, that the Mendoza family should bear no love to Pérez, because in the feuds which had arisen he was taking the Princess's side. The Prince of Melito had threatened to run him through the body. The Marques de Fabara and the Conde de Cifuentes called one day on the Princess, and were kept waiting because she was closeted with the Secretary. Both of them thought that such a fellow was not fit to live. Escovedo, it came out, had taken the opposite side to Pérez. He, too, had been brought up by Ruy Gomez, and claimed a right to interfere in defence of his old master's honour. He had disapproved of the acquaintance; he had said that it must and should be put an end to; and he had spoken to the Princess with so rude a tongue, that she called him a foul-mouthed villain.

The quarrel of this kind explains the ease with which Pérez consented to kill Escovedo. We know no actual good of Pérez, and there would have been nothing surprising if, out of revenge, he really had misled the King into thinking Escovedo more guilty than he was. But the attempt to prove it broke down; Philip had been influenced by Don John's and Escovedo's own despatches, which had been diciphered by another hand; and never to the last felt certain that his Secretary had in this matter deceived him.

Some personal resentment there was, and the Princess was in some way the occasion of it, but in fact Philip's conduct requires no secret passion to make it intelligible. He did not doubt, at least at first, that he had done right, but he was unwilling to admit the truth. He had to maintain his respectability, and, therefore, would not try to prevent the Escovedos and their friends from prosecuting their complaints, while he was not ill-pleased that their suspicions should run wide of himself, and fasten in a quarter where he knew that there was nothing to be discovered. It was just the course which commonplace cunning would naturally pursue. The Marques de los Velez could not understand

---

1. There is no evidence for it except what is supposed to lie in the letter of Antonio Pérez 'à un Gran Personage,' which formed part of his public defence. What that letter means it is impossible to say, or even what it was intended to suggest. Pérez says that the King disapproved of the intimacy between himself and the Princess, and there was a mystery connected with this. But a mystery was not necessarily a love affair, nor does it follow that there was a mystery because such a person as Pérez wished to make himself interesting by hinting at one.

it; he did not like the look of things, and applied for the governorship of Peru: Pérez offered to retire from the public service and satisfy his enemies thus: but the King refused to accept Pérez's resignation. He said that he could not spare him; he reiterated, on the word of a gentleman, 'that he would never forsake him, and that Pérez knew his word could be depended on.'

More and more loudly Matteo Vasquez and the Escovedos demanded a trial. The King could not directly refuse. Pérez himself advised acquiescence; the actual assassins, he said, were beyond reach of discovery; there was no evidence; he was ready to face the prosecution; the name of the Princess need not be mentioned. Philip, however, had a conscience above perjury; he was known only to discreet persons who could be safely trusted. The case was to be heard before the High Court of Castile. The King sent for Don Antonio de Pazos, who was then President, told him everything, and asked his advice. The President thought that the prosecution must be silenced; he informed young Escovedo that if he insisted on justice he should have it, but he was accusing persons of high rank in the state; his charge, if he failed to make it good, would recoil on himself; and he assured him on the word of a priest that Pérez and the Princess were as innocent as himself. With Matteo Vasquez the President was more peremptory. Vasquez, he said, was no relation of Escovedo's; his interference, especially as he was a priest, was gratuitous and unbecoming; on the facts he was mistaken altogether. The Escovedos yielded and promised to go no further; Vasquez was obstinate, and persisted. Public curiosity had been excited; it was felt instinctively that the King was in the secret, and there was now a widespread desire to know what that secret was. Vasquez hated Pérez and the Princess also, and made himself the representative of the popular anxiety.

Philip had been contented that opinion should run in a false direction; and he had hoped to prevent too close an inquiry by his confidence with the President. He had failed, and he had seemed to wish in consequence to silence Vasquez, and, if possible, to reconcile him with the Princess whom he had calumniated. But now the difficulty was on her side. She, the greatest lady in Spain after the Queen, had been insulted and slandered; it was not for her to leave a cloud upon her name by stooping to take the hand of her accuser. The Cardinal Archbishop of Toledo was sent to reason with her, but the Archbishop was too much of her own opinion to make an impression on her indignation. She had already a long catalogue of grievances, and this last insult was too much. She wrote to Philip a letter which he showed to Pérez, and Pérez preserved it.

SEÑOR, – Your Majesty has commanded the Cardinal of Toledo to speak with me in the matter of Antonio Pérez. Matteo Vasquez and his friends have said openly that all who enter my house lose your favour. They have stated also that Antonio Pérez killed Escovedo on my account; that he was under so many obligations to my family, that he would do whatever I asked him. They have published abroad these speeches; and I require your Majesty, as the king and a gentleman, to take such notice of this conduct as the world shall hear of. If your Majesty declines, if the honour of my house is to be sacrificed, as our property has been sacrificed, if this is to be the reward of the long and faithful services of my ancestors, be it so. I have discharged my conscience; self-respect forbids me to say more.

I write to your Majesty in resentment at the offences which I have received, and I write in confidence, supposing myself to be addressing a gentleman.

The President presses me about a letter, which I wrote to your Majesty, touching bribes taken by — (word omitted). I am charged with having said something of the Duke of —. My character suffers from these tokens of your Majesty's good-will. Though justice is on my side, my suit is before a tainted tribunal; I shall lose it and be put out of possession. When I ask the President why he acts thus towards me, he says that your Majesty will have it so. Melchior de Herrera (?) allows that I am right; but he swears me to this and that, and pretends that it is your pleasure. You have sent him a memorial from Don Inigo.[1] Why am I to be twice memorialised? It is important to me to withdraw the security under which I and my children are bound for Don Inigo. He has broken his obligations, and may leave Valladolid. Antonio de Padilla confesses that it is so; but your Majesty forbids him to interfere. If this is true, I may as well abandon my suit, and my children too. This is the natural conclusion from the position which you assume towards me. When I reflect what my husband's merits were, such treatment would make me lose my senses did I not need them all to guard myself from this Moorish cur (Matteo Vasquez) whom your Majesty keeps in your service. I demand that neither I nor any of mine may be placed in that man's power.

---

1. Inigo de Mendoza, Marquis of Almenara.

I have given this letter, though it strays beyond our immediate subject, because it shows how imperfectly the circumstances are known to us which surround the story; and how idle it is for us to indulge imagination beyond what is written. Long avenues of questions lie open before us, which must remain unanswered, yet in the answer to which alone can lie a complete explanation of the relations between the Princess of Eboli and the King of Spain.

Submit to be reconciled with the 'Moorish cur' it was plain she would not. He had circulated slanders against her in the court, and she insisted that he should withdraw them.[1] Pérez was obstinate too, for his honour was touched. The Archbishop of Toledo and the King's special preacher, Fray Hernando de Castillo, stood by them, and the quarrel had gone into a new form. Philip's position was a ridiculous one. If Vasquez persisted in prosecuting Pérez before the judge who was acquainted with the truth, it was scarcely possible that the truth would be unrevealed. Secretary Vasquez is a dark figure. The letter of the Princess shows that Philip was secretly employing this man in various matters in which she supposed herself to be wronged, and there were reasons for his conduct at which it is idle to guess.

Consulting no one but his confessor, the King gave orders for the arrest both of Pérez and of the Princess also, and on July 29, 1579, they were ordered into separate confinement. The lady's relations, it is likely, required no explanations, but for form's sake Philip offered them. The same night he wrote to the Duke of Infantado and to Medina Sidonia. A dispute had arisen, he said, between his two secretaries, Antonio Pérez and Matteo Vasquez, with which the Princess was concerned. She had complained to him unreasonably, and his confessor had vainly endeav-

---

1. This article had been written, and was partly in type, before I had seen the interesting work, lately published, on the Princess of Eboli, by Don Gaspar Moro. Although the documents discovered by Don Gaspar have added largely to our knowledge of the secret history of the Princess, I have found it unnecessary to withdraw or alter any opinion which I had formed. I have had the pleasure of finding my own conjectures for the most part confirmed and converted into certainties by evidence not open to dispute. Don Gaspar has disproved conclusively the imagined *liaison* between the Princess and Philip the Second.

    Don Gaspar has proved that the jealousy of which Pérez speaks, as having governed Philip's conduct, was no jealousy of the preference of Pérez to himself by the Princess, but a jealousy of the influence of a woman, with whom he was on the worst possible terms, over his own secretary. The Crown was in some way interested in the great law-suits which the Princess was carrying on. In all that related to her Matteo Vasquez was as deep in Philip's confidence as Antonio Pérez in the wider world of

oured to persuade her to be reconciled to Vasquez. She had been committed, therefore, to the fortress of Pinto, and he had thought it right to give them immediate information. The resentment of the Duke of Infantado was not likely to be deep; Medina Sidonia replied coolly that so wise a sovereign had doubtless good reasons for his actions. He was himself laid up with gout, and the pain was in his mind as well as in his body. He trusted that his Majesty would be gracious to the Princess, and that the grace would be even more marked than the punishment.

The Archbishop of Toledo called the next morning on Juana de Coello, Pérez's wife. He told her from the King that she was not to be alarmed. Her husband's life was in no danger, nor his honour either. The imprisonment was a mere matter of precaution to prevent other mischiefs.

The Princess now drops out of the scene. Philip informed her that if she would undertake to hold no more communication with Pérez, she would be received to favour, and might return to the court. She replied that if Pérez ever wrote to her or sent her a message, the King should know of it. But this was not sufficient. After a brief confinement she was allowed to retire to her castle at Pastraña, and there without further disturbance she remained to the end of her life.

Meanwhile, if Philip's object had been to stop the prosecution for Escovedo's murder, and to divert suspicion from himself, both purposes had been attained. Matteo Vasquez must have been satisfied, for his name was never mentioned again. Popular opinion had accused Pérez of having committed the murder at the Princess's instigation. Their simultaneous arrest led to a general belief that the suspicion was not

politics. His relations with each of them were carefully concealed from the other.

Pérez might know that Matteo Vasquez was employed by his master against the Princess; but Matteo Vasquez never guessed that his master had ordered Pérez to assassinate Escovedo: and thus Philip himself, by his passion for secrecy, and for what he regarded as skilful management, had entangled his two secretaries in a furious antagonism.

Pérez had no knowledge how far Philip had engaged himself in the Eboli litigation. The King was irritated at Pérez for unconsciously thwarting him by taking up the Princess's cause. Matteo almost succeeded in dragging into light his master's complicity with Escovedo's murder, by his innocent belief that Pérez and the Princess were the guilty parties, and that the cause of the murder was resentment at the part which Escovedo had taken in attempting to separate the Princess from Pérez. Not a hint, not a suggestion of any love-scandal appears in the whole of the correspondence. Some great question was at issue on which the court was divided, and which was enveloped in a network of intrigue – the King sitting in the middle of it, playing the part of Providence with the best intentions and with the most unfortunate results – for he affected especially to imitate Providence in the secrecy of its methods.

unfounded. If the King had made a second confidant of Vasquez, and had concerted the details of the comedy with him, the result, at least for a time, did credit to his ingenuity. Pérez's fault, whatever it had been, was not to appear unpardonable. He was left four months in charge of the alcalde of the court. He was treated with kindness, and even distinction, and was permitted to have his children with him.

In the November following he became unwell, and was permitted further to return to his own house, though still as a prisoner. Next he was required to sign a bond of *pleytohomenage,* by which he and Matteo Vasquez engaged as king's vassals not to injure each other. The guard was then removed. He recovered his freedom and resumed his duties as secretary to the Council of State, though no longer as confidential secretary to the King. The whole matter seemed to have been thus wound up, and public interest was soon directed on worthier objects. The death of Don Sebastian in Africa had left vacant the Portuguese throne. Philip took possession of the succession as the nearest heir. The Duke of Alva with a few skilful movements disposed of the pretender. Philip went to Lisbon to be installed as sovereign, and in the glory of this grand achievement Escovedo's assassination might have gone the way of other scandals.

But, as Pérez said, 'it was a thing which had no beginning and could have no end.' A cloud still hung over him, and his slightest movements were watched. The Princess of Eboli sent him presents from Pastraña. It was immediately reported to Philip. He had many friends, the Archbishop of Toledo, and 'grandees' of highest rank. They came often to see him, but he was forbidden to return their visits. Philip evidently chose that a sinister suspicion should still remain attached to him. Antonio de Pazos, the President of Castile, knew the whole story, for the King had told him. Juana de Coello complained to him of her husband's treatment, and insisted that his reputation ought to be cleared. The President was of the same opinion, and so informed the King. 'If Antonio Pérez has committed a crime,' he said, 'give him a formal trial and hang him. If he is innocent, let him go on his good behaviour, and if he offends again, punish him.'

The King answered: 'If the matter were of a kind which would allow a judicial process, it should have been ordered from the first day. You must tell the woman to be quiet; no change is possible at present.'

'Time,' Philip used to say, 'cures all evils.' 'Time and I never fail.' And so he went on trusting to time when time could not help him.

Pérez had friends, but he had enemies also. Matteo Vasquez had withdrawn, but others had taken his place, and Philip's ambiguities encouraged them. Among these were the powerful Mendozas. Pérez had managed the Princess's money affairs. He had jewels in his charge and other things also which they conceived to belong to them. His habits were luxurious, and remained so in spite of his semi-disgrace. His palace, his plate, his furniture, his equipments, and entertainments were the most splendid in Madrid. He gambled also; perhaps he won, perhaps he lost; in either case it was a reproach. How, men asked, could Antonio Pérez support such a vast expenditure? and the answer suggested was, of course, corruption or malversation. He had six thousand ducats a year from his offices; but the Archbishop of Seville, a friendly witness, said that he must be spending fifteen or twenty thousand. The King was advised to order an inquiry into the accounts of all the public offices, and of Pérez's, of course, among them.

A 'lion's mouth,' like that at Venice, was opened for secret information, and was not long in want of sustenance. Accusations poured in as venomous as hatred could distil. Rodrigo Vasquez de Arce,[1] who afterwards became President of the High Court, conducted the investigation of them, and the result was not favourable to Pérez. Undoubtedly he had received sums of money from all parts of the empire to expedite business, just as Bacon did in England, and as high officials everywhere were then in the habit of doing. They looked on such things as recognised perquisites so long as nothing was said about them; but gratuities were formally prohibited, and, when exposed, were incapable of defence.

On the Report being presented, Philip allowed Pérez to be prosecuted for corrupt practices, and it was then that, at a venture, he was accused further of having altered ciphered despatches.

No one knew better than Philip that, under the arrangements of his cabinet, the alteration of despatches without his own knowledge was impossible. Pérez wrote to Philip to remonstrate. 'He would not answer such a charge,' he said, 'without producing his papers,' and among them the King's own notes upon Escovedo's death. The confessor was sent to see these papers, and, having read them, could only recommend his master to let the charge fall. As to corrupt practices, he advised Pérez to make no defence, and assured him that he should not be condemned in the value of a pair of gloves. The sentence went beyond the pair of gloves. Pérez was suspended from his office for ten years. He

1. It does not appear whether he was a relation of Matteo Vasquez.

was to suffer two years' imprisonment, and was to pay besides thirty thousand ducats, half to the Crown, and half to the family of the Princess of Eboli, as property belonging to them which he had unlawfully appropriated.

This judgment was delivered on January 23, 1585. It was not published; nor is it certain how much of it was enforced. But there were reasons why, at that moment, the sentence of imprisonment was convenient. The Escovedo business was bursting up again. Enriquez, the page, who had assisted at the murder, had let fall incautious speeches. The president, Rodrigo Vasquez, took the subject into the scope of his inquiries. He sent for Enriquez and examined him. On his evidence Diego Martinez was arrested also. If these two could be induced to tell the truth, the proofs against Pérez would be complete. He might produce his papers, but in a close court the judges might refuse to receive or look at them to save the King's credit; and Pérez would certainly be executed.

The King was just then going down to Aragon for the opening of the Cortes. In Aragon trials were public, with equal justice between king and subject. Pérez, himself an Aragonese, if left free might follow the King thither, and put himself under the protection of the laws of the Province. There certainly, if not in Madrid, his exculpation would be heard. It was therefore determined that he should be at once arrested, and a guard was sent to his house to take him.

Pérez from first to last had an honest friend at the court, Cardinal Quiroga, Archbishop of Toledo. The Archbishop saw, or feared, that Pérez was about to be sacrificed, and his sense of equity, though he was Grand Inquisitor, was outraged. He recommended Pérez to take sanctuary. He would then be a prisoner of the Church, and his case would be heard in the Holy Office. The Inquisition had already denounced Philip's method of removing doubtful subjects. It would stand by Pérez now and prevent a scandalous crime.

Pérez took the Cardinal's advice and fled to the nearest church. But the Crown officials were determined to have him, and the sanctuary was not respected. The church door was burst in; he was torn out of his hiding-place, and carried off again to a state prison. His property was sequestrated, his papers siezed, and the Nuncio, when he protested, was threatened with dismissal. Henry the Eighth himself could not have been more peremptory in his contempt of sacred privileges than the ministers of the Most Catholic King. The documents were at once examined. The secret correspondence was found to have been abstracted. Juana de Coello was supposed to have it; and, to extort it from her, she and her children were carried off also, and confined in the same castle with her husband.

It was true that she had some part of the private papers, and threats of torture could not wring them from her till she had ascertained that those of most special consequence were not among them. She found some one who would take a note to her husband. Being without ink she wrote it with her blood. The answer came back that she might deliver the papers without fear, the Escovedo notes being secured elsewhere. She mentioned where the boxes would be found. The King's confessor himself came to her to receive the keys. He, too, had some sense remaining of right and wrong, and he told her that if Pérez was troubled any further, he would himself go 'como un loco,' like a madman, into the Plaza, and proclaim the truth to all the world.

The boxes being surrendered, Juana de Coello and the children were sent home, there being no longer occasion for keeping them. As the confessor was going off, she could not help telling him that there were still a few papers reserved. The King, when he came to look, must have discovered that this was fatally true. All else was in its place, even to the most secret ciphered correspondence; but the fifty or sixty especial letters, which he knew himself to have written, about Escovedo, and knew also that Pérez had preserved – these were not to be discovered. That, if he had got possession of these letters, Philip would have allowed Pérez to be tried and executed, is not certain; but it may have been well for him that he was not exposed to the temptation. As matters stood, the judges might refuse to admit the letters, and might pass sentence on the evidence. But Juana de Coello could carry the damning records into Aragon, or across the frontier, and publish them; and all Europe would cry out 'Shame!'

Nor was the Church idle. The Church authorities, with the Pope behind them, demanded that Pérez should be restored to sanctuary. Worried, impatient, cursing the day that he had ever blundered into so detestable a quagmire, the King again paused. Once more the prison doors were opened; once more Pérez was brought back to Madrid, and lodged in a handsome house with his family. Evidently the unfortunate King was at his wits' end, and could not determine what course to choose. Pérez went to church for mass. The great people came as before to show him countenance. He himself addressed many letters to the King, which were carefully read, if not answered. The Archbishop of Toledo, in particular, was confident that all would be well. The attitude of the Church alone, he said, would suffice to protect Pérez.

The President Rodrigo would have gone on gladly with the trial, but obstacles were continually arising. Some one asked him what was to be done. 'How can I tell you?' he replied. 'One day the King says go on, the next he says hold back. There is a mystery which I cannot make out.'

Fourteen months thus drifted away. At the end of them the King could hold out no longer. There was still but a single witness, for Diego Martinez had so far continued staunch. He might confess, perhaps, if he was tortured, but torture could not be used without the King's permission. Philip wrote to Pérez telling him generally that he might rely on his protection, but without saying what steps he was prepared to take. Pérez was brought to trial at last before President Rodrigo. He stood upon his innocence, denied that he had murdered Escovedo, and denied all knowledge of the matter. Enriquez gave evidence with correctness; but Diego Martinez, who was confronted with him, said he was a liar, and his story a fabrication. Conviction on such terms was not to be had. Pérez's papers were handed to President Rodrigo to be examined. He searched them through, but found nothing to the purpose.

Pérez, after all, would probably have been acquitted, but for the intervention of a 'Deus ex machinâ,' Philip himself, who interposed in a manner the most unlooked for. This is the most extraordinary feature in the whole story. Philip, it might have been thought, would have welcomed Pérez's acquittal as the happiest escape from his embarrassments; but it seems that his conscience was really disturbed at the success of deliberate perjury. Just as it became clear that the prosecution had failed, and that Pérez, whether guilty or not, could not be pronounced guilty without a violation of the laws, Philip's confessor, as if from himself, but of course with his master's sanction, wrote to him to say that although he had killed Escovedo, he had a complete defence for it.

When the truth was known, his character would be cleared; he advised him, therefore, to make a complete confession, and at once say that he had acted by the King's order.

This was written on September 3, the year after the defeat of the Armada. Through all that famous enterprise, from its first conception to the final catastrophe, this business had simmered on, and was at last at boiling-point.

Well as Pérez knew his master, he was not prepared for this last move. What could it mean? The King had promised to stand by him.

But if he confessed, his guilt would be clear. He might say what he pleased, but the judges might hang him notwithstanding. There was Diego Martinez, too, to be thought of. He would be hanged at any rate. So long as the proof was deficient, confession would be insanity. The King, besides, had positively ordered that the motives for the murder were not to be introduced.

In this tone he replied to Diego de Chaves; but the confessor stood to his opinion. Evidently he had consulted Philip again.

'The plain course for you,' he answered, 'is to say directly that you had the King's orders for Escovedo's death. You need not enter on the reasons. You ought not to make a false oath in a court of justice; and if you have done so already you ought not to persevere in it. Where there has been no fault there can be no punishment, and confession will only show the innocence of yourself and your accomplice. When the truth is out, the wound will heal, and his Majesty will have given the Escovedo family the justice which they demand. If they persist after this, they can be silenced or banished. Only, once more, the causes which led the King to act as he did are not to be mentioned.'

Both Philip and the confessor were aware that the compromising letters were still in possession of either Pérez or his wife. Pérez, who was not troubled about perjury, thought it safer to risk an uncertainty than to act as the confessor advised. To confess was to place his life in the judges' hands. He could feel no certainty that the King's orders would be held a sufficient authority. Philip's conduct had been strange from the beginning, and kings' consciences are not like the consciences of private individuals. They may profess to wish one thing, while their duty as sovereigns requires another. There was another alternative; the Escovedos, who were now the only prosecutors, might agree to compromise. Pérez proposed it to the confessor; the confessor permitted Pérez to try, if the King was not to be party to the transaction: overtures were made, and were successful. The Escovedo family consented to withdraw their suit on receiving twenty thousand ducats.

This seemed like the end; and if there had been nothing more in Escovedo's death than an ordinary murder, the compensation would have been held sufficient, and the end would have really come. But behind the private wrong there was a great question at issue, whether the sovereign had or had not a right to make away with his subjects when he believed them criminal, because for reasons of state it was inexpedient to bring them to trial. Though Castile had no longer constitutional rights like Aragon, a high-minded people (as the

Castilians were) had a regard for their own security. The doctrine had been condemned by the Holy Office, and the judges can have liked it as little.

The opportunity of bringing the matter to a point was not to be lost. The President Rodrigo wrote to Philip that his reputation was at stake. The prosecution had been dropped, but the world was convinced, notwithstanding, that the murder had been committed by his order. It concerned his honour that Pérez should explain why that order had been given. He begged the King to send him an instruction in the following terms: 'Tell Antonio Pérez, in my name, that, as he knows the causes for which I commanded him to kill Escovedo, I desire him to declare what those causes were.'

M. Mignet adheres to his opinion that Pérez was to be betrayed; that, being without his papers, he must fail to prove what he was required to reveal, and could then be executed as a slanderer and an assassin. It would be difficult for him and perhaps impossible to recall satisfactorily a condition of things which was now buried under the incidents of twelve eventful years. But there is no occasion to suspect Philip of such deliberate treachery. The stages through which his mind had passed can easily be traced. He never doubted the righteousness of Escovedo's execution; but he had been afraid to irritate his brother, and had therefore wished his own part in it to be concealed. Therefore, when Pérez was first suspected, he had not come forward to protect him; and therefore also he had connived at the direction of the suspicion on the Princess of Eboli. A long time had passed away, Don John was gone, the aspect of Europe had changed. He had no longer the same reluctance to admit that he had ordered the murder; but he had bidden Pérez be silent about the causes, because, though sufficient for his own conscience, it would be hard, when circumstances were so much altered, to make them intelligible to others. The Spaniards of 1590, smarting under the destruction of the Armada, might well have thought if Don John and the Duke of Guise had tried the 'enterprise' together, when the Queen of Scots was alive, so many of their homes would not then have been desolate.

But public opinion was excited. The compromise of the prosecution seemed to imply that there was something disgraceful behind. A secret half revealed is generally more dangerous than the truth; and thus, when called on by the judges to direct Pérez to make a full confession, the King felt that it was better to consent.

This explanation seems sufficient, without looking for sinister motives. The order was written, and Pérez was required to obey.

It might have been thought that he would have seen in such an order the easiest escape from his troubles. To speak was to be acquitted (at least morally) of a worse crime than of having been a too faithful servant. But it is likely that he did feel it would be difficult for him to make out a satisfactory case. He could produce the King's instructions, and could describe the motive in general terms. But state reasons for irregular actions are always looked askance at, and loyal subjects are inclined to excuse their sovereigns at the expense of their advisers. Pérez might naturally fear that he would be accused of having misled the King, perhaps through malice. This view was taken of the case by the Archbishop of Toledo. 'Señor,' he said to the confessor when he heard of this fresh command, 'either I am mad or this whole affair is mad. If the King bade Pérez kill Escovedo, why does he ask for the causes? The King knew them at the time. Pérez was not Escovedo's judge. He placed before the King certain despatches. The King directed a course to be taken upon them, and Pérez obeyed. Now after twelve years, without his papers, with so many persons gone who could have given evidence, he is asked for explanations. Give him back his papers, bring back five hundred persons now dead out of their graves; and even then he will not be able to do it.'

The Archbishop protested, the Nuncio protested. Juana de Coello and Pérez's children wept and clamoured; but President Rodrigo, with the King's orders in his hand, persisted that Pérez should speak. Three times successively, in the course of a month, he was brought into court, and he remained stubborn. He says that he would not confess, because the King had personally ordered him to be silent, and that a written form could not supersede an immediate direction, without a private intimation that it was to be obeyed. This is evidently an insufficient explanation. He must have felt that if he detailed the causes for the murder he admitted the fact; and that if he admitted the fact he might be sacrificed.

But the King was determined that the whole truth should be told at last, and that, as he could not tell it himself, it should be told by Pérez. After a month's resistance, the question was applied in earnest. Pérez was tortured. He broke down under the pain, and told all. It was then that Doña Juana appealed to God against Diego de Chaves in the Dominican chapel. It was then that Doña Gregoria dared President Rodrigo in his hall. What the King or the judges had intended to do next, is mere conjecture. Diego Martinez, when his master had spoken,

189

confessed also. He was not punished, and Pérez perhaps would not have been punished either. The judges might have been contented with the exposure. But Pérez did not care to tempt fortune or Philip's humours further. His wife was allowed to visit him in prison. He escaped disguised in her clothes. Horses were waiting, he rode for his life to Aragon, and the next day was safe beyond the frontier.

So ends the first part of the tragi-comedy. The next opened on another stage and with wider issues.

The Fueros or 'Liberties' of Aragon were the only surviving remnant of the free institutions of the Peninsula. At the beginning of the sixteenth century, the two Castiles, Valencia, Granada, and Aragon had their separate administrations and their separate legislatures. The great cities had their municipal corporations, while Portugal till within ten years had been an independent kingdom. One by one they had been absorbed. Aragon remained still free, but with a freedom which had been found inconvenient at Madrid, and was unvalued by the most powerful of the Aragonese nobles themselves. The tendency of the age was towards centralisation, and the tenure of the Fueros had been growing yearly more precarious. Queen Isabella had been impatient for a revolt which would give her an excuse for extinguishing them. The Duke of Alva more lately, on some provocation, said that with three or four thousand of his soldiers he would make the King's authority supreme.

Such as it was, however, the Constitution still subsisted, being supported chiefly by the populace of the towns, who, as long as noise and clamour were sufficient, were the enthusiastic champions of their national privileges. A council for the administration of the province sat at Madrid, but its powers were limited to advice. The Cortes met annually at Saragossa to vote the taxes, but the King could neither prorogue nor dissolve them without their own consent. A Committee of the Cortes carried on the government, and in the intervals of the sessions remained in office. The Aragonese had their own laws, their own judges, their own police, their own prisons: and no 'alien' armed force was permitted within their boundaries. The Grand Justiciary, the highest executive officer, was nominated by the King, but could not be deprived by him. A Royal Commissioner resided in Saragossa, to observe and to report, to act in cases to which the Crown was a party, perhaps irregularly to distribute favours and influence opinion. But this was the limit of his interference. The Commissioner in the year 1590 was Inigo de Mendoza, Marquis of Almenara, the cousin and the chief antagonist of the Princess of Eboli.

Such was Aragon when Antonio Pérez sought an asylum in the land of his fathers. He professed to have been tortured till his limbs were disabled, but he was able to ride without resting till he had crossed the frontier and had reached Calatayud. He made no effort, perhaps he was too weak, to go further, and he took refuge in a Dominican convent. Within ten hours of his arrival an express came in from Madrid to a private gentleman, Don Manuel Zapata, with orders to take him, dead or alive, and send him back to his master. Pérez says that when his flight was known at the court, there was general satisfaction. 'Uncle Martin,' the palace jester, said to Philip the next morning, 'Sir, all the world rejoices at the escape of Antonio Pérez; he cannot be very wicked; you should rejoice too.'

Philip did not rejoice at all. He had put himself in the power of one of his subjects, and he did not choose to remain any longer in so degrading a position. When he had been himself willing to submit his conduct to a judicial inquiry, Pérez, who had less to fear if he had been acting uprightly, had shown so much unwillingness that possibly Philip may have now doubted whether Escovedo's conduct had after all been properly represented to him. Pérez had fled, carrying the compromising documents along with him; he was probably on his way to France, to delight Philip's enemies with the sight of them, and with the tale of his own wrongs.

Anticipating pursuit, Pérez had sent a friend, Gil de Mesa, to the Grand Justiciary, to signify his arrival, and to put himself under the protection of the law. Meanwhile, the town mob at Calatayud rose in his defence, and when Don Manuel arrived at the monastery he found the priests and students in arms to protect their sanctuary. Fifty soldiers arrived immediately after from Saragossa. The orders of the Justiciary were to bring Pérez at once to the national prison of the Manifestacion, where he was to be detained till the King could be communicated with. The King's reply was an order to the Marquis of Almenara to prosecute him immediately in the Court of Aragon on three charges.

1. For having caused the death of Escovedo, falsely pretending the King's authority.
2. For having betrayed secrets of state and tampered with ciphered despatches.
3. For having fled from justice when his conduct was being judicially inquired into.

If Pérez had been wholly innocent, he would have felt that he had at last an opportunity of setting himself clear in the face of the world. The court would be open, the trial public, and his defence could neither be garbled nor suppressed. His reluctance was as vehement as ever, and was not concealed by his affectation of a desire to spare his master. From Calatayud, and from Saragossa afterwards, he wrote letter upon letter both to Philip and to Diego de Chaves, protesting his loyalty, entreating to be left in quiet with his wife and children; indicating that he had the means of defending himself, but hoping that he might not be forced to use them.

These letters being left unanswered, he took into his confidence a distinguished Aragonese ecclesiastic, the Prior of Gotor. He showed the Prior the mysterious papers which he had brought with him, with Philip's notes upon them, and desired him to go at once to Madrid and demand an audience of Philip. 'His Majesty,' Pérez said in his instructions to the Prior, 'must know that I possess these documents. They contain confidential secrets affecting others besides Escovedo; let his Majesty judge whether it is desirable that evidences should be produced in court which touch the reputation of distinguished persons, which will create a scandal throughout Europe, and will reflect on the prudence and piety of his Majesty himself. Though the confessor has taken most of my papers from me, Providence has been pleased that I should retain these, and these will suffice for my defence. If brought to trial I shall certainly be acquitted, but I prefer to save the King's reputation; my case is now notorious, and it will not be wise to challenge the world's opinion. I have been shorn like a lamb for eleven years, and I have held my peace. My blood had been shed. I have been tortured in a dungeon, and I have remained faithful. In eight or ten days I must give in my answer. Some people tell me that I ought rather to lose my head than speak; but if I am driven to it the truth must be told.'

The Prior went. Philip saw him more than once, and heard what he had to say. There could be no doubt that Pérez had the compromising letters, for the Prior had seen them. Yet Philip's courage did not fail him. After Pérez's flight the Court of Castile had given judgment against him in default. He was to be dragged through the streets and hanged. His head was to be cut off and exposed, and all his property was to be confiscated. The answer to the mission of the Prior of Gotor was the publication of his sentence.

Pérez thus driven to bay took up the challenge. He drew a memorial containing his own account of the causes of Escovedo's murder. He attached it to such notes as sufficed to prove the King's complicity, reserving others in case of future necessity; and this was publicly presented as his reply to the Marquis of Almenara. The King had probably expected that the judges of Aragon would not lightly accept so grave a charge against their sovereign; that they would respect the sentence of the better-informed Court of Castile, and would understand that there was something behind which was left unexplained. But Aragon was excited, and chose to show its independence. After the admission of the memorial Don Inigo sent word to the King, that if no further evidence were produced, Pérez would certainly be acquitted.

The King believed that he had other resources at his disposition by which complete defeat could be avoided, and at the last moment directed that the case before the Grand Justiciary should be abandoned. 'If,' said Philip, 'it was possible to reply with the same publicity which Pérez has given to his defence, his guilt would be proved, and he would be condemned. Throughout this whole affair I have considered only the public good. The long imprisonment of Pérez, the entire course which the cause has taken, has had no other object. Abusing my clemency, and afraid of the issue, he so defends himself that to answer him I must publish secrets which ought not to be revealed, and involve persons whose reputation is of more consequence than the punishment of a single offender. Therefore, I shall go no further with the prosecution in the Court of Aragon. I declare Pérez to have sinned worse than ever vassal sinned before against his sovereign – both in time, form, and circumstance; and I desire this my declaration to be entered with my notice of withdrawal. Truth, which I have always maintained, must suffer no injury. And I reserve such rights as appertain, or may appertain to me, of bringing the offender to account for his crimes in any other manner.'

The 'other manner' was through the Court of Enquesta. In the Constitution of Aragon, a special reservation excluded from protection the King's servants and officials. Over these the law of the province had no more authority than the King was pleased to allow – and the King under this clause claimed to have Pérez surrendered to himself. The local lawyers, however, interpreted 'servants' to mean only servants in Aragon and engaged in the affairs in Aragon, not persons belonging to other countries or other provinces. Aragonese, who accepted Crown employment, undertook it with their eyes open and at their own risk, and might be supposed to have consented to their exemption; but such a case as that of Pérez had not been contemplated when the clause in the Constitution was allowed. But the King had one more resource.

Though acquitted, the prisoner was still detained, as if the authorities were unsatisfied of his real innocence.

Pérez had grown impatient, and, in his loose, vain way, had babbled to his companions in the Manifestacion, and his language had been so extravagant that it had been noted down and forwarded to the court. He had threatened to fly to France or Holland, when he would make the King repent of his treatment of him. He had compared himself to Marius, who had been driven into exile and had returned to the consulship. He said that he would raise a revolt in Castile; he would bring in Henry the Fourth; he would make Aragon into a Free Republic like Venice. He spoke of Philip as another Pharaoh. He had ventured into more dangerous ground, and had called into question the mysteries of the faith. Some of these rash expressions had been noted down in writing, with the solemn reflections on them of the King's confessor. The impatient wretch had said, that 'if God the Father had allowed the King to behave so disloyally to him he would take God the Father by the nose.' The confessor observes, 'This proposition is blasphemous, scandalous, offensive to pious ears, and savouring of the heresy of the Vadiani, who affirmed that God was corporeal and had human members. Nor was it an excuse to say that Christ, being made man, had a nose, since the words were spoken of the First Person.'

Again, Pérez had said, 'God is asleep in this affair of mine. If He works no miracle for me, it will go near to destroy the faith.' 'This proposition,' the confessor noted, 'is scandalous. The prisoner has been accused of the greatest enormities; he has been tried by course of law and condemned to death, and he speaks as if he was without fault.' Worse still. Pérez had gone on, 'God sleeps! God sleeps! God is an idle tale; there cannot be a God!' The confessor observes, 'This proposition is heretical, as if God had no care for human things, when the Bible and the Church affirm that He does care. To say that there cannot be a God *is* heresy, for though it be said in doubt, yet doubt is not allowed in matters of faith; we must believe without doubt.' Lastly, Pérez had said, 'If things pass thus, I cannot believe in God.' The confessor notes, 'This is blaphemous, scandalous, and offensive, and savours of heresy also.' The confessor's ears had no doubt been outraged. Many a poor sinner had gone to the stake for less audacious utterances. For nine months after the failure with the Enquesta, Pérez remained in the Manifestacion, pouring out these wild outcries. At the end of them an order came from the Holy Office at Madrid to the three Inquisitors at Saragossa to take possession of his person and remove him to their own prison in the old Moorish palace of the Aljaferia.

The Inquisitor-General of Spain was his old friend the Archbishop of Toledo. In Madrid the Inquisition had been well disposed towards him, and once he had thrown himself on its protection. Had he now submitted voluntarily, he would probably have been safe from serious injury, and an impartial decision would have been arrived at. The Inquisition, be it remembered, was no slave of the Crown, and, though a cruel guardian of orthodoxy, would not have looked too narrowly at the fretful words of a man whom the Archbishop believed to have been ill used. The judges of Aragon were by this time satisfied that Pérez was not entirely the martyr which he pretended to be, and that the King had something to say for himself. Philip, who appears to Protestant Europe a monster of injustice, was in Spain respected and esteemed. The Grand Justiciary did not wish to quarrel with the Crown in a case so doubtful, still less to quarrel with the Holy Office, and was preparing quietly to comply.

But Pérez would not have it so, and preferred to trust to popular jealousy. A mob is always ready to listen when it is told that Liberty is in danger. A story was circulated in Saragossa that the Marquis of Almenara had bribed the prisoners in the Manifestacion to send in a false account of Pérez's language, and that the Inquisition was claiming a right which did not belong to it, that the Fueros were being betrayed, and that the Aragonese were to be made slaves of the Castilians. Symptoms showed themselves of an intended rising, and the Justiciary and Don Inigo, after a night's conference, agreed that Pérez should be removed at once and without notice to the Inquisition prison. At noon on May 24, 1591, he was quietly placed in a carriage at the Manifestacion Gate. A knot of young men tried to stop the horses, and clamoured for the Constitution; but they were told that it was *cosa de fey*, an affair of religion, and that they must mind their own business. The carriage reached the Aljaferia without interruption, and Pérez was in the Inquisitors' hands.

But on the instant Saragossa was in arms. The alarm bell boomed out. The market-place swarmed with a furious multitude shouting 'Fueros, Fueros! Libertad, Libertad!' Their plans had been already laid. Half the mob went to attack the Aljaferia, the others to the house of Philip's representative, the Marquis of Almenara. He, too, it is likely, had remembered that Pérez was the friend of the Princess of Eboli, and had thrown himself into the quarrel with some degree of personal animosity. He was now to expiate his eagerness. He was urged to fly.

The Mendozas, he answered, never fled. The palace door was dashed in. The Justiciary, who had hurried to protect him, was thrown down and trampled on. Don Inigo was seized, dragged out, and borne away among cries of 'Muera, muera! Kill him, kill him!' Stripped naked, his clothes torn off, his arms almost forced out of their sockets, struck and pelted with stones, he was at last rescued by a party of police, who carried him into the city prison. There, a fortnight after, he died of his injuries, so ending his lawsuit with the widow of Ruy Gomez.

The Inquisitors at the Aljaferia had a near escape of the same fate. The walls were strong and the gates massive. But the fierce people brought faggots in cartloads, and raised a pile which would have reduced the palace and all in it to dust and ashes. The Inquisitors, they said, had burnt others; they should now burn themselves unless Pérez was instantly released. The Inquisitors would have held out, but the Archbishop of Saragossa, Almenara's brother, insisted that they must yield. Pérez, four hours only after they had siezed him, was given back to his friends, and borne away in triumph.

But the mob had risen for the rights of Aragon, and not, after all, for a prisoner of whose innocence even they were unconvinced. Pérez imagined himself a national hero. He had expected that the Cortes would take up his case, that he would be allowed to present himself at the bar, and detail the story of his wrongs in Philip's own presence. The leaders of the people had formed a cooler estimate of its merits. They contented themselves with taking him back to the Manifestacion. The officials of the province went up to Madrid, to deliberate with the court what was next to be done.

For Pérez personally there was no enthusiasm. If the Inquisition would acknowledge the Fueros, the sensible people of Saragossa were ready to surrender him. The Inquisition made the necessary concessions, and Pérez's own supporters now advised him to submit unreservedly. But this he did not dare to do; he tried to escape from the Manifestacion and failed. He appealed again to the mob. Broad-sheets were printed and circulated declaring that the officials were betraying the Fueros, and though the chiefs of the first insurrection had withdrawn, the multitude could still be wrought upon. Unfortunately for Aragon, the Grand Justiciary, Don Juan de Lanuza, a wise and prudent man, suddenly died. Had he lived a few weeks longer he might have saved his country, but it was not so to be. The nomination of his successor belonged to the King, but the office had by custom become hereditary in the Lanuza family; Don Juan's son, a generous hot-headed youth, claimed to act without waiting for the King's sanction, and, fatally for himself, was ruled or influenced by his uncle, Don Martin, who was Pérez's most intimate ally. The officials had returned from the court. The Council of Saragossa had decided that Pérez should be restored to the Holy Office.

The removal was to be effected on the following morning, September 24; but when the morning came the mob were out again. The manifestacion was broken open, the council room was set on fire, and Pérez was again released. It was understood, however, that he was not to remain any longer at Saragossa to be a future occasion of quarrel. He was escorted a league out of the city on the road to the Pyrenees, and he was made to know that if he returned he would not be protected. He did return; he pretended that the roads were unsafe, but he came back in secret, and in the closest disguise, and lay concealed in Don Martin's house till it could be seen how the King would act.

Constitutional governments which cannot govern are near their end. When the intelligent and the educated part of the population are superseded by the mob, they cannot continue zealous for forms of freedom which to them are slavery. The mob has usurped the power; if it can defend its actions successfully, it makes good the authority which it has seized; if it fails, the blame is with itself. The Aragon executive had protected Pérez on his arrival in the province, they had given him the means of making an open defence, and, so far as their own council could decide in his cause, they had pronounced him acquitted. But there were charges against him which could not be openly pleaded, and his innocence was not so clear that it would be right as yet to risk a civil war in the case so ambiguous. The judges considered that enough had been done. The mob and the young Justiciary thought otherwise, and with them the responsibility rested.

Philip was in no hurry. Ten thousand men were collected quietly on the frontier under Don Alonzo de Vargas. The sentiments of the principal persons were sounded, and it was ascertained that from those who could offer serious resistance there was none to be anticipated. Liberty had lost its attractions when it meant the protection of criminals by the town rabble. That the mob had shaken themselves clear of Pérez made little difference to Philip, for they had taken him by force out of prison. The middle-class citizens, who still prized their Constitution, believed, on the other hand, or at least some of them believed, that the King had no longer an excuse for interfering with them. Philip so far respected their alarm that before he ordered the advance of the troops he sent out a proclamation that the Constitution would not be disturbed; and possibly, if there had been no opposition, he would have found his course less clear. But the more eager spirits could not be restrained; the nobles held aloof; the young Justiciary, however, was ardent and enthusiastic – he was compromised besides, for he had taken office without waiting for the King's permission. The invasion was an open breach of the Fueros. He called the citizens of Saragossa to arms, and sent appeals for help to Barcelona and the other towns.

There was no response – a sufficient proof either that the province was indifferent, or that the cause was regarded as a bad one. Lanuza led out a tattered multitude of shopkeepers and workmen to meet the Castilians; but, though brave enough in a city insurrection, they had no stomach for fighting with a disciplined force. They turned and scattered without a blow, and Alonzo de Vargas entered Saragossa on November 12, 1591.

The modern doctrine, that political offences are virtues in disguise, was not yet the creed even of the most advanced philosophers. The Saragossa rabble had resisted the lawful authorities of the province. They had stormed a prison; they had murdered the King's representative; worst of all, they had taken arms for liberty, and had wanted courage to fight for it. The Justiciary was executed, and fifteen or twenty other persons. The attack on the Aljaferia was an act of sacrilege, and the wrongs of the Inquisition were avenged more severely. A hundred and twenty-three of the most prominent of the mob were arrested. Of these, seventy-nine were burnt in the market-place. The ceremony began at eight in the morning; it closed at night, when there was no light but from the blazing faggots; the last figure that was consumed was the effigy of Antonio Pérez, the original cause of the catastrophe. The punishment being concluded, the Constitution was abolished. The armed resistance was held to have dispensed with Philip's promises, and the Fueros of Aragon were at an end.

Pérez himself escaped on the night on which the Castilians entered, and made his way through the Pyrenees to Pau. He published a narrative of his sufferings – that is, his own version of them, with the further incriminating documents which the Protestant world at once received with greedy acclamation. Much of what he said was probably true; much might have worn another complexion if the other side had been told. But Philip never condescended to reply. Pérez was taken up by Henry the Fourth, pensioned, trusted, and employed so long as the war with Spain continued. He was sent into England. He was received by Elizabeth; entertained by Essex, and admitted into acquaintance by Francis Bacon – not with the approval of Bacon's mother, who disliked him from the first. He was plausible; he was polished; he was acute. He had been so long intimately acquainted with Spanish secrets, that his information was always useful and often of the highest value. But he was untrue at the heart. Even his own *Relacion* is in many points inconsistent with itself, and betrays the inward hollowness; while his estimate of his own merits went beyond what his most foolish friends could believe or acknowledge. Gradually he was seen through both in Paris and London. When peace came he was thrown aside, and sank into neglect and poverty. He attempted often, but always fruitlessly, to obtain his pardon from Philip the Third, and eventually died miserably in a Paris lodging, a worn-out old man of seventy-two, on November 3, 1611.

So ends the story of a man who, if his personal merits alone were concerned, might have been left forgotten among the unnumbered millions who have played their chequered parts on the stage of the world. Circumstances, and the great religious revolution of the sixteenth century, converted Philip in the eyes of half Europe into a malignant demon. The darkest interpretations were thrown upon every unexplained action which he committed; and Antonio Pérez became the hero of a romance more fit for a theatre than the pages of accredited history. The imaginative features of it have now disappeared, but there remains an instructive picture of Philip's real character. He said that he had been guided throughout by no motive save concern for the public welfare, and there is no reason to suppose that he was saying anything except what he believed to be true; yet he so acted as to invite suspicion in every step which he took.

Escovedo, as his conduct was represented by Pérez, deserved to be punished, perhaps to be punished severely. To prosecute him publicly would have been doubtless inconvenient; and Philip, without giving him an opportunity of defending himself, undertook the part of a secret Providence, and allowed him to be struck in the dark without explaining his reasons. Providence does not permit vain mortals, even though they be Catholic kings, to usurp a jurisdiction which is reserved for itself. It punished Philip by throwing him into the power of an unscrupulous intriguer, who had, perhaps, in some measure really misled him on the extent of Escovedo's faults.

He tried to extricate himself, but he was entangled in the net which his own hands had woven; and, when Pérez refused to assist him, and preferred to keep him struggling at his mercy, he was driven to measures which could be represented to the world as a base persecution of the instrument of his own crime. Thus out of an unwise ambition to exercise the attributes of omniscience, the King laid himself open to accusation, and the worst motives which could be supposed to have actuated him were those which found easiest credit.

But the legend of the loves of Philip the Second and the Princess of Eboli was not of Spanish growth. The *Relacion* of Pérez was read in the Peninsula, but it did not shake the confidence with which Philip was regarded by his subjects. The Fueros of Aragon perished, but they perished only because constitutional liberties which degenerate into anarchy are already ripe for an end.

The Spanish Story of the Armada

The fate of the great expedition sent by Philip the Second to restore the Papal authority in England has been related often in prose and verse. It is the most dramatic incident in our national history, and the materials for a faithful account of it in the contemporary narratives are unusually excellent. The English nature on that occasion was seen at its best. The days had not yet come of inflated self-praise; and the spirit which produces actions of real merit is usually simple in the description of such actions. Good wine needs no bush; the finest jewels need least a gaudy setting; and as the newspaper correspondent was not yet born, and the men who did the fighting wrote also the reports, the same fine and modest temper is equally seen in both.

Necessarily, however, Englishmen could only tell what they themselves had seen, and the other side of the story has been left untold. The Spanish historians have never attempted to minimise the magnitude of their disaster, but they have left the official records to sleep in the shades of their public offices, and what the Spanish commanders might have themselves to say of their defeat and its causes has been left hitherto unprinted. I discovered myself at Simancas the narrative of the Accountant-General of the Fleet, Don Pedro Coco Calderon, and made use of it in my own history. But Don Pedro's account showed only how much more remained to be discovered, of which I myself could find no record either in print or MS.

The defect has now been supplied by the industry and patriotism of an officer in the present Spanish Navy, who has brought together a collection of letters and documents bearing on the subject which are signally curious and interesting.[1] Captain Fernandez Duro deserves grateful thanks and recognition, as enabling us for the first time really

---

1. *La Armada Invencible.* Por el Capitan Fernandez Duro.

to understand what took place. But more than that, he reproduces the spirit and genius of the time; he enables us to see, face to face, the De Valdez, the Recaldes, the Oquendos, the De Leyvas, who had hitherto been only names to us. The 'Iliad' would lose half its interest if we knew only Agamemnon and Achilles, and knew nothing of Priam and Hector. The five days' battle in the English Channel in August 1588 was fought out between men on both sides of a signally gallant and noble nature; and when the asperities of theology shall have mellowed down at last, Spanish and English authorities together will furnish materials for a great epic poem.

Until that happy and still far-distant time shall arrive, we must appropriate and take up into the story Captain Duro's contribution. With innocent necromancy he calls the dead out of their graves, and makes them play their drama over again. With his assistance we will turn to the city of Lisbon on April 25 of the *Annus Mirabilis*. The preparations were then all but completed for the invasion of England and the overthrow of the Protestant heresy. From all parts of Catholic Europe the prayers of the faithful had ascended for more than a year in a stream of passionate entreaty that God would arise and make His power known. Masses had been said day after day on a thousand altars; and devout monks and nuns had bruised their knees in midnight watches on the chapel pavements. The event so long hoped for was to come at last. On that day the consecrated standard was to be presented in state to the Commander-in-Chief of the Expedition. Catholics had collected from every corner of the world: Spanish and Italian, French and Irish, English and German, owning a common nationality in the Church. The Portuguese alone of Catholic nations looked on in doubt. Portugal had been recently annexed by force to Spain. The wound was still bleeding, and even religion failed to unite the nobles and people in common cause with their conquerors. But Lisbon had ceased to be a Portuguese city. Philip dealt with it as he pleased, and the Church of Portugal, at least, on this occasion, was at Philip's disposition.

There was something of real piety in what was going on; and there was much of the artificial emotion which bore the same relation to piety which the enthusiasm of the Knight of la Mancha bore to true chivalry. Philip himself in certain aspects of his character was not unlike Don Quixote. He believed that he was divinely commissioned to extirpate the dragons and monsters of heresy. As the adventure with the enchanted horse had been specially reserved for Don Quixote, so the 'Enterprise of England,' in the inflated language of the time, was said to have been reserved for Philip; and as analogies are apt to complete themselves, the short, good-humoured, Medina Sidonia, who had been selected for commander-in-Chief, had certain resemblance to Sancho.

The Duke of Medina had no ambition for such adventures; he would have greatly preferred staying at home, and only consented to take the command out of a certain dog-like obedience to his master. The representatives of the imaginary powers had been called in to bring him to accept the dangerous responsibility. A pious hermit told him that he had been instructed by the Almighty to promise him victory. The Prioress of the Annuciata, Maria de la Visitacion, who had received the five wounds and was punished afterwards as a detected impostor, had seen Sant Iago and two angels smiting Drake and his unbelieving comrades, and she assured the Duke of glory in both worlds if he went. The Duke's experience of English Admirals had been, so far, not glorious to him at all. He had been in command at Cadiz a year before when the English fleet sailed up the harbour, burnt eighteen large ships, and went off without fighting, taking six more away with them. Spain had cried shame and had called the Duke a coward, but Philip had refused to be displeased, and had deliberately chosen him for an undertaking far more arduous than the defence of a provincial port. On this April 25 he was to receive his commission, with the standard under which he was to go into action, and the Catholic Church was to celebrate the occasion with its imposing splendours and imperious solemnities.

The Armada lay in the Tagus waiting the completion of the ceremony. It was the most powerful armament which had ever been collected in modern Europe, a hundred and thirty ships – galleons from a thousand to thirteen hundred tons; galeasses manned by three hundred slaves, carrying fifty guns; galleys almost as formidable, and other vessels, the best appointed which Spain and Italy could produce. They carried nine thousand seamen, seasoned mariners who had served in all parts of the world, and some ten or twelve thousand soldiers, who were to join the Prince of Parma and assist in the conquest of England. Besides them were some scores of nobles and gentlemen who, with their servants and retinues, had volunteered for the new crusade, gallant, high-spirited youths, quite ready to fight with Satan himself in the cause of Spain and Holy Church. In them all was a fine profession of enthusiam – qualified, indeed, among the seamen by a demand for wages in advance, and a tendency to desert when they received them.

But a regiment of priests dispersed through the various squadrons kept alive in most the sense that they were going on the most glorious expedition undertaken by man.

The standard which was to be presented itself indicated the sacred character of the war. Into the Royal Arms of Spain there had been introduced as supporters on one side Christ on the Cross, on the other the Virgin Mother; and on the scroll below was written: 'Exsurge Deus et vindica causam tuam,' 'Arise, O Lord, and avenge thy cause.' 'Philip, by the grace of God King of Castile, of Leon, of Aragon, the Two Sicilies, Jerusalem, Portugal, Navarre, Granada, Toledo, Valencia, Galicia, Majorca, Sardinia, Cordova, Corsica, Murcia, Jaen, Algarves, Algesiras, Gibraltar, the Canary Islands, the East and West Indies, the Isles and Continents of the Ocean; Archduke of Austria, Duke of Burgundy, of Brabant and Milan, Count of Hapsburgh, Count of Flanders, Tirol, and Barcelona; Lord of Biscay and Molina,' &c; the monarch, in short, whose name was swathed in these innumerable titles, had determined to commit the sacred banner to his well-beloved Don Alonzo de Guzman, surnamed El Bueno, or the Good, and under its folds to sweep the ocean clear of the piratical squadrons of the English Queen.

The scene was the great metropolitian church of Lisbon, the Iglesia Major. It was six o'clock in the morning; streets and squares were lined with troops who had been landed from the ships. The King was represented by his nephew, the Cardinal Archduke, who was Viceroy of Portugal. The Viceroy rode out of the Palace with the Duke on his right hand, followed by the gentlemen adventureres of the expedition in their splended dresses. At the church they were received by the Archbishop. The standard was placed on the altar. Mass was sung. The Viceroy then led the Duke up the altar steps, lifted a fold of the standard and placed it in his hands, while, as the signal was passed outside, the ships in the river and the troops in the streets fired a salute – quna pe'ueña salva,' a small one, for powder was scarce and there was none to waste. The scene was not impressive; and the effect was frittered away in a complexity of details. The Archbishop took the holy sacrament and passed out of the church, followed by a stream of monks and secular clergy.

The Archduke and the newly-made Admiral went after them, the standard being borne by the Duke's cousin, Don Luis of Cordova, who was to accompany him to England. In this order they crossed the great square to the Dominican Convent, where the scene in the Iglesia

Major was repeated. The Dominicans received the procession at the door. The standard was again laid on the altar, this time by the Duke of Medina himself, as if to signify the consecration of his own person to the service of the beings whose forms were embroidered upon it. The religious part of the transaction finished, they returned to the Palace, and stood on the marble stairs while the troops fired a second volley. The men were then marched to their boats, with an eye on them to see that none deserted, and His Royal Highness and the Captain-General of the Ocean, as the Duke was now entitled, went in to breakfast.

The presentation had wanted dignity and perhaps seriousness. There was no spontaneous enthusiasm. The Portuguese aristocracy were pointedly absent, and the effect was rather of some artificial display got up by the clergy and the government. And yet the expedition of which this scene was the preliminary had been the dream of Catholic piety, and the discharge of a duty with which the Spanish nation appeared to be peculiarly charged. The Reformation in England had commenced with the divorce of a Spanish Princess. As England became the stronghold of heresy, Catholics, the Popes, the clergy universally had entreated Charles, and Philip after him, to strike at the heart of the mischief and take a step which, if successful, would punish the Protestant rebellion and give peace to Europe. The great Emperor and Philip too had listened reluctantly. Rulers responsible for the administration of kingdoms do not willingly encourage subjects in rebellion, even under the plea of religion. The divorce of Catherine had been an affront to Charles the Fifth and to Spain, yet it was not held to be a sufficient ground for war, and Philip had resisted for a quarter of a century the supplications of the suffering saints to deliver them from the tyranny of Elizabeth. It was an age of revolt against established authority. New ideas, new obligations of duty were shaking mankind. The intellect of Europe was outgrowing its creed. Part of the world had discovered that doctrines and practices which had lasted for fifteen hundred years were false and idolatrous. The other and larger part called the dissentients rebels and children of the Devil, and set to work to burn and kill them. At such times kings and princes have enough to do to maintain order in their own dominions, and even when they are of opposite sides have a common interest in maintaining the principle of authority. Nor when the Pope himself spoke on the Catholic side were Catholic princes completely obedient. For the Pope's pretensions to deprive kings and dispose of kingdoms were only believed in by the clergy.

No secular sovereign in Europe admitted a right which reduced him to the position of a Pope's vassal. Philip held that he sufficiently discharged his own duties in repressing heresy among his own subjects without interfering with his neighbours. Elizabeth was as little inclined to help Dutch and French and Scotch Calvinists. Yet the power of princes, even in the sixteenth century, was limited, and it rested after all on the good will of their own people. Common sympathies bound Catholics to Catholics and Protestants to Protestants, and every country in Europe became a cauldron of intrigue and conspiracy. Catholics disclaimed allegiance to Protestant sovereigns, Protestants in Catholic countries looked to their fellow-religionists elsewhere to save them from stake and sword. Thus between all parties, in one form or another, there were perpetual collisions, which the forbearance of statesmen alone prevented from breaking out into universal war.

Complete forbearance was not possible. Community of creed was a real bond which could not be ignored, nor in the general uncertainty could princes afford to reject absolutely and entirely the overtures made to them by each other's subjects. When they could not assist they were obliged to humour and encourage. Charles the Fifth refused to go to war to enforce the sentence of Rome upon Henry the Eighth, but he allowed his ambassadors to thank and stimulate Catherine's English friends. Philip was honestly unwilling to draw the sword against his sister-in-law, Elizabeth; but he was the secular head of Catholic Christendom, bound to the maintenance of the faith. He had been titular King of England, and to him the English Catholics naturally looked as their protector. He had to permit his De Quadras and his Mendozas to intrigue with disaffection and to organise rebellion. To kill dangerous or mischievous individuals was held permissible as an alternative for war, or as a means of ending disturbance. It was approved of even by Sir Thomas More in his *Utopia*. William the Silent was murdered in the Catholic interest. Henri Quartre was murdered in the Catholic interest, and any one who would do the same to the English Jezebel would be counted to have done good service.

Elizabeth had to defend herself with such resources as she possessed. She could send secret help to the Prince of Orange; she could allow her privateers to seize Spanish treasures on the high seas or plunder Philip's West Indian cities. She could execute the traitorous priests who were found teaching rebellion in England. Philip in return could let the Inquisition burn English sailors as heretics when they could catch them. And thus the two nations had drifted on, still nominally at peace, and each unwilling to declare open war; but peace each year had become more difficult to preserve, and Philip was driven on by the necessities of things to some open and decided action.

Several times a Catholic invasion of England had been distinctly contemplated. The Duke of Alva was to have tried it. Don John of Austria was to have tried it. The Duke of Guise was to have tried it. The nearest and latest occasion had been after the Conquest of Portugal and the great defeat of the French at the Azores in 1583. The Spanish Navy was then in splendid condition, excited by a brilliant victory, and led by an officer of real distinction, Alonzo de Bazan, Marques de Santa Cruz. A few English privateers had been in the defeated fleet at the Battle of Terceira; and Santa Cruz, with the other naval commanders, was eager to follow up his success and avenge the insults which had been offered for so many years to the Spanish flag by the English corsairs.

France, like all Northern Europe, was torn into factions. The Valois princes were anti-Spanish. The House of Guise was fanatically Catholic, and too powerful for the Crown to control. Santa Cruz was a diplomatist as well as a seaman. In Guise he had a friend and confederate. The plan of action had been secretly arranged. Santa Cruz and the Spanish Navy were to hold the Channel. Guise was to cross under their protection and land an army in Sussex. The Catholics were to rise, set free Mary Stuart, and make her Queen. This was the scheme. The fleet was ready. Guise was ready; and only Philip's permission was waited for. Santa Cruz was a rough old sailor, turned seventy, who meant what he said and spoke his mind plainly. Like his countrymen generally, he was tired of seeing his master for ever halting on his leaden foot (*pié de plomo*); and on August 9, 1583, while still at the Azores, he wrote to stimulate him to follow up his success by still more splendid achievement. Philip was now master of the Portuguese Empire. He (Santa Cruz) was prepared, if allowed, to add England to his dominions. The Low Countries would then surrender.

Now was the time. The troops were ready, the fleet was in high condition. Philip talked of expense and difficulty. If difficulty was an objection, the bold admiral said that nothing grand could ever be achieved; and for money, great princes could find money if they wished. The King should have faith in God, whose work he would be doing; and if he was himself permitted to try, he promised that he would have as good success as in his other enterprises.

Charles the Fifth, among his other legacies to his son, had left him instruction to distrust France and to preserve the English alliance. The passionate Catholics had assured Philip over and over again that the way to keep England was to restore the faith. But plot after plot had failed, Elizabeth was still sovereign, and Catholic conspiracies so far had only brought their leaders to the scaffold. Mary Stuart was a true believer, but she was herself half a Frenchwoman, and Guise's father had defeated Philip's father at Metz; Guise and Mary masters of France and England both was a perilous possibility. Philip did not assent; he did not refuse. He thanked Santa Cruz for his zeal, but said that he must still wait a little and watch. His waiting did not serve to clear his way. Elizabeth discovered what had been designed for her, and as a return Sir Francis Drake sacked St. Domingo and Carthagena. More than that, she had sent open help to his insurgent provinces, and had taken charge, with the consent of the Hollanders, of Flushing and Brill.

Santa Cruz could not but admire the daring of Drake and the genius of the English Queen. They were acting while his own master was asleep. He tried again to rouse him. The Queen, he said, had made herself a name in the world. She had enriched her own subjects out of Spanish spoil. In a single month they had taken a million and a half of ducats. Defensive war was always a failure. Once more the opportunity was his own. France was paralysed, and Elizabeth, though strong abroad, was weak at home. To delay longer would be to see England grow into a power which he would be unable to deal with. Spain would decline, and would lose in mere money more than four times the cost of war.[1]

This time Philip listened more seriously. Before, he had been invited to act with the Duke of Guise, and Guise was to have the spoils. Now, at any rate, the lead in the campaign was to be his own. He bade Santa Cruz send him a plan of operations and a calculation in detail of the ships and stores which would be required. He made him Lord High Admiral, commissioned him to collect squadrons at Cadiz and Lisbon, take them to sea, and act against the English as he saw occasion. Santa Cruz would probably have been allowed his way to do what he pleased in the following year but for a new complication, which threw Philip again into perplexity. The object of any enterprise led by Santa Cruz would have been the execution of the Bull of Pope Pius, the dethronement of Elizabeth, and the transference of the crown to Mary Stuart, who, if placed on the throne by Spanish arms alone, might be

1.   Santa Cruz to Philip the Second, January 13, 1586.

relied on to be true to Spanish interests. Wearied out with Mary's perpetual plots, Elizabeth, when Santa Cruz's preparations were far advanced, sent her to the scaffold. There was no longer a Catholic successor in England to whom the crown could go on Elizabeth's deposition, and it was useless to send an army to conquer the country till some purpose could be formed for disposing of it afterwards. Philip had been called King of England once. He was of the blood of the House of Lancaster. He thought, naturally, that if he was to do the work, to him the prize should belong.

Unfortunately, the rest of the world claimed a voice in the matter. France would certainly be hostile. The English Catholics were divided. The Pope himself, when consulted, refused his assent. As Pope Sixtus the Fifth, he was bound to desire the reduction of a rebellious island; as an Italian prince, he had no wish to see another wealthy kingdom added to the enormous empire of Spain. Mary Stuart's son was natural heir. He was a Protestant, but gratitude might convert him. At any rate, Philip was not to take Elizabeth's place. Sixtus was to have given a million crowns to the cost of the armament; he did not directly withdraw his promise, but he haggled with the Spanish ambassador at the Holy See. He doubted the possibility of Philip's success, and even his personal sincerity. He declined to advance a ducat till a Spanish army was actually on English soil. The Prince of Parma, who was to cross from Flanders and conduct the campaign in England itself, was diffident, if not unwilling; and Philip had to feel that even the successful occupation of London might prove the beginning of greater troubles. He had been driven forward himself against his inclination.

The chief movers in the enterprise, those who had fed the fire of religious animosity through Europe, and prevented a rational arrangement between the Spanish and English nations, were the Society of Jesus, those members of it especially who had been bred at Oxford in the Anglican Church, and hated it with the frenzy of renegades. From them came the endless conspiracies which Spain was forced to countenance, and the consequent severities of the English government; and Philip, half a bigot and half a cautious statesman, wavered between two policies till fate decided for him. Both on Philip's part and on Elizabeth's part there was a desire for peace if peace could be had. Philip was weary of the long struggle in the Low Countries, which threatened to be endless if Elizabeth supported it. Elizabeth herself wished to be left in quiet, relieved of the necessity of supporting insurgent Protestants and hanging traitorous priests. An arrangement was possible, based on principles of general toleration.

The Pope was right in not wholly trusting Philip. The Spanish King was willing to agree that England should remain Protestant if England wished it, provided the Catholics were allowed the free exercise of their own religion, and provided Elizabeth would call in her privateers, surrender to him the towns which she held in Holland, and abandon her alliance with the Dutch States. It was true that Flushing and Brill had been trusted to her charge by the States, and that if she withdrew her garrison she was bound in honour to replace them in the States' hands. But she regarded the revolt of the Low Countries as only justified by the atrocities of the Blood Council and the Inquisition. If she could secure for the Dutch Confederation the same toleration which she was willing herself to concede to the English Catholics, she might feel her honour to be acquitted sufficiently, and might properly surrender to Philip towns which really were his own.

Here only, so far as the two sovereigns were concerned, the difficulty lay. Philip held himself bound by duty to allow no liberty of religion among his own subjects. On the other hand, if peace was made the Spanish garrisons were to be withdrawn from the Low Countries; the executive government would be left in the hands of the States themselves, who could be as tolerant practically as they pleased. On these terms a general pacification was within reach. The Prince of Parma strongly advised it. Philip himself wished for it. Half Elizabeth's council recommended it and she herself wished for it. With this purpose a conference was being held at Ostend between Elizabeth's and Parma's commissioners. The terms were rational. The principal parties, it is now possible to see – even Philip himself – were sincere about it.

How long the terms of such a peace would have lasted, may be fairly questioned. Bigotry and freedom of thought had two centuries of battle still before them till it could be seen which was to prevail. But an arrangement might then have been come to at Ostend, in the winter of 1587–8, which would have lasted Philip's and Elizabeth's lifetime, could either party have trusted the other. In both countries there was a fighting party and a peace party. In England it was said that the negotiations were a fraud, designed only to induce Elizabeth to relax her preparations for defence. In Spain it was urged that the larger and more menacing the force which could be collected, the more inclined Elizabeth would be to listen to reason.

The preparations at Cadiz and Lisbon were no secret. All Europe was talking of the enormous armament which Spain was preparing, and which Santa Cruz was to convoy to the English Channel. Both the Tagus and Cadiz Harbour were reported to be crowded with ships, though as yet unprovided with crews for them. With some misgivings, but in one of her bolder moments, the Queen in the spring of 1587 allowed Drake to take a flying squadron with him down the Spanish coast. She hung about his neck a second in command to limit his movements; but Drake took his own way, leaving his vice-admiral to go home and complain. He sailed into Cadiz Harbour, burnt eighteen galleons which were lying there, and, remaining leisurely till he had finished his work, sailed away, intending to repeat the operation at Lisbon.

It might have been done with the same ease. The English squadron lay at the mouth of the river within sight of Santa Cruz, and the great admiral had to sit still and fume, unable to go out and meet him *por falta de gente* – for want of sailors to man his galleons. Drake might have gone in and burnt them all, and would have done it had not Elizabeth felt that he had accomplished enough, and that the negotiations would be broken off if he worked more destruction. He had singed the King's beard, as he called it; and the King, though patient of affronts, was moved to a passing emotion. Seamen and soldiers were hurried down to the Tagus. Orders were sent to the Admiral to put to sea at once and chase the English off the shore. But Philip, too, on his side was afraid of Santa Cruz's too great audacity. He, too, did not wish for a collision which might make peace impossible. Another order followed. The fleet was to stay where it was to continue its preparations. It was to wait till the next spring, when the enterprise should be undertaken in earnest if the peace conference at Ostend should fail in finding a conclusion.

Thus the winter drove through. Peace perhaps was not really possible, however sincerely the high contracting parties might themselves desire it. Public opinion in Spain would have compelled Philip to leave the conqueror of Terceira in command of the expedition. Santa Cruz would have sailed in March for the English Channel, supported by officers whom he had himself trained; and, although the Armada might still have failed, history would have had another tale to tell of its exploits and its fate. But a visible coldness had grown up between the King and the Admiral. Philip had confidence in his own powers of management. He chose to regulate everything, to the diet and daily habits of every sailor and soldier on board. He intended to direct and limit the action of the Armada even when out and gone to its work. He had settled perhaps in his own mind that, since he could not himself be King of England, the happiest result for him would be to leave Elizabeth where she was, reduced to the condition of his vassal, which she would become if she consented to his terms. With the presence of an overpowering fleet in the Channel, a moderate but not too excessive use of force, an avoidance of extreme and violent measures, he conceived that he could bring Elizabeth to her knees.

For such a purpose Santa Cruz was not the most promising instrument; he required some one of more malleable material who would obey his own instructions, and would not be led either by his own ambition or the enthusiasm and daring of his officers into desperate adventures. It was probably, therefore, rather to his relief than regret that in February, when the Armada was almost ready to sail, the old Admiral died at Lisbon. Santa Cruz was seventy-three years old. He had seen fifty years of service. Spanish tradition, mourning at the fatal consequence, said afterwards that he had been broken-hearted at the King's hesitation. Anxiety for the honour of his country might have worn out a younger man. He came to his end, and with him went the main chance of a successful issue of the expedition. He was the ablest seaman that Spain possessed, and had studied long the problems with which he would have had to deal. Doubtless he had left men behind among those who had served under him who could have taken his place, and have done almost as well. But Philip had determined that, since the experiment was to be made, he would himself control it from his room in the Escurial, and in his choice of Santa Cruz's successor he showed that naval capacity and patriotic enthusiasm were the last qualities for which he was looking.

Don Alonzo de Guzman, Duke of Medina Sidonia, was the richest peer in Spain. He was now thirty-eight years old, and his experience as a public man was limited to his failure to defend Cadiz against Drake. He was a short, broad-shouldered, olive-complexioned man, said to be a good rider; but, if his wife was to be believed, he was of all men in Spain the least fitted to be trusted with the conduct of any critical undertaking. The Duchess, Doña Aña de Mendoza, was the daughter of Philip's Minister, Ruy Gomez, and of the celebrated Princess of Eboli, whom later scandal called Philip's mistress.

Something is known at last of the history of the lady. If there was a woman in Spain whom Philip detested, it was the wife of Ruy Gomez. If there was a man whom the Princess despised, it was the watery-blooded King. An intrigue between a wild cat of the mountain and a narrow-minded, conscientious sheep-dog would be about as probable as a love-affair between Philip and the Princess of Eboli; and at the time of her son-in-law's appointment she was locked up in a castle in defiant disgrace. The Duke had been married to her daughter when he was twenty-two and his bride was eleven, and Doña Aña, after sixteen years' experience of him, had observed to her friends that he was well enough in his own house among persons who did not know what he was; but that if he was employed on business of state the world would discover to its cost his real character. That such a man should have been chosen to succeed Alonzo de Bazan astonished every one. A commander of Gold, it was said, was taking the place of a commander of Iron. The choice was known to Santa Cruz while he still breathed, and did not comfort him in his departure.

The most astonished of all, when he learnt the honour which was intended for him, was the Duke himself, and he drew a picture of his own incapacity as simple as Sancho's when appointed to govern his island.

'My health is bad,' he wrote to Philip's secretary, 'and from my small experience of the water I know that I am always sea-sick. I have no money which I can spare. I own a million ducats, and I have not a real to spend on my outfit. The expedition is on such a scale and the object is of such high importance that the person at the head of it ought to understand navigation and sea-fighting, and I know nothing of either. I have not one of those essential qualifications. I have no acquaintances among the officers who are to serve under me. Santa Cruz had information about the state of things in England; I have none. Were I competent otherwise, I should have to act in the dark by the opinion of others, and I cannot tell to whom I may trust. The Adelantado of Castile would do better than I. Our Lord would help him, for he is a good Christian and has fought in naval battles. If you send me, depend upon it, I shall have a bad account to render of my trust.'[1]

The Duchess, perhaps, guided her husband's hand when he wrote so faithful an account of himself. But his vanity was flattered. Philip persisted that he must go. He and only he would answer the purpose in view, and so he allowed himself to be persuaded. 'Since your Majesty still desires it, after my confession of incompetence,' he wrote to Philip, 'I will try to deserve your confidence. As I shall be doing God's work, I may hope that He will help me.'

Philip gratefully replied: 'You are sacrificing yourself for God's service and mine. I am so anxious, that if I was less occupied at home I would accompany the fleet myself, and I should be certain that all would go

1.   Medina Sidonia to Secretary Idiaquez, Feb. 16, 1588. Duro, vol. i. p. 414.

well. Take heart; you have now an opportunity of showing the extraordinary qualities which God, the author of all good, has been pleased to bestow upon you. Happen what may, I charge myself with the care of your children. If you fail, you fail; but the cause being the cause of God, you will not fail.'

Thus the Duke was to command the Armada and to sail at the earliest possible moment, for the commissioners were sitting in Ostend, and his presence in the Channel was of pressing consequence. Santa Cruz besides had fixed on the end of March as the latest date for the departure, on account of the north winds which later in the season blow down the coast of Portugal. The Duke at the time of his nomination was at his house at San Lucar. He was directed to repair at once to Lisbon, where his commission would reach him. An experienced but cautious Admiral, Don Diego Flores de Valdez, was assigned to him as nautical adviser, and Philip proceeded to inflict upon him a series of instructions and advice as wise and foolish as those with which Don Quixote furnished his squire. Every day brought fresh letters as suggestions rose in Philip's mind. Nothing was too trifling for his notice, nothing was to be left to the Duke's discretion which could possibly be provided for.

In a secret despatch to the Prince of Parma, the King revealed alike his expectations and his wishes. He trusted that the appearance of the Armada and some moderate victory over the English fleet would force Elizabeth to an agreement. If the Catholic religion could be tolerated in England, and if Flushing and Brill were given up to him, he said that he was prepared to be satisfied. To Medina Sidonia he reported as his latest advice from England that the Queen was inclining to the treaty, but was dissuaded by Leicester and Walsingham, and he gave him a list of the English forces which he might expect to meet, which was tolerably accurate and inferior to his own.

So far Philip wrote like a responsible and sensible prince, but the smallest thing and the largest seemed to occupy him equally. He directed the Duke to provide himself with competent Channel pilots, as if this was a point which might be overlooked. He laid down regulations for the health of the crews, he fixed himself the allowances of biscuit and wine, salt fish and bacon. Beyond all, he charged the Duke to attend to their morals. They were in the service of the Lord, and the Lord must not be offended by the faults of His instruments. The clergy throughout Spain were praying for them and would continue to pray, but soldiers and sailors must do their part and live like Christians.

214

They must not swear; they must not gamble, which led to swearing. If they used low language God would be displeased. Every man before he embarked must confess and commend himself to the Lord. Especially and pre-eminently, loose women must be kept away, and if any member of the expedition fell into the *pecado nefando* he must be chastised to the example of the rest.

This was well enough also, but from morals the King went next to naval details, of which he could know nothing. He had heard, he said, that the gentlemen adventurers wanted state-rooms and private berths. It would encumber the ships, and the Duke was not to allow it. As the Duke was ignorant of navigation, the King held himself competent to instruct. He was to make straight for the English Channel, advance to the North Foreland, and put himself in communication with Parma. If foul weather came and the ships were scattered, they were to collect again, first at Finisterre, and then at the Scilly Isles. In the Channel he must keep on the English side, because the water was deeper there. Elizabeth's fleet, Philip understood, was divided, part being under Drake at Plymouth, and part in the Straits of Dover. If the Duke fell in with Drake he was to take no notice of him unless he was attacked, and was to keep on his course. If he found the two squadrons united, he would still be in superior force and might join battle, being careful to keep to windward.

There were limits even to Philip's confidence in his ability to guide. He admitted that he could not direct the Duke specifically how to form the ships for an engagement. Time and opportunity would have to determine. 'Only,' he said, 'omit no advantage, and so handle the fleet that one part shall support another. The enemy will try to fight at a distance with his guns. You will endeavour to close. You will observe that their practice is to shoot low into the hulls rather than into the rigging. You will find how to deal with this. Keep your vessels together, allow none to stray or go in advance. Do not let them hurry in pursuit of prizes after victory. This fault has often caused disaster both on sea and land. Conquer first, and then you will have spoil enough. The Council of War will order the distribution of it.

'What I am now saying implies that a battle will have to be fought; but if the enemy can be got rid of without an action, so much the better. The effect will be produced without loss to yourself. Should the Prince be able to cross, you will remain with the Armada at the mouth of the Thames, lending such assistance as you can. Consult with the Prince, and land none of your forces without his approval. Remember that your only business is to fight at sea. Differences between leaders are injurious, and always to be avoided. I am confident that you will co-operate cordially with the Prince as my service demands; but I must charge you to follow these injunctions of mine strictly according to the exact words. I have similarly directed the Prince on his own conduct, and if you two acting together can succeed in your undertaking, there will be honour to spare for both of you. You will remain at the Thames' mouth till the work is done.

'You may then, if the Prince approves, take in hand Ireland, in which case you will leave your Spanish troops with him and exchange them for Germans and Italians. You will be careful in what you spend. You know how costly the Armada has been to me. You will also see that I am not cheated in the muster rolls, and that the provisions are sound and sufficient. You will watch the conduct of the officers and keep them attentive to their duties. This is all which occurs to me at present. I must leave the rest to your own care and prudence, and for any further advices which I may have to send you.'[1]

Much of all this was no doubt reasonable and true. But generals chosen to conduct great enterprises do not require to be taught the elements of their duties. That Philip thought it necessary to write all these details was characteristic both of himself and of the Duke. But it was characteristic of Philip also, that he had not made up his mind what the fleet was after all to do, or what he himself wished it to do. The first set of instructions was followed by a second, addressed both to the Duke and the Prince of Parma. The orginal purpose was that the fleet should make its way to the North Foreland. Parma was to use its presence in the Channel, to cross at once with the army, advance to London and take possession of the government.

This, however, implied that the English squadrons should have been first destroyed, or driven off the sea into their harbours. It was possible, as Philip foresaw, that the victory at sea might be less complete. He assumed that the English would be overmatched, but they were bold and skilful, and, even if defeated, might be left in a condition to be troublesome. The passage of the army might in that case be dangerous; and Parma was left on his own responsibility to resume the negotiations at Ostend. Medina Sidonia was to gain and fortify the Isle of Wight, and the presence of the Armada in the Solent was to be used as an instrument to extort favourable terms from Elizabeth's government. It

1.　Philip the Second to the Duke of Medina Sidonia, April 1. Duro, vol. ii. pp. 5–13.

would be no longer possible to demand the restoration of Catholicism in England, but the free exercise of the Catholic religion was to be insisted on. As the first point, and for the sake of the toleration of the Catholics, Philip would be willing to abandon his claim to compensation for the plundering expeditions of Francis Drake. The next condition was to be the restoration to the King of the towns which Elizabeth held in the Low Countries. It was possible that, before consenting, the Queen would demand the same liberty of religion for the Protestants of the Low Countries which she was required to grant to her own Catholics. To this, however, Parma was in no case to consent. The English might argue that the Huguenots were tolerated under the Edicts in France. Parma was to answer that the example was not to the point, that the King, at any rate, would not give way. The Isle of Wight would be in his own hands. The fleet would be safe in the Solent. Other fortresses could be seized along the coast, and Elizabeth would be forced to consent to a peace, under which she would be virtually reduced into the position of Philip's vassal.

Accidents, however, might happen, and the Prince of Parma also was perplexed with minute conditional instructions.

Disaster, it is evident, Philip did not anticipate. Something less than complete success he probably did anticipate, and on the whole might prefer it. Satisfied with having provided for all contingencies, he was now only anxious to see the Armada on its way. The nuns and hermits, meanwhile, had removed the alarms of Medina Sidonia, had convinced him that God could not neglect a business in which He was so peculiarly concerned, and that, in the fine language of theological knight-errantry, the service which he was to execute had been specially reserved by Providence for the the King to achieve.[1]

Such thoughts and such experiences were doubtless indications of a high-wrought frame of mind; but men may dwell too exclusively on the conviction that God is on their side. While the priests were praying and the King and the Duke were calculating on the Divine assistance, they were omitting the most obvious precautions by which moderate success could be looked for. Santa Cruz had reported that the fleet was almost ready to sail. The stores of provisions had been laid in while he was still alive, and the water-casks had been filled. But after his death

---

1. 'Y que lo tiene guardado á V. Md. para que por su mano y con su gran zelo y christiandad, se reduzca aquel Regno al gremio y obediencia de su Iglesia.' Medina Sidonia to Philip, April 11.

there was no responsible person left in Lisbon to see to anything. Great naval expeditions were nothing new in Spain. The West Indies and Mexico and Peru had not been conquered by men in their sleep; and what ships and ships' crews required for dangerous voyages was as well understood at Lisbon and Cadiz as in any harbour in the world.

But the Armada was surrounded by a halo of devout imagination which seemed to paralyse ordinary sense. It was to have sailed in March, but, even to the inexperienced eye of Medina Sidonia when he arrived at his command, the inadequacy of the preparations was too obvious. The casks of salt meat were found to be putrefying; the water in the tanks had not been renewed, and had stood for weeks, growing foul and poisonous under the hot Lisbon sun. Spare rope, spare spars, spare anchors – all were deficient. The powder-supply was short. The balls were short. The contractors had cheated audaciously, and the soldiers and mariners so little liked the look of things that they were deserting in hundreds, while the muster-masters drew pay for the full numbers and kept it.

Instead of sailing in March, as he had been ordered, the Duke was obliged to send to Madrid a long list of indispensable necessaries, without which he could not sail at all. Nothing had been attended to save the state of the men's souls, about which the King had been so peculiarly anxious. They at any rate had been sent to confession, had received each his ticket certifying that he had been absolved and had duly commended himself to the Lord. The loose women had been sent away, the cards and dice prohibited, the moral instructions punctually complied with. The rest had been left to chance. The short powder-supply was irremediable. The Duke purchased a few casks from merchant ships, but no more was to be had. For the rest, the King wrote letters, and the Duke, according to his own account, worked like a slave, and the worst defects were concealed if not supplied. Not, however, till the end of April were the conditions advanced sufficiently for the presentation of the standard, and even then the squadron from Andalusia had not arrived.

All was finished at last, or at any rate seemed so. The six squadrons were assembled under their respective commanders. Men and officers were on board, and sailing orders, addressed to every member of the expedition, were sent round, in the Duke's name, to the several ships, which, remembering the fate to which all these men were being consigned by their crusading enthusiasm, we cannot read without emotion.

'From highest to lowest you are to understand the object of our expedition, which is to recover countries to the Church now oppressed by the enemies of the true faith. I therefore beseech you to remember your calling, so that God may be with us in what we do. I charge you, one and all, to abstain from profane oaths dishonouring to the names of our Lord, our Lady, and the Saints. All personal quarrels are to be suspended while the expedition lasts, and for a month after it is completed. Neglect of this will be held as treason. Each morning at sunrise the ship boys, according to custom, shall sing "Good Morrow" at the foot of the mainmast,[1] and at sunset the "Ave Maria." Since bad weather may interrupt the communications, the watch-word is laid down for each day in the week:– Sunday, Jesus; the days succeeding, the Holy Ghost, the Holy Trinity, Santiago, the Angels, All Saints, and our Lady. At sea, every evening, each ship shall pass with a salute under the lee of the Commander-in-Chief, and shall follow at night the light which he will carry in his stern.'

So, as it were, singing its own dirge, the doomed Armada went upon its way, to encounter the arms and the genius of the new era, unequally matched with unbelievers. On May 14 it dropped down the river to Belem, and lay there waiting for a wind. A brief account may here be given of its composition and its chief leaders. The fleet consisted of a hundred and thirty ships. Seven of them were over a thousand tons and sixty-seven over five hundred. They carried two thousand five hundred guns, chiefly small, however – four, six, and nine-pounders. Spanish seamen understood little of gunnery. Their art in their sea-battles was to close and grapple and trust to their strength and courage in hand-to-hand fighting. Large for the time as the galleons were, they were still overcrowded. Soldiers, sailors, officers, volunteers, priests, surgeons, galley-slaves, amounted, according to the returns, to some twenty thousand men. The soldiers were the finest in Europe; the seamen old trained hands, who had learnt their trade with Santa Cruz. They were divided into six squadrons, each with its Vice-Admiral and Capitana or flag-ship. The Duke carried his standard in the *San Martin*, of the squadron of Portugal, the finest vessel in the service, and, as the Spaniards thought, in the world. The other five, of Biscay, Castile, Andalusia, Guypuscoa, and the Levant, were led by distinguished officers.

As the names of these officers recur frequently in the account of what

1. 'Los pajes, segun es costumbre, daran los buenos dias al pié del mástil major.'

followed, some description may be given of each.

The Vice-Admiral of the Biscay squadron was Juan Martinez de Recalde, a native of Bilbao, an old, battered sea-warrior, who had fought and served in all parts of the ocean. He knew Ireland; he knew the Channel; he had been in the battle at Terceira, and in the opinion of the service was a second only to Santa Cruz. His flagship was the *Santa Aña*, a galleon of eight hundred tons; he sailed himself in the *Gran Grin*, of eleven hundred; so far fortunate, if any one in the expedition could be called fortunate, for the *Santa Aña* was disabled in a storm at the mouth of the Channel.

The leaders of the squadrons of Castile and Andalusia were two cousins, Don Pedro and Don Diego de Valdez. Don Diego, whom Philip had chosen for the Duke's mentor, was famous as a naval architect, had been on exploring expeditions, and had made a certain reputation for himself. He was a jealous, suspicious, cautious kind of man, and Philip had a high opinion of him. Don Pedro was another of the heroes of Terceira, a rough, bold seaman, scarred in actions with English corsairs, and between the two kinsmen there was neither resemblance nor affection. Don Pedro's misfortune in the Channel, which will soon be heard of, brought him more honour than Don Diego earned by his timidity. He lived long after, and was for eight years governor of Cuba, where the Castle of the Moro at Havana still stands as his monument.

Two other officers deserve mention: Miguel de Oquendo, who sailed in the *Señora de la Rosa*, of Guypuscoa, and Alonzo de Leyva, who had a ship of his own, the *Rata Coronada*. Oquendo's career had been singularly distinguished. He had been the terror of the Turks in the Mediterranean. At Terceira, at a critical point in the action, he had rescued Santa Cruz when four French vessels were alongside of him. He had himself captured the French Admiral's flagship, carrying her by boarding, and sending his own flag to her masthead above the smoke of the battle. He was an excellent seaman besides, and managed his ship as was said, as easily as a horse. Alonzo de Leyva held no special command beyond his own vessel; but he had been named by Philip to succeed Medina Sidonia in case of misadventure. With him, and under his special charge, were most of the high-born adventurous youths who had volunteered for the crusade. Neither he nor they were ever to see Spain again, but Spanish history ought not to forget him, and ought not to forget Oquendo.

Of priests and friars there were a hundred and eighty; of surgeons, doctors, and their assistants, in the entire fleet, not more than eighty-five. The numbers might have been reversed with advantage.

Meanwhile, the winds were unpropitious. For fourteen days the fleet lay at anchor at the mouth of the Tagus unable to get away. They weighed at last on May 28, and stood out to sea; but a northerly breeze drove them to leeward, and they could make no progress, while almost instantly on their sailing the state of the stores was brought to light. The water had been on board for four months! the casks were leaking, and what was left of it was unfit to drink. The provisions, salt meat, cheese, biscuit, were found to be half putrid, and a remarkable order was issued to serve out first what was in worse condition, that the supplies might hold out the longer. As the ships were to keep together, the course and speed were necessarily governed by those which sailed the worst. The galleons, high built, and with shallow draught of water, moved tolerably before the wind, but were powerless to work against it. The north wind freshened. They were carried down as low as Cape St. Vincent, standing out and in, and losing ground on each tack. After a fortnight's labour they were only in the latitude of Lisbon again.

Tenders were sent in every day to Philip, with an account of their progress. Instead of being in the mouth of the Channel the Duke had to report that he could make no way at all, and, worse than that, the entire ships' companies were on the way to being poisoned. Each provision cask which was opened was found worse than the last. The biscuit was mouldy, the meat and fish stinking, the water foul and breeding dysentery. The crews and companies were loud in complaint; the officers had lost heart, and the Duke, who at starting had been drawing pictures in his imagination of glorious victories, had already begun to lament his weakness in having accepted the command. He trusted God would help him, he said. He wished no harm to any one. He had left his quiet, and his home, and his children, out of pure love to his Majesty, and he hoped his Majesty would remember it.[1] The state of the stores was so desperate, especially of the water, that it was held unsafe to proceed. The pilots said that they must put into some port for a fresh supply. The Duke feared that if he consented the men, in their present humour, would take the opportunity and desert.

At length, on June 10, after three weeks of ineffectual beating up and down, the wind shifted to the south-west, and the fleet could be laid upon its course. The anxiety was not much diminished. The salt

1. Medina Sidonia to Philip the Second, May 30.

meat, salt fish, and cheese were found so foul throughout that they were thrown overboard for fear of pestilence, and the rations were reduced to biscuit and weevils. A despatch was hurried off to Philip that fresh stores must instantly be sent out, or there would be serious disaster. The water was the worst of all, as when drunk it produced diarrhoea. On June 13 matters mended a little. The weather had cooled. The south-west wind had brought rain. The ships could be aired and purified. They were then off Finisterre, and were on a straight course for the Channel. Philip's orders had been positive that they were not to delay anywhere, that they were to hurry on and must not separate. They had five hundred men, however, down with dysentery, and the number of sick was increasing. A council was held on board the *San Martin*, and the Admirals all agreed that go on they could not. Part of the fleet, at least, must make into Ferrol, land the sick, and bring off supplies. The Duke could not come to a resolution, but the winds and waves settled his uncertainties.

On the 19th it came on to blow. The Duke, with the Portugal squadron, the galleys and the larger galleons, made in at once for Corunna, leaving the rest to follow, and was under shelter before the worst of the gale. The rest were caught outside and scattered. They came in as they could, most of them in the next few days, some dismasted, some leaking with strained timbers, the crews exhausted with illness; but at the end of a week a third part of the Armada was still missing, and those which had reached the harbour were scarcely able to man their yards. A hospital had to be established on shore. The tendency to desert had become so general that the landing-places were occupied with bodies of soldiers. A despatch went off to the Escurial, with a despairing letter from the Duke to the King.

'The weather,' he said, 'though it is June, is as wild as in December. No one remembers such a season. It is the most strange since we are on the business of the Lord, and some reason there must be for what has befallen us. I told your Majesty that I was unfit for this command when you asked me to undertake it. I obeyed your orders, and now I am here in Corunna with the ships dispersed and the force remaining to me inferior to the enemy. The crews are sick, and grow daily worse from bad food and water. Most of our provisions have perished, and we have not enough for more than two months' consumption. Much depends on the safety of this fleet. You have exhausted your resources to collect it, and if it is lost you may lose Portugal and the Indies. The men are out of spirit. The officers do not understand their business. We are no longer strong. Do not deceive yourself into thinking that we are equal to the work before us.

You remember how much it cost you to conquer Portugal, a country adjoining Castile, where half the inhabitants were in your favour. We are now going against a powerful kingdom with only the weak force of the Prince of Parma and myself. I speak freely, but I have laid the matter before the Lord; you must decide yourself what is to be done. Recollect only how many there are who envy your greatness and bear you no goodwill.'[1]

On the 27th thirty-five ships were still absent, and nothing had been heard of them. The storm, however, after all had not been especially severe, and it was not likely that they were lost. The condition to which the rest were reduced was due merely to rascally contractors and official negligence, and all could easily be repaired by an efficient commander in whom the men had confidence. But the Duke had no confidence in himself nor the officers in him. Four weeks only had passed since he had left Lisbon and he was already despondent, and his disquieted subordinates along with him. He had written freely to Philip, and advised that the expedition should be abandoned. He again summoned the Vice-Admirals to his cabin and required their opinions. Should they or should they not go forward with their reduced force?

The Inspector-General, Don George Manrique, produced a schedule of numbers. They were supposed, he said, to have twenty thousand men besides the galley-slaves. The Vice-Admirals were less easily frightened than their leader. None were for giving up. Most of them advised that they should wait where they were till the ships came in, repairing damages and taking in fresh stores. Pedro de Valdez insisted that they should go on as soon as possible. While they remained in harbour fresh meat and vegetables might be served out, and the crews would soon recover from a sickness which was caused only by bad food. With vigour and energy all that was wrong could be set right. The missing ships were doubtless ahead expecting them, and would be fallen in with somewhere.

Don Pedro was addressing brave men, and carried the council along with him. He wrote himself to Philip to tell him what had passed. 'The Duke,' he said, 'bore him no goodwill for his advice, but he intended to persist in a course which he believed to be for his Majesty's honour.'

A day or two later the wanderers came back and restored the Duke's courage. Some had been as far as Scilly, but none had been lost and none had been seriously injured. The fresh meat was supplied as Don Pedro advised. The sick recovered; and all were soon in health again. Fresh supplies were poured down out of the country. The casks were

1. Medina Sidonia to Philip the Second from Corunna, June 24.

refilled with pure water. In short, the sun began to shine once more, and the despondency fit passed away. Philip wrote kindly and cheerily. 'Everything would be furnished which they could want. The Duke might spend money freely, and need spare nothing to feed the men as they ought to be fed. If they had met with difficulties in the beginning they would have greater glory in the end. There were difficulties in every enterprise. They must overcome them and go on.' The Duke still hesitated. He said truly enough that other things were wanting besides food: powder, cordage, and the thousand minor stores which ought to have been provided and were not. But the rest of the chief officers were now in heart again, and he found himself alone. Recalde only, like a wise man, begged Philip to modify his instructions and allow him to secure Plymouth or Dartmouth on their advance, as, although they might gain a victory, it was unlikely to be so complete as to end the struggle, and they might require a harbour to shelter the fleet.

Philip, unfortunately for himself, paid no attention to Recalde's suggestion, but only urged them to be gone at their best speed. The ships were laid on shore to be scraped and tallowed. The gaps in the crews were filled up with recruits. Another ship was added, and at the final muster there were a hundred and thirty-one vessels, some seven thousand sailors and ten or twelve thousand infantry, two thousand slaves, and fourteen hundred officers, priests, gentlemen, and servants. With restored health and good-humour they were again commended to the Lord. Tents were set up on an island in the harbour, with an altar in each and friars in sufficient number to officiate. The ships' companies were landed and brought up man by man till the whole of them had again confessed and again received the sacrament.

'This,' said the Duke, 'is great riches, and the most precious jewel which I carry with me. They now are all well, and content, and cheerful.'

Two months of summer were still left when the Armada made its second start out of Corunna on Friday, July 22, with fresh heart and better provision. On the 23rd the last vessel in the fleet had passed Cape Ortegal, and the wind, as if to make amends for past persecution, blew fair and moderate from the south. Saturday, Sunday, and Monday the galleons swept easily along across the Bay of Biscay, and on the Monday night, the 25th the Duke found himself with all his flock about him at the mouth of the English Channel. Tuesday broke calm and cloudy, with a draft of northerly air. Heavy showers fell. One of the galleys had sprung a leak, and was obliged to go home. On Wednesday the wind backed to the west, and rose into a gale, blowing hard with a high sea. The waves broke into the stern galleries of the galleons, and the fleet was hove to. On Friday the storm was over, but there was still a long, heavy roll.

The ships were unmanageable, and from the maintop of the *San Martin* forty sail were again not to be seen. The remaining galleys, finding that in such weather they were like to be swamped, had made away for the coast of France; the *Santa Aña*, the Capitana of the Biscay squadron, had disappeared completely and was supposed to have been sunk. She had in fact lost her reckoning, and at last found her way into Havre. The rest of the missing ships proved only to be a few miles ahead. After a slight flutter, the Armada, shorn of its galleys and the *Santa Aña*, was again complete, and with the sky clearing from south-west went on upon its way. As yet they had seen nothing – not a sail or a boat; but being on the enemy's coast they put themselves into fighting order. They were in three divisions. The Duke was in the centre with the main battle. Alonzo de Leyva led the advance as the post of honour. The rear was under Martinez de Recalde, the formation being like an oblique crescent, or like the moon when it lies on its back, De Leyva and Recalde being at the two horns.

In this order they sailed slowly on through the day, still with nothing in sight, but knowing by observation and soundings that they were coming up to land. The sun on Friday, at noon, gave them 50 degrees, and the lead 56 fathoms. At four in the afternoon the grey ridge of the Lizard rose above the sea three leagues off. They were now in sight of the den of the dragon which they were come to slay, and Medina Sidonia ran up to his masthead a special flag of his own, which had been embroidered for the occasion – Christ on the Cross, and Our Lady and the Magdalen on either side of Him. As the folds unrolled in the breeze, each ship in the fleet fired a broadside, and the ships' companies gathered and knelt on the deck to give thanks to the Almighty.

That evening the Duke despatched the last letter to the King which for a month he had leisure to write. So far, he said, the enemy had not shown himself, and he was going forward in the dark; no word had come from Parma; before him was only the silent sea, and the long line of the Cornish coast, marked at intervals by columns of smoke which he knew to be alarm beacons. The sea that was so silent would soon be noisy enough. With a presentiment of danger, the Duke told the King that he must so far disregard his orders that, until Parma had communicated with him, he proposed to halt at the Isle of Wight and to go no further. Sail was taken in that night. On the Saturday morning a despatch boat was sent away with the letter to the King, and the fleet crept on slowly and cautiously.

They had hoped to fall in with a fishing-smack, but none were to be discovered; nor was it till Saturday night, or rather at one o'clock on the Sunday morning, that they were able to gather any information at all. At that hour, and not before, a pinnace that had gone forward to observe came back with four Falmouth fishermen who had been fallen in with at sea. From them the Duke and the admirals learnt that Drake and Howard had come out that morning from Plymouth harbour, and were lying in the Sound, or outside it, waiting for them. The burning beacons had brought notice on the Friday evening that the Armada was in sight, and the English had instantly got under way. The Spanish records and diaries say distinctly that from these fishermen they had gathered their first and only knowledge of the English movements.

The charge afterwards brought against the Duke, therefore, that he had learnt that Plymouth was undefended, that Oquendo and Recalde urged him to go in and take it, and that he refused and lost the opportunity, is proved to be without foundation. Very likely a council of admirals did advise that Plymouth should be attacked if they found Howard and Drake still in the Sound, for in the narrow space the ships would be close together, and the superior numbers of the Spaniards and their superior strength in small arms and musketry would be able to assert themselves. Medina Sidonia may have agreed, but the opportunity was never allowed him. The English fleet was already outside, and the Duke could not enter till he had fought an action.

An hour after midnight, on the Sunday morning, the Falmouth boatmen gave their information. Four hours later, directly off Ramehead, the two fleets were engaged. The air through the night had been light from the west. The water was smooth. At five o'clock, just after sunrise, eleven large vessels were seen from the deck of the *San Martin* three miles to leeward, outside the Mewstone, manoeuvring to recover the wind, which was beginning to freshen. Forty others were counted between the Armada and the land to the west of the Sound. The squadron first seen consisted of the Queen's ships under Lord Howard; the others were Drake and the privateers. The breeze rose rapidly. The Duke flew the consecrated standard, and signalled to the whole fleet to brace round their yards and hold the wind between the two English divisions. Howard, however, with apparent ease, went on to windward and joined Drake.

Both of them then stood out to sea behind the whole Armada, firing heavily into Recalde and the rearward Spanish squadron as they passed. Recalde tried hard to close, but Sir John Hawkins had introduced new lines into the construction of the English ships. The high castles at poop and stern had been reduced, the length increased, the beam diminished. They could sail perhaps within five points of the wind. They showed powers, at any rate, entirely new to Recalde, for they seemed to be able to keep at any distance which they pleased from him. They did not try to break his line or capture detached vessels. With their heavy guns, which he found to his cost to be of weightier metal and to carry farther than his own, they poured their broadsides into him at their leisure, and he could make no tolerable reply. Alonzo de Leyva and Oquendo, seeing that Recalde was suffering severely, went to his assistance, but only to experience themselves the effects of this novel method of naval combat and naval construction.

To fight at a distance was contrary to Spanish custom, and was not held worthy of honourable men. But it was effective; it was perplexing, it was deadly. The engagement lasted on these conditions through the whole Sunday forenoon. The officers of the Armada did all that gallant men could achieve. They refused to recognise where the English superiority lay till it was forced upon them by torn rigging and shattered hulls. Recalde's own ship fired a hundred and twenty shot, and it was thought a great thing. But the English had fired five to the Spanish one, and the effect was the greater because, as in Rodney's action at Dominica, the galleons were crowded with troops, among whom shot and splinter had worked havoc. The Castilians and Biscayans were brave enough; there were no braver men in the world; but they were in a position where courage was of no use to them. They were perplexed and disturbed; and a gentleman present who describes the scene observes that 'este dia mostraronse de nuestra Armada algunos officiales medrosos' – this day some of the officers of our fleet showed cowardice.

No prizes were taken. Drake and Howard understood their business too well to waste life upon single captures. Their purpose was to harass, shatter, and weaken the entire Armada, as opportunity might offer, with the least damage to themselves, till shot and weather, and the casualties likely to occur under such conditions, had reduced the fleets to something nearer to an equality. Tactics so novel baffled the Spaniards. They had looked for difficulties, but they had counted with certainty on success if they could force the English into a general engagement. No wonder that they were unpleasantly startled at the result of the first experiment.

227

The action, if such it could be called when the Armada had been but a helpless target to the English guns, lasted till four in the afternoon. The south-west wind then was blowing up, and the sea was rising. The two fleets had by that time driven past the opening into the Sound. The Duke could not have gone in if he had tried, nor could De Leyva himself, under such circumstances, have advised him to try; so, finding that he could do nothing, and was only throwing away life, he signalled from the *San Martin* to bear away up Channel. The misfortunes of the day, however, were not yet over. The Spanish squadrons endeavoured to resume their proper positions, De Leyva leading and Recalde covering the rear. The English followed leisurely, two miles behind, and Recalde's own vessel had suffered so much in the engagement that she was observed to be dropping back, and to be in danger of being left alone and overtaken. Pedro de Valdez, in the Capitana of the Andalusian squadron, one of the finest ships in the fleet, observing his old comrade in difficulties, bore up to help him.

After such a day, the men, perhaps, were all of them disturbed, and likely to make mistakes in difficult manoeuvres. In turning, the Capitana came into collision with the *Santa Catalina* and broke her own bowsprit; the fore-topmast followed, and the ship became an unmanageable wreck. She had five hundred men on board, besides a considerable part of the money which had been sent for the use of the fleet. To desert such a vessel, and desert along with it one of the principal officers of the expedition, on the first disaster, would be an act of cowardice and dishonour not to be looked for in a Spanish nobleman.

But night was coming on. To bear up was to risk a renewal of the fighting, for which the Duke had no stomach. He bore Don Pedro a grudge for having opposed him at Corunna, when he had desired to abandon the expedition; Diego Florez, his adviser, had also his dislike for Don Pedro, and, to the astonishment of every one, the signal was made that the fleet was not to stop, and that Don Pedro was to be left to his fate. De Leyva and Oquendo, unable to believe the order to be serious, hastened on board the *San Martin* to protest. The Duke hestitated; Diego Florez, however, said that to wait would be to risk the loss of the whole fleet, and by Diego Florez Philip had directed the Duke to be guided. Boats were sent back to bring off the Capitana's treasure and the crew, but in the rising sea boats could do nothing. Don Pedro was deserted, overtaken, and of course captured, after a gallant resistance. The ship was carried into Dartmouth, and proved a valuable prize. Besides the money, there was found a precious store of powder, which the English sorely needed. Among other articles was a chest of swords, richly mounted, which the Duke was taking over to be presented to the English Catholic peers. Don Pedro himself was treated with the high courtesy which he deserved, to be ransomed at the end of a year, and to be spared the ignominy of further service under his extraordinary commander-in-chief.

The loss of Don Pedro was not the last, and not the worst, calamity of the night. Soon after dark the air was shaken and the sky was lighted by an explosion in the centre of the Spanish fleet. Oquendo's ship, *Our Lady of the Rose*, was blown up, and two hundred men, dead and wounded, were hurled into the sea. The wreck that was left was seen to be in a blaze, in which the rest on board were like to perish. Oquendo himself was absent. Some said it was an accident, others that there had been some quarrel, and that one of the parties in a rage had flung a match into the magazine and sprung overboard. This time the Armada was rounded to; the burning ship was covered by the main body. The money on board, for each galleon had its own treasury, was taken out with the survivors of the crew. The hull was then abandoned to the English. A few casks of stores were still found in her hold which had escaped destruction. Shortly afterwards she sank.

From the day on which it sailed the fleet had been pursued by misfortune. Two such disasters following on the unexpected and startling features of the first engagement struck a chill through the whole force. The officers had no longer the least trust in a commander-in-chief whom they had ill liked from the first. The national honour was supposed to be touched by the desertion of Pedro de Valdez, who was universally loved and respected.

The next morning, August 1, broke heavily. The wind was gone, and the galleons were rolling in the swell. The enemy was hull down behind them, and the day was spent in repairing damages, knotting broken ropes, and nailing sheets of lead over the shot-holes. Recalde's ship had been so roughly handled that the disposition of the squadrons was altered. De Leyva took charge of the rear in the *Rata Coronada*, where the danger was greatest. Don Martinez was passed forward into the advance, where he could attend to his hurts out of harm's way. The Duke in sour humour found fault all round. Orders were issued that each ship should keep a position definitely laid down; and any captain found out of his place was to be immediately hanged. Severity at such a moment was resented as ill-timed and undeserved. The day passed without incident. With the sunset the sea fell smooth, and not an air was stirring. The English fleet had come up, but was still a league behind. Both fleets were then off Portland.

An hour after midnight De Leyva, Oquendo, and Recalde came on board the *San Martin*, woke the Duke out of his sleep, and told him that now was the time for him to repair his credit. By the light of the rising moon the English ships could be seen drifted apart with the tide, and deprived in the breathless calm of their superior advantages. The galeasses, with their oars, should be sent out instantly to attack single vessels. The dawn it was likely would bring a breeze from the east, when the galleons could gather away and support them. The Duke roused himself. Oquendo himself carried the orders to the captain of the galeasses, Don Hugo de Monçada. The galeasses prepared for action. The easterly air came up as was expected, and with the first clear light Howard was seen dead to leeward standing in for the land, and endeavouring, as he had done at Plymouth, to recover the weather-gauge. The galeasses proved of small service after all, for the wind was soon too fresh; and they were useless. They could do nothing except in a calm. But the *San Martin* and her leading consorts bore down with all sail set.

Howard, being near the shore, had to tack and stand off to sea. He had thus to pass out through the centre of the whole Spanish fleet. The ships became intermixed, the *Ark Raleigh* was surrounded with enemies, and every Spanish captain's heart was bounding with the hope of boarding her. If they could once grapple they were justly confident in the numbers and courage of their men. So near the chances were at one moment, that Martin de Bretandona, the Levantine commander, might have closed with one of the largest of the English ships 'if he could have been contented with less than the vessel which carried Howard's flag.' But the wind freshened up with the day, and Don Martin and his friends saw vessels handled in a style which they had never seen before.

It has been often confidently urged, as a reason for reducing the naval estimates, that Howard's fleet was manned by volunteers. It is true that the English crews were not composed of men who were in the permanent service of the Crown, but never were a body of sailors gathered together more experienced in sailing ships and fighting them. They were the rovers of the ocean. To navigate the wildest seas, to fight Spaniards wherever they could meet them, had for thirty years been their occupation. Tacking, wearing, making stern way where there was no room to turn, they baffled every attack by the swiftness of their movements, and cleared their way out of the throng. Once more they drew away to windward, took at their leisure such positions as suited them, and, themselves beyond the reach of the feeble Spanish artillery, fired into the galleons with their long heavy guns till five o'clock in the afternoon.

This day the Duke personally behaved well. The *San Martin* was in the thickest of the fight, and received fifty shots in her hull. The famous standard was cut in two. The leaks were so many and so formidable that the divers were again at work all night plugging and stopping the holes. But the result was to show him, and to show them all, that the English ships were superior to theirs in speed and power and weight of artillery, and that to board them against their will was entirely hopeless. Another observation some of them made which was characteristic of the age. The galleons which had no gentlemen on board had been observed to hold off and keep out of range. In the evening the wind fell. With the last of it, Howard and Drake bore away and left them, as, with the calm, the galeasses might again be dangerous. Wednesday was breathless. The English wanted powder besides, having used what they had freely; and they were forced to wait for fresh supplies, which came up in the course of the afternoon.

August 4, Thursday, was St. Dominic's Day. The house of Guzman de Silva claimed St. Dominic as a member of their family; and St. Dominic, the Duke was assured, would now lend a hand to his suffering kinsman. The Isle of Wight, where he had announced to Philip that he intended to stop, was directly under his lee. Once anchored in St. Helen's Roads he would have the Armada in a safe shelter, where, if the English chose to attack him, they must come to closer quarters, as there would not be sea room for the manoeuvres which had been so disastrous to him.[1] If he could land ten thousand men he might take the island; and, perplexed, agitated, and harassed by the unexpected course which events had taken with him, he probably still intended to act on this resolution, which was the wisest which he could have formed. He would have another action to fight before he could get in, but with St. Dominic's help he might this time have better fortune.

Howard and Drake seemed willing to give St. Dominic an oppor-

---

1. The Duke's intention of stopping at the Isle of Wight was expressed by him as clearly as possible. Writing on July 30 to the King, he said he must advance 'poco a poco con toda el Armada junta en mis escuadrones hasta isla D'Wich y *no pasar* adelante hasta tener aviso del Duque de Parma. Porque si yo saliese de alli con esta, la costa de Flandes no habiendo en toda ella puerto ni abrigo ninguno para estas naves, con el primer temporal que les diese lose charia á los bancos, donde sin ningun remedio se habrian de perder; y por excusar este peligro tan evidente, me ha parecido no pasar adelante de aquella isla hasta saber lo que el Duque hace,' etc. – Duro, vol. ii., p. 221.

tunity of showing what he could do. They had received their powder. They had been reinforced by a few privateers who had come out from the Needles, and they showed a disposition to engage at a nearer distance than they had hitherto ventured. They were so far at a disadvantage that the wind was light, but, using what there was of it, the *Ark Raleigh* led straight down on the *San Martin*, ranged alongside, and opened a furious fire from her lower ports, as it appeared to the Spaniards, with heavier guns than she had used in the previous actions. Again the *San Martin* was badly cut up. Many of her men were killed and more were wounded.

Seeing her hard pressed, Recalde and Oquendo came to the Duke's support. Oquendo drove his own ship between the *Ark* and the *San Martin*, receiving the broadside intended for her, and apparently causing some confusion on board the *Ark* by a shot of his own. At this moment the wind dropped altogether. An eddy of the tide carried off the other English ships, leaving Howard surrounded once more by the enemy and in worse difficulties than in the fight off Portland. Three large galleons were close on board of him, with Oquendo, the boldest officer of the Armada, in one of them. Eleven boats, to the amazement of the Spaniards, dropped over the *Ark*'s side. Scores of men sprang into them, seized their oars, and took the *Ark* in tow, careless of the storm of musketry which was rattling upon them. She was already moving when the breeze rose again. Her sails filled and she flew away, dragging her own boats, and leaving behind the swiftest of the pursuing galleons as if they were at anchor.[1]

Again the experience was the same. A long day of fighting at disadvantage ended as usual. The ammunition of the Armada, which the Duke knew from the first to be insufficient, was giving out under the unprecedented demands upon it. Had he been wise he would still have made a desperate attempt to force his way into St. Helen's. His strength was not very much reduced. Though the loss of life had been considerable, Pedro de Valdez's ship was the only one which had been taken. To prevent him from entering the Solent the English must have closed with him, which they still hesitated to do, as they could not now tell how much hurt they had inflicted. The Duke had still this single chance of recovering his credit. He might have gone in. Had he done it, he might have taken the Wight, have even taken Portsmouth or

1. 'Se fué saliendo con tanta velocidad que el galeon *San Juan* de Fernando y otro ligerísimo, con ser los mas veleros de la Armada, que le fuéron dando caça, en comparacion se quedaron surtos.'

232

Southampton; at all events, he would have placed the Armada in a position out of which it would have been extremely difficult to dislodge it.

But the unfortunate man determined to stick to Philip's own instruction, go on to the Straits of Dover as he had been told to do, send Parma notice of his arrival, and leave the rest to fate. He despatched a messenger to tell the Prince to expect him and to have his army embarked ready to cross on the instant of his arrival. He asked for a supply of fly-boats, gun-boats worked with oars, which Parma could not send him, and for ammunition of which the Prince had none to dispose, expecting himself rather to be furnished from the fleet. Then he signalled to his flock to follow him, and pursued his way up Channel, followed by the English as before.

The Isle of Wight once passed, the worst danger to England was over. Lord Henry Seymour's squadron was in the Downs. Howard and Drake would soon join hands with him, and they could then concert what was next to be done.

The Armada drifted on before a light west wind through Thursday night, all Friday, and till Saturday afternoon. They were then at Calais and dropped anchor in the roads. Like a shadow which they could not shake off, the English clung to them behind. As they anchored, the English anchored also, a mile and a half astern, as if the infernal devils, *esta endemoniada gente,* had known what the Duke was going to do. Philip's advice had been to avoid the French coast, to keep the other side, and to bring up behind the North Foreland. The Duke, like Sancho in the night adventure with the fulling-hammers, was flying for safety under the skirts of Parma's coat, and thought that the nearer he could be to him the better it would be. He had thus brought his charge to the most dangerous roadstead in the Channel, with an enemy close to him who had less cause to fear the weather than he, and almost within gunshot of the French shore, when he did not know whether France was friend or foe. For the moment he thought himself secure. The wind was off the land. He looked to see the Prince of Parma and his boats coming out of Dunkirk at latest on the Monday morning.

The French governor came off to call before dark, expressed his surprise to see him in a position where a shift of weather might be inconvenient, but offered him, meanwhile, the hospitalities of the port. On the Sunday morning, August 7, the purveyor of the fleet went on shore to buy vegetables. The men were employed cleaning up the guns and setting the ships in order after the confusion of the past week, and so much work had to be done that the daily rations were not served out, and the Sunday holy day was a harassed fast. As the day wore on messengers came in from Parma. His transports were lying in Dunkirk, but nothing was ready, and the troops could not be embarked for a fortnight. He was himself at Bruges, but promised to hurry down to the port and to use all possible expedition.

This was not consoling intelligence. In the uncertain weather the Calais roadstead was no place to linger in; and the Duke's anxieties were not diminished when the English squadron of the Downs under Seymour and Sir John Hawkins sailed in and anchored with their consorts. Hawkins – Achines they called him – was an object of peculiar terror to the Spaniards from his exploits in the West Indies. Next to Drake, he was more feared than any other English seaman. The galleons were riding with two anchors on account of the tide. An English pinnace, carrying a light gun, ran down in the afternoon, sailed up to the *San Martin*, lodged a couple of shots in her hull, and went off again. Hugo de Monçada sent a ball after her from the *Capitana* galeass which cut a hole in her topsail, but she flew lightly away. The Spanish officers could not refuse their admiration for such airy impertinence.

If the Duke was uneasy the English commanders did not mean to give him time to recover himself. Calais Roads might be an awkward anchorage, but the weather might settle. August weather in the Channel often did settle. There had been a week of fighting and the Armada had got the worst of it, but still there it was, to outward appearance, not much damaged and within touch of the Prince of Parma. The backward state of Parma's preparations was unknown and unsuspected by the English commanders. Any morning he might be looked for, issuing out of Dunkirk with his fleet of gunboats, his army on board his barges, and making his way across the Straits with the Armada to protect him. That Sunday evening Howard, Drake, Hawkins, Seymour, and Martin Frobisher held a consultation in the *Ark's* main cabin. The course which they intended to follow had probably been resolved on generally when Howard anchored so near the enemy on the previous evening, and the meeting must have been only to arrange the method and moment of action.

After nightfall, the flood tide would be running strong along the coast, and an intermittent but rising wind was coming up from the west. The Duke observed lights moving soon after dark among the English vessels. He expected mischief of some kind and had ordered a strict lookout. About midnight eight large hulks were seen coming slowly down with tide and wind. Spars, ropes, and sails had been steeped in pitch, and as they approached nearer they burst out into flame and smoke. Straight on they came, for they had crews on board to direct the course, who only retreated to their boats when it was impossible to remain longer. The Spaniards, already agitated by the strange tricks of their English foes, imagined that the fire-ships were floating mines like those which had blown to pieces so many thousands of men at the bridge at Antwerp. The Duke, instead of sending launches to tow them clear, fired a signal for the whole fleet to get instantly under way. In the hurry and alarm, and with two anchors down, they had no time to weigh. They cut their cables, leaving buoys by which to recover them at daylight, and stood out into the Channel, congratulating themselves for the moment at having skilfully and successfully avoided a threatening danger.

Medina Sidonia's intention had been to bring up again outside. He himself let go an anchor two miles off, and the best-appointed galleons followed his example. The main body, unfortunately, had been sent to sea so ill-provided that their third anchors, where they had any, were stowed away below and could not be brought up in time. Thus, when day dawned, the Duke found himself with less than half his force about him. The rest had drifted away on the tide and were six miles to leeward. The purpose of his enemy's 'traicon,' treason, as the Spaniards regarded it, was now apparent. The *San Martin*, and the vessels which remained with her, hoisted anchor and signalled to return to the roadstead. Seventy of the Duke's ships were far away, unable to obey if they had tried. The wind had drawn into the north-west; they were driving seemingly on the fatal banks, and when the Duke proposed to go after them, the pilots told him that if he did they would probably be all lost together.

The spectacle on the shore was yet more dispiriting. The *Capitana* galeass, in clearing out from the fire-ships, had fouled the cable of another vessel. Monçada, who commanded her, knew as little of seamanship as his commander-in-chief. Her helm was jammed. She had drifted ashore under the town, and as the tide had gone back, was lying on her side on the sands, defending herself desperately against the crews of six English ships, one of them Howard's *Ark*, who were attacking her in their boats. Monçada fought like a hero till he was killed by a musket-shot, the slaves jumped overboard, the surviving sailors and soldiers followed their example, and the galeass was taken and plundered.

To the Duke such a sight was sad enough; but he had little time to attend to it. While Howard was losing time over the galeass, Drake and Hawkins had stooped on a nobler quarry. The great fleet was parted; forty ships alone were present to defend the consecrated banner of Castile which was flying from the mainmast of the *San Martin*. But in those forty were Oquendo, De Leyva, Recalde, Bretandona, all that was best and bravest in the Spanish service. The first burst of the storm fell on the *San Martin* herself. Drake, determined to make the most of his opportunity, no longer held off at long range, but closed up, yardarm to yardarm; not to make prizes of the galleons, but to destroy, sink, or disable them.

The force which the English brought into the action was no longer unequal to that of the enemy. The air was soon so full of smoke that little could be seen from one ship of what was passing in another part of the action. Each captain fought his own vessel as he could, Medina giving no orders. He was accused afterwards of having shown cowardice. It was said that his cabin was stuffed with woolpacks, and that he lay himself during the fight in the middle of them. It was said, also, that he charged his pilot to take his ship where the danger was least. If he did, his pilot disobeyed his orders, for the *San Martin* was in the hottest part of the battle. Though the *San Martin*'s timbers were of double thickness, the shot at close range went through 'enough to shatter to pieces a rock.' Her deck became a slaughter-house. Half her crew were killed or wounded, and she would have sunk altogether had not Oquendo and De Leyva dashed in and forced the English to turn their guns upon them, and enabled the unhappy Duke to crawl away and stop his leaks again.

This was about noon; and from that time he himself saw no more till the engagement was over. Even from his maintop nothing could be made out for the smoke; but the air was shaking with the roar of the artillery. The Spanish officers behaved with the heroism which became the countrymen of Cortez and Santa Cruz. There was no flinching, though blood was seen streaming out of the scuppers. Priests went up and down under the hottest fire, crucifix in hand, confessing and absolving the dying. Not a ship struck her colours. They stood to their guns till their powder was all gone, and in half the ships not a round was left.

Happily for them, the English were not better furnished; Howard's ammunition was all but exhausted also, and the combat ended from mere incapacity to continue it. But the engagement from the first preserved the same character which had been seen in those which had preceded it. The Spaniards' courage was useless to them. Their ships could not turn or sail; their guns were crushed by the superior range of the English artillery; they were out-matched in practical skill, and, close as the ships were to one another, they could not once succeed in fixing a grappling-iron in an English rigging. Thus, while their own losses were terrible, they could inflict but little in return. They had endured for five hours to be torn to pieces by cannon-shot – and that was all.

Before sunset the firing had ceased; the wind rose, the smoky canopy drifted away, and the *San Martin* and her comrades were seen floating, torn and tattered, *casi sin poder hacer mas resistencia,* almost powerless to resist longer. A galleon in Recalde's squadron had gone down with all hands on board. The *San Philip* and the *San Matteo* were falling away dismasted and helpless towards the Dutch coast, where they afterwards went ashore. The condition of the rest was little better. The slaughter had been appalling from the crowd of soldiers who were on board. They had given themselves up as lost, when it pleased God, for they could give no other explanation, that the enemy ceased to fire, drew off, and left them to bring their vessels to the wind. They were so crippled that they could not bear their canvas, and unless they could repair their damages swiftly, the north-west wind which was rapidly rising would drive them on the banks above Dunkirk.

From the day on which they left Lisbon an inexorable fatality had pursued them. The night passed miserably in examining into injuries, patching up what admitted of being mended and discovering other hurts which could not be mended. The fresh water which they had brought from Corunna had been stowed on deck. The casks had been shot through in the action, and most of it was gone. Yet seventy vessels out of the great fleet were still entire. They had not come up to join in the fight, because they could not. The situation was not really desperate, and a capable chief with such a force at his disposition might have done something still to retrieve his country's credit, if only these ships could be made use of. Yet when day broke it seemed that a common fate would soon overtake those who had fought and those who so far had escaped.

They came together in the night. The dawn found them dragging heavily into the North Sea. The north-west wind was blowing hard, and setting them bodily on the banks. The bad sailers could not go to windward at all. Those which had been in the fight could not bear sail enough to hold a course which, when sound, they might have found barely possible. The crews were worn out. On the Sunday they had been dinnerless and supperless. All Monday they had been fighting, and all Monday night plugging shot-holes and fishing spars. The English fleet hung dark and threatening a mile distant on the weather quarter. The water was shoaling every moment. They could see the yellow foam where the waves were breaking on the banks. To wear round would be to encounter another battle, for which they had neither heart nor strength, while the English appeared to be contented to let the elements finish the work for them.

The English vessels drew more water, and would have grounded while the galleons were still afloat. It was enough for them if they could prevent the Armada from turning round, and could force it to continue upon a course of which an hour or two would probably see the end. The *San Martin* and Oquendo's ship, the *San Juan*, were furthest out. The sounding-line on the *San Martin* gave at last but six fathoms; the vessels to leeward had only five. Some one, perhaps Diego Florez, advised the Duke to strike his flag and surrender. Report said that a boat was actually lowered to go off to Howard and make terms, and that Oquendo had prevented it from pushing off, by saying savagely that he would fling Diego Florez overboard. The Duke's friends, however, denied the charge, and insisted that he never lost his faith in God and God's glorious mother. Certain it is, that with death staring them in the face and themselves helpless, men and officers betook themselves to prayer as the only refuge left, and apparently the prayer was answered.

A person who was on the *San Martin* describes the scene. Every one was in despair, he said, and only looking for destruction. Had the enemy known the condition in which they were, and borne down and attacked them, they must all have given in, for they were without power to defend themselves. At the last extremity somewhere about noon, 'God was pleased to work a miracle.' The wind shifted, backing to the south-west, and ceased to jam them down upon the sands. With eased sheets they were able to point their heads northwards and draw out into the deep water. The enemy followed, still keeping at the same distance, but showed no further disposition to meddle with them; and the Armada breathed again, though huddled together like a flock of frightened sheep. A miracle they thought it. They began to think that God's anger was spent, and that He would now be propitious. He had brought the survivors of them 'through the most terrible cannonade ever seen or written of' (la mas fuerte bateria y major que los nacidos han visto ni los escriptores han escrito). This Tuesday, August 9, was the day of Philip's patron saint, St. Lawrence, whose arm he had lately added to his sacred treasures in the Escurial. In the afternoon a council of war was again held on board the flag-ship, consisting of the Duke, Alonzo de Leyva, Recalde, Don Francisco de Bobadilla, and Diego

Florez. They had little pleasant to say to each other. Oquendo was at first absent, but came in while they were still deliberating. 'O Señor Oquendo,' they cried, 'que haremos?' 'What shall we do?' 'Do!' he replied, 'bear up and fight again.' It was the answer of a gallant man who preferred death to disgrace.

But the Duke had to consider how to save what was left of his charge, and the alternatives had to be considered. They were before the wind, running right up the North Sea. The Duke explained that every cartridge had been spent in the vessels which had been engaged, and that, although some were left in the rest of the fleet, the supply was miserably short. Half the sailors and half the artillerymen were killed or wounded. The Prince of Parma was not ready, and they had found by experience that they were no match for the English in fighting. The coast of Spain was at present unprotected, and unless they could carry the fleet home in safety would be in serious danger. The Duke's own opinion was that they ought to make haste back, and by the sea route round the North of Scotland and Ireland. To return through the Straits implied more battles, and in their battered state it was doubtful whether they could work their way as the wind stood, even if the enemy left them alone.

Flight, for it was nothing else, after such high expectations and loud prayers and boastings, flight after but a week's conflict, seemed to the old companions of Santa Cruz an intolerable shame. De Leyva was doubtful. He admitted, as the Duke said, that the English were too strong for them. They had done their best and it had not availed. His own ship would hardly float, and he had not thirty cartridges left. Recalde and Bobadilla supported Oquendo, and insisted that, at whatever risk, they must endeavour to recover Calais Roads. They were old sailors, who had weathered many a storm. The chances of war had been against them so far, but would not be against them always. If the English fleet could go down Channel, it was not to be supposed that a Spanish fleet could not, and if they were to return home the Channel was the nearest road.

Spanish history has accused Medina Sidonia of having been the cause that the bolder course was rejected. Independent contemporary witnesses say that it was made impossible by the despondency of the men, who could not be induced to encounter the English again.

Though he determined against returning through the Channel, more than one alternative was still open to him. The harbours of Holland and Zealand were in the hands of Dutch rebels. But there was the Elbe, there was the Baltic, there was Norway. If the Duke had been a man of daring and genius there was the Firth of Forth. Had he anchored off Leith and played his cards judiciously, there was still a possibility for him to achieve something. The Duke, however, probably knew that his master had intended to exclude the King of Scots from the English succession, and may have doubted the reception which he might meet with.

Thus forlorn and miserable, the great Armada was set upon its course for the Orkneys, from thence to bear away to the West of Ireland, and so round to Spain. Drake and Howard, not conceiving that their object would be so lightly abandoned, and ignorant of the condition to which the enemy was reduced, followed them at a distance to see what they would do, and on the Wednesday had almost taken Recalde, whose disabled ship was lagging behind. The Duke, however, did not dare to desert a second admiral. He waited for Recalde to come up, and the English did not interfere. In fact they could not. Their magazines were hardly better furnished than the Spanish. In pursuing the Armada they acknowledged that they were but 'putting on a brag' to frighten the Duke out of turning back.

On Friday the 12th the Armada passed the mouth of the Forth. Howard had followed so far, expecting that it might seek shelter there. But it went by with a leading wind. He knew then that till another season they would see no more of it, so put about and returned to Margate.

Relieved of his alarming presence, the Spaniards were able to look into their condition and to prepare for a voyage which might now be protracted for several weeks. The Duke himself was short and sullen, shut himself in his state-room, and refused to see or speak with any one. Diego Florez became the practical commander, and had to announce the alarming news that provisions taken in at Corunna had been wholly inadequate, and that at the present rate of consumption they would all be starving in a fortnight. The state of the water supply was worst of all, for the casks had most of them been destroyed by the English guns. The salt meat and fish were gone or spoilt. The rations were reduced to biscuit. Half a pound of biscuit, a pint of water, and half a pint of wine were all that each person could be allowed. Men and officers fared alike; and on this miserable diet, and unprovided with warm clothing, which they never needed in their own sunny lands, the crews of the Armada were about to face the cold and storms of the northern latitudes.

They had brought with them many hundreds of mules and horses. They might have killed and eaten them, and so mitigated the famine.

But they thought of nothing. The wretched animals were thrown overboard to save water, and the ships in the rear sailed on through floating carcases – a ghastly emblem of the general wreck. The Duke felt more than the officers gave him credit for. In a letter which he despatched to Philip on August 21, in a forlorn hope that it might reach Spain somehow, he described the necessity which had been found of cutting down the food, and the consequent suffering.[1] That alone would have been enough, for the men were wasting to a shadow of themselves, but besides there were three thousand sick with scurvy and dysentery, and more with wounds uncured.

But if he sympathised with the men's distresses he did not allow his sympathy to be seen. He knew that he was blamed for what had happened, that he was distrusted and perhaps despised; and while keeping aloof from every one, he encouraged their resentment. It pleased him, while secluded in his cabin, to order an inquiry into the conduct of the commanders who had lost their anchors at Calais, and had failed to support him in the action which followed. He accused them of cowardice. He held a court-martial on them and ordered twenty to be executed. Death with most was exchanged for degradation and imprisonment, but two poor wretches were selected on whom the sentence was to be carried out, as exceptionally culpable.

When he had decided to fly, the Duke had ordered that the whole fleet should follow and not go in advance of the *San Martin*. A Captain Cuellar and a Captain Christobal de Avila had strayed for a few miles ahead, intending, as the Duke perhaps supposed, to desert. Don Christobal, to the disgust of the fleet, was executed with a parade of cruelty. He was hanged on the yard of a pinnace, which was sent round the squadrons with Don Christobal's body swinging upon it before it was thrown into the sea.

Cuellar's fate was to have been the same. He commanded a galleon called the *San Pedro*. He had been in the action and had done his duty. His ship had been cut up. He himself had not slept for ten days, having been in every fight since the Armada entered the Channel. When all was over, and the strain had been taken off, he had dropped off exhausted. His sailing-master, finding the *San Pedro* leaking, had gone in advance to

---

1. 'Por ser tan pocos los bastimentos que se llevan, que, para que puedan durar un mes, y el agua, se han acortado las raciones generalmente sin exceptuar persona, porque no perezcan, dando se media libra de biscocho, y un cuartillo de agua, y medio de vino sin ninguna otra cosa, con que se va padeciendo lo que V.M. podra juzgar.' – Medina Sidonia to Philip, August 21. Duro, vol. ii. p. 226.

lay-to and examine her hurts. Exasperated at the disobedience to his directions, the Duke sent for Cuellar, refused to listen to his defence, and ordered him to be hanged. Don Francisco de Bobadilla with difficulty obtained his life for him, but he was deprived of his ship and sent under arrest to another galleon, to encounter, as will be seen, a singular adventure.

The fleet held together as far as the Orkneys. The intention was to hold a northerly course till the 60th parallel. Assuming the wind to remain in the west, the pilots held that from this altitude the galleons could weather the Irish coast at sufficient distance to be out of danger – to weather Cape Clear, as they described it, but the Cape Clear which they meant – a glance at the map will show it – was not the point so named at present, but Clare Island, the extreme western point of Mayo. The high-built, broad and shallow galleons were execrable sailers, but some sailed worse than others, and some were in worse condition than others.

They passed the Orkneys together, and were then separated in a gale. The nights were lengthening, the days were thick and misty, and they lost sight of each other. Two or three went north as far as the Faroe Islands, suffering pitifully from cold and hunger. Detachments, eight or ten together, made head as they could, working westward, against wind and sea, the men dying daily in hundreds. The *San Martin*, with sixty ships in company, kept far out into the Atlantic, and they rolled down towards the south dipping their mainyards in the tremendous seas.

On August 21, the day on which the Duke wrote to Philip, they were two hundred miles west of Cape Wrath, amidst the tumult of the waters. 'The Lord,' he said, 'had been pleased to send them a fortune different from that which they had looked for; but since the expedition had been undertaken from the beginning in the Lord's service, all doubtless had been ordered in the manner which would conduce most to the King's advantage and the Lord's honour and glory. The fleet had suffered so heavily that they had considered the best thing which they could do would be to bring the remains of it home in safety. Their finest ships had been lost, their ammunition had been exhausted, and the enemy's fleet was too strong for what was left. The English guns were heavier than the Spanish; their sailing powers immeasurably superior. The sole advantage of the Spaniards was in small arms, and these they could not use, as the enemy refused to close. Thus, with the assent of the vice-admirals, he was making for home round the Scotch Isles. The food was short; the dead were many; the sick and wounded more. He himself could but pray that they might soon reach a port, as their lives depended on it.'

This letter, though sent off out of the Western Ocean, did eventually reach the King's hands. Meanwhile the weather grew wilder and wilder. The number of vessels which could bear up against the gales diminished daily, and one by one they fell to leeward on the fatal Irish shore. Leaving Medina Sidonia and the survivors which reached home along with him, the story must follow those which were unequal to the work required of them. The Spaniards were excellent seamen. They had navigated ships no worse than those which were lumbering through the Irish seas, among West Indian hurricanes and through the tempests at Cape Horn. But these poor wretches were but shadows of themselves; they had been sickened at the outset with putrid provisions; they were now famished and ill; their vessels' sides were torn to pieces by cannon-shot and leaking at a thousand holes, their wounded spars no longer able to bear the necessary canvas; worst of all, their spirits were broken. The superstitious enthusiasm with which they started had turned into a fear that they were the objects of a malignant fate with which it was useless to struggle. Some had been driven among the Western Islands of Scotland; the ships had been lost; the men who got on shore alive made their way to the Low Countries. But these were the few. Thirty or forty other vessels had attempted in scattered parties to beat their way into the open sea. But, in addition to hunger, the men were suffering fearfully for want of water, and perhaps forced the pilots either to make in for the land, or else to turn south before they had gained sufficient offing.

Thus, one by one all these drove ashore, either on the coast of Sligo or Donegal, or in Clew Bay or Galway Bay, or the rocks of Clare and Kerry, and the wretched crews who escaped the waves found a fate only more miserable. The gentlemen and officers, soiled and battered though they were, carried on land such ornaments as they possessed. The sailors and soldiers had received their pay at Corunna, and naturally took it with them in their pockets. The wild Irish were tempted by the plunder. The gold chains and ducats were too much for their humanity, and hundreds of half-drowned wretches were dragged out of the waves only to be stripped and knocked on the head, while those who escaped the Celtic skenes and axes, too weak and exhausted to defend themselves, fell into the hands of the English troops who were in garrison in Connaught. The more intelligent of the Irish chiefs hurried down to prevent their countrymen from disgracing themselves. They stopped the robbing and murdering, and a good many unfortunate victims found shelter in their castles.

Such Spaniards as were taken prisoners by the English met a fate of which it is impossible to read with regret. Flung as they were upon shore, ragged, starved, and unarmed, their condition might have moved the pity of less generous foes. But the age was not pitiful. Catholic fanaticism had declared war against what it called heresy, and the heretics had to defend their lives and liberties by such means as offered themselves. There might be nothing to fear from the Spanish prisoners in their present extremity, but if allowed to recover and find protection from Irish hospitality, they might and would become eminently dangerous. The number of English was far too small to enable them to guard two or three thousand men. With the exception, therefore, of one or two officers who were reserved for ransom, all that were captured were shot or hanged on the spot.

The history of these unfortunates must be looked for in the English records rather than the Spanish. They never returned to Spain to tell their own story, and Captain Duro has little to say about them beyond what he has gathered from English writers. Among the documents published by him, however, there is an extraordinary narrative related by the Captain Cuellar who so nearly escaped hanging, a narrative which not only contains a clear account of the wreck of the galleons, but gives an authentic picture of the Ireland of the time.

The scene of the greatest destruction among the ships of the Armada was Sligo Bay. It is easy to see why. The coast on the Mayo side of it trends away seventy miles to the west as far as Achill and Clare Island, and ships embayed there in heavy south-westerly weather had no chance of escape. On one beach, five miles in length, Sir Jeffrey Fenton counted eleven hundred dead bodies, and the country people told him, 'the like was to be seen in other places.' Sir William Fitzwilliam saw broken timber from the wrecks lying between Sligo and Ballyshannon, 'sufficient to have built five of the largest ships in the world,' besides masts and spars and cordage, and boats bottom uppermost. Among the vessels which went ashore at this spot to form part of the ruin which Fitzwilliam was looking upon was a galleon belonging to the Levantine squadron, commanded by Don Martin de Aranda, to whose charge Cuellar had been committed when Bobadilla saved him from the yard-arm.

Don Martin, after an ineffectual struggle to double Achill Island, had fallen off before the wind and had anchored in Sligo Bay in a heavy sea with two other galleons. There they lay for four days, from the first to the fifth of September, when the gale rising, their cables parted, and

244

all three drove on shore on a sandy beach among the rocks. Nowhere in the world does the sea break more violently than on that cruel shelterless strand. Two of the galleons went to pieces in an hour. The soldiers and sailors, too weak to struggle, were most of them rolled in the surf till they were dead and then washed up upon the shingle. Gentlemen and servants, nobles and common seamen, shared the same fate. Cuellar's ship had broken in two, but the forcastle held a little longer together than the rest, and Cuellar, clinging to it, watched his comrades being swept away and destroyed before his eyes. The wild Irish were down in hundreds stripping bodies. Those who had come on shore with life in them fared no better. Some were knocked on the head, others had their clothes torn off and were left naked to perish of cold.

Don Diego Enriquez, a high-born patrician, passed, with the Conde de Villafranca and sixty-five others, into his ship's tender carrying bags of ducats and jewels. They went below, and fastened down the hatchway, hoping to be rolled alive on land. A huge wave turned the tender bottom upwards, and all who were in it were smothered. As the tide went back the Irish came with their axes and broke a hole open in search of plunder; while Cuellar looked on speculating how soon the same fate would be his own, and seeing the corpses of his comrades dragged out, stripped naked, and left to the wolves. His own turn came at last. He held on to the wreck till it was swept away, and he found himself in the water with a brother officer who had stuffed his pockets full of gold. He could not swim, but he caught a scuttle board as it floated by him and climbed up upon it. His companion tried to follow, but was washed off and drowned.

Cuellar a few minutes later was tossed ashore, his leg badly cut by a blow from a spar in the surf. Drenched and bleeding as he was, he looked a miserable figure. The Irish, who were plundering the better dressed of the bodies, took no notice of him. He crawled along till he found a number of his countrymen who had been left with nothing but life, bare to their skins, and huddled together for warmth. Cuellar, who had still his clothes, though of course drenched, lay down among some rushes. A gentleman, worse off than he, for he was entirely naked, threw himself at his side too spent to speak. Two Irishmen came by with axes who, to Cuellar's surprise, cut some bushes, which they threw over them for a covering, and went on to join in the pillage on the shore. Cuellar, half dead from cold and hunger, fell asleep. He was woke by a troop of English horsemen galloping by for a share in the spoil. He called his comrade but found him dead, while all round the crows and wolves were busy over the naked carcases. Something like a monastery was visible not far off. Cuellar limped along till he reached it. He found it deserted. The roof of the chapel had been lately burnt. The images of the saints lay tumbled on the ground. In the nave twelve Spaniards were hanging from the rafters. The monks had fled to the mountains.

Sick at the ghastly spectacle, he crept along a path through a wood, when he came upon an old woman who was hiding her cattle from the English. Her cabin was not far distant, but she made signs to him to keep off, as there were enemies in occupation there. Wandering hopelessly on, he fell in with two of his countrymen naked and shivering. They were all famished, and they went back together to the sea, hoping to find some fragments of provisions washed on land. On the way they came on the body of Don Enriquez and stopped to scrape a hole in the sand and bury it. While they were thus employed a party of Irish came up, who pointed to a cluster of cabins and intimated that if they went there they would be taken care of. Cuellar was dead lame. His companions left him. At the first cottage which he reached, there was an old Irish 'savage,' an Englishman, a Frenchman, and a girl. The Englishman struck at him with a knife and gave him a second wound. They stripped him to his shirt, took a gold chain from him, which they found concealed under it, and a purse of ducats. They would have left him *en cueros*, like the rest, without a rag upon him, had not the girl interposed, who affected to be a Christian, 'though she was no more a Christian than Mahomet.' The Frenchman proved to be an old sailor who had fought at Terceira. In him the Spanish captain found some human kindness, for he bound up his leg for him and gave him some oatcakes with butter and milk. The Frenchman then pointed to a ridge of distant mountains. There, he said, was the country of the O'Rourke, a great chief, who was a friend of the King of Spain. O'Rourke would take care of him; many of his comrades had already gone thither for protection.

With his strength something restored by the food, Cuellar crawled along, stick in hand. At night he stopped at a hut where there was a lad who could speak some Latin. This boy talked with him, gave him supper and a bundle of straw to sleep upon. About midnight the boy's father and brother came in, loaded with plunder from the wrecks. They, too, did him no hurt, and sent him forward in the morning with a pony and a guide. English soldiers were about, sent, as he conjectured, probably with truth, to kill all the Spaniards they could fall in with. The first party that he met did not see him. With the second he was less fortunate. His guide saved his life by some means which Cuellar did not understand. But they beat him and took his shirt from him, the last of his garments that had been left. The boy and pony went off, and he thought then that the end was come, and prayed God to finish with him and take him to His mercy. Forlorn as he was, however, he rallied his courage, picked up a piece of old matting, and with this and some plaited ferns made a shift to cover himself: thus costumed he went on to a hamlet at the side of a lake; the hovels of which it consisted were all empty; he entered the best-looking of them, found some fagots of oat-straw, and was looking about for a place to sleep among them, when three naked figures sprang suddenly up. He took them for devils, and in his extraordinary dress they thought the same of him; but they proved to have belonged to the wrecked galleons; one of them a naval officer, the other two soldiers. They explained mutually who they were, and they buried themselves in the oat-sheaves and slept. They remained there for warmth and concealment all the next day.

At night, having wrapped themselves in straw, they walked on till they reached the dominions of the chief to whom they had been directed. O'Rourke himself was absent 'fighting the English,' but his wife took them in, fed them, and allowed them to stay. As a particular favour she bestowed an old cloak upon Cuellar, which he found, however, to be swarming with lice. The hospitality was not excessive. A report reached him that a Spanish ship had put into Killybegs harbour, was refitting for sea, and was about to sail. He hurried down to join her, but she was gone. He learned afterwards that she had been wrecked and that all on board had perished.

He was now like a hunted wolf. The English Deputy had issued orders that every Spaniard in the country must be given up to the government. The Irish did not betray Cuellar, but they did not care to risk their necks by giving him shelter, and he wandered about through the winter in Sligo and Donegal, meeting with many strange adventures. His first friend was a poor priest, who was performing his functions among the Irish, in spite of the law, disguised as a layman. From this man he met with help. He worked next as a journeyman with a blacksmith, whose wife was a brute. The priest delivered him from these people, and carried him to a castle, which, from the description, appears to have been on Lough Erne, and here, for the first time, he met with hearty hospitality, in the Irish understanding of the term.

The owner of the castle was a gentleman. He recognised an ally in every enemy of England. He took Cuellar into his troop of retainers, and dressed him in the saffron mantle of the Irish gallowglass. For some weeks he was now permitted to rest and recover himself, and he spent the time in learning the manners of the people. The chief's wife was beautiful, unlike the blacksmith's, and the handsome and unfortunate Spanish officer was an interesting novelty. Besides the lady there were other girls in the castle, who came about him perhaps too ardently, asked him a thousand questions, and at length insisted that he should examine their hands and tell their fortunes. He had learnt palmistry from the gipsies in his own land. His invention was ready. He spoke Latin, and he gathered from their lips broken fragments of their own Irish. At length, with his art and his attractiveness, he gives the reader to understand that he was inconveniently popular; men and women persecuted him with demands and attentions, and he had to throw himself on the protection of the chief himself. He describes the habits and character of the people as if he was writing of a fresh discovered island in the New World.

They lived, he said, like mere savages about the mountains. Their dwelling-places were thatched hovels. The men were large-limbed, well-shaped, and light as stags (*sueltos como corzos*). They took but one meal a day, and that at night. Their chief food was oatmeal and butter; their drink sour milk, for want of anything better, and never water, though they had the best in the world. The whiskey Cuellar does not mention. On feast days they dined on undone boiled meat, which they ate without bread or salt. The costume of the men was a pair of tight-fitting breeches with a goatskin jacket; over this a long mantle. Their hair they wore low over their eyes. They were strong on their legs, could walk great distances, and were hardy and enduring. They, or such of them as he had known, paid no obedience to the English. They were surrounded by swamps and bogs, which kept the English at a distance, and there was a constant war between the races.

Even among themselves they were famous thieves. They robbed from each other, and every day there was fighting. If one of them knew that his neighbour had sheep or cow, he would be out at night to steal it, and kill the owner. Occasionally a fortunate robber would have collected large herds and flocks, and then the English would come down on him, and he had to fly to the hills with wife, and children, and stock. Sheep and cattle were their only form of property. They had no clothes and no furniture. They slept on the ground on a bed of rushes, cut fresh as they wanted them, wet with rain or stiff with frost. The women were pretty, but ill dressed. A shift or a mantle, and a handkerchief knotted in front over the forehead, made their whole toilet; and on the women was thrown all the homework, which, after a fashion, they managed to do.

The Irish professed to be Christians. Mass was said after the Roman rule. Their churches and houses of religion had been destroyed by the English, or by such of their own countrymen as had joined the English. In short, they were a wild lawless race, and every one did as he liked. They wished well to the Spaniards because they knew them to be enemies of the English heretics, and had it not been for the friendliness which they had shown, not one of those who had come ashore would have survived. It was true at first they plundered and stripped them naked, and fine spoils they got out of the thirteen galleons which were wrecked in that part of the country; but as soon as they saw that the Spaniards were being killed by the English, they began to take care of them.

Such was Cuellar's general picture, very like what was drawn by the intruding Saxon, and has been denounced as calumny. Cuellar was, at any rate, impartial, and rather liked his hosts than otherwise. The Lord Deputy was alarmed at the number of fugitives who were said to be surviving. As the orders to surrender them had not been attended to, he collected a force in Dublin and went in person into the West to enforce obedience. Cuellar's entertainer had been especially menaced, and had to tell his guests that he could help them no further. He must leave his castle and retreat himself with his family into the mountains, and the Spaniards must take care of themselves. Cuellar calls the castle Manglana; local antiquaries may be able to identify the spot. It stood on a promontory projecting into a long, deep, and broad lake, and was covered on the land side by a swamp. It could not be taken without boats or artillery, and the Spaniards offered to remain and defend it if the chief would leave them a few muskets and powder, with food for a couple of months. There were nine of them. The chief agreed, and let them have what they wanted; and, unless Cuellar lies, he and his friends held 'Manglana' for a fortnight against a force of English, when God came to their help by sending such weather that the enemy could not any longer keep the field.

The chief, finding the value of such auxiliaries, wished to keep them permanently at his side, and offered Cuellar his sister for a wife. Cuellar, however, was longing for home. He supposed that if he could reach Scotland he could cross easily from thence to Flanders. One night after Christmas he slipped away and made for Antrim, travelling, seemingly, only in the dark, and hiding during the day. He was in constant danger, as the tracks were watched, and suspected persons were seized and searched.

He got as far as the Giant's Causeway; there he heard particulars of the wreck of the ship which he had tried to join at Killybegs. It was a galeass with Alonzo de Leyva on board and two or three hundred others with him. They were all dead, and Cuellar saw the relics of them which the people had collected on the shore. Alonzo de Leyva was the best loved of all the Spaniards in the fleet, and the sight of the spot where he had perished was a fresh distress. He was afraid to approach a port lest he should be siezed and hanged. For six weeks he was hid away by some women, and after that by a bishop, who was a good Christian, though dressed like a savage. This bishop had a dozen Spaniards with him, fed, clothed, and said Mass for them, and at last found a boat to carry them across the Channel.

They went, and after three days' struggle with the sea contrived to land in Argyllshire. They had been led to hope for help from James. Cuellar says that they were entirely mistaken. James never gave them a bawbee [one halfpenny], and would have handed them over to the English if he had not been afraid of the resentment of the Scotch Catholic nobles. The Calvinist Lowlanders showed them scanty hospitality. The Prince of Parma was informed of their condition, and agreed with a Flemish merchant to bring over to him all the Spaniards, now numerous, who were on Scotch soil, at five ducats a head. Even yet misfortune had not tired of persecuting them. In their passage they were chased and fired on by a Dutch frigate. They had to run ashore, where they were intercepted by the Hollanders, and all but Cuellar and two of his companions were killed.

So ends the Spanish captain's story. The wide calamities involving multitudes are but the aggregate of the sufferings of each individual of whom the multitude is composed. Cuellar came off luckily compared with most of his companions.

The sixty galleons which remained with the Duke till the end of August were parted again by a south-westerly gale, off the point of Kerry. The Duke himself passed so far out to sea that he did not see the Irish coast at all. Recalde, with two large ships besides his own, had come round Dunmore Head, near the land. His crews were dying for want of water. He seems to have known Dingle. Dr. Sanders, with the Pope's contingent, had landed there eight years before, and a statement in an account of Recalde's life that he had once carried a thousand men to the coast of Ireland, refers probably to that occasion. At all events, he was aware that there was a harbour in Dingle Bay, and he made for it with his consorts.

One of them, *Our Lady of the Rosary*, was wrecked in Blasket Sound. She carried seven hundred men when she sailed out of Lisbon. Two hundred out of the seven were alive in her when she struck the rock, and every one of them perished, save a single lad. Recalde, with the other galleon, anchored in the Dingle estuary, and sent in to the town a passionate entreaty to be allowed to fill his water-casks. The fate of the Papal troops, who had been all executed a few miles off, had so frightened the Irish there that they did not dare to consent. The English account states that Recalde had to sail as he was, to live or die. The belief in Spain was that he took the water that he wanted by force. Perhaps the inhabitants were not entirely inhuman, and did not interfere. He saved the lives for the moment of the wretched men under his charge, though most of them perished when they reached their homes; he brought back his ship to Corunna, and there died himself two days after his arrival, worn out.

Oquendo also reached Spain alive. The persevering west winds drove him down the Bay of Biscay, and he made his way into St. Sebastian, where he had a wife and children: but he refused to see them; he shut himself into a solitary room, turned his face to the wall, and ended like Recalde, unable to outlive the disgrace of the grand Armada. They had done all that men could do. On the miserable day when their commander decided to turn his back and fly they would have forced him upon a more honourable course, and given the forlorn adventure an issue less utterly ignominious. But their advice had been rejected. They had sailed away from an enemy whose strength at most was not greater than theirs. They had escaped from a battle with a human foe to a more fatal war with the elements, and they had seen their comrades perish round them. The tremendous catastrophe broke their hearts, and they lay down and died.

Oquendo's *Capitana* had been blown up after the fight at Plymouth. By a strange fatality the ship which brought him home blew up also in the harbour at St. Sebastian. The explosion may have been the last sound which reached his failing sense. The stragglers came in one by one; sixty-five ships only of the hundred and thirty who, in July, had sailed out of Corunna full of hope and enthusiasm. In those hundred and thirty had been twenty thousand human creatures, freshly dedicated to what they called the service of their Lord. Nine or ten thousand only returned; a ragged remnant, shadows of themselves, sinking under famine and fever and scurvy, which carried them off like sheep with the rot. When they had again touched Spanish soil, a wail of grief rose over the whole peninsula, as of Rachel weeping for her children; yet above it all rose the cry, Where was Alonzo de Leyva? Where was the flower of Spanish chivalry?

Cuellar knew his fate; but Cuellar was with his Irish chief far away. Weeks, even months, passed before certain news arrived, and rumour invented imaginary glories for him. He had rallied the missing galleons, he had fallen in with Drake, had beaten and captured him, and had sunk half the English fleet. Vain delusion! De Leyva, like Oquendo and Recalde, had done all that could be done by man, and God had not interposed to help him. He had fought his *Rata Coronada* till her spars were shot away and her timbers pierced like a sieve. She became water-logged in the gales on the Irish coast. A second galleon and a surviving galeass were in his company. The *Rata* and the galleon drove ashore. De Leyva, in the galeass, made Killybegs harbour, and landed there with fourteen hundred men. It was the country of the O'Neil. They were treated with the generous warmth which became the greatest of the Irish chieftains. But their presence was known in Dublin. O'Neil was threatened, and De Leyva honourably refused to be an occasion of danger to him. He repaired the galeass at Killybegs. The October weather appeared to have settled at last, and he started again with as many of his people as the galeass would carry to make the coast of Scotland. She had passed round the north of Donegal, she had kept along the land and had almost reached the Giant's Causeway, when she struck a rock and went to pieces, and De Leyva and his companions went the way of the rest.

The men who came back seemed as if they had been smitten by a stroke from which they could not rally. One of them describes pathetically the delight with which, after those desperate storms, and hunger and cold and thirst, they felt the warmth of the Spanish sun again; saw Spanish grapes in the gardens at Santander, and the fruit hanging on the trees; had pure bread to eat and pure water to drink. But the change brought no return of health. For the first weeks they were left on board their ships, no preparation on shore having been made to receive them. When the mortality was found rather to increase than diminish, they were moved to hospitals, but they died still by hundreds daily, as if destiny or Providence was determined to sweep off the earth every innocent remnant of the shattered expedition, while those who were really to blame escaped unpunished.

Medina Sidonia had been charged by Philip to report his progress to
him as often as messengers could be sent off. He had written when off
the Lizard before his first contact with the enemy. He had written again
on August 21 among the Atlantic rollers, when he believed that he was
bringing home his charge at least safe if not victorious. On September
22 he arrived at Santander, and on the 23rd reported briefly the close of
the tragedy so far as it was then known to him.[1] The weather, he said,
had been terrible since he last wrote. Sixty-one vessels were then with
him. They had held tolerably well together till September 18, when
they were caught in another gale, and fifty of them had gone he knew
not where. Eleven only had remained with himself. They had made the
coast near Corunna, and had signalled for help, but none had come off.

They had then struggled on to Santander and were lying there at
anchor. He had himself gone on shore, being broken down by suffering.
The miseries which they had experienced had exceeded the worst that
had ever before been heard of. In some ships there had not been a drop of
water for fourteen days. A hundred and eighty of the crew of the San
Martin had died, the rest were down with putrid fever. Of his personal
attendants all were dead but two. There was not food enough left on
board for those who were alive to last two days. The Duke 'blessed the
Lord for all that He had ordained;' but prayed the King to see instantly to
their condition, and to send them money, for they had not a maravedi[2]
in the fleet. He was himself too ill to do anything. There was no person
whose duty it was to help them, neither inspector, purveyor, nor
paymaster. They could obtain nothing that they wanted. He had written
to the Archbishop of Burgos for assistance in establishing a hospital.

The opinion in Spain was savagely hostile to the Duke. It was thought
that if he had possessed the feelings of a gentleman, he would have died
of the disgrace like Oquendo and Recalde. The Duke, so far from feeling
that he was himself to blame, considered that he above the rest had most
reason to complain of having been forced into a position which he had
not sought and for which he had protested his unfitness. Being Lord High
Admiral, his business was to remain with the fleet, however ill he might
be, till some other responsible officer could be sent to relieve him. His
one desire was to escape from the sight of ships and everything belonging
to them, and hide himself and recover his spirits in his palace at San
Lucar. Not Sancho, when he left his island, could be in greater haste to

1. The Duke of Medina Sidonia to Philip, September 23, from Santander.
2. Spanish coin.

rid himself of his office and all belonging to it.

On September 27, before an answer could arrive from Philip, he wrote again to Secretary Idiaquez. Almost all the sailors were dead, he said. Many of the ships were dismasted; no one could believe the state in which they were. Idiaquez must look to it. For himself, his health was broken; he was unfit for further duty, and even if he was perfectly well he would never go on shipboard again. He was absolutely without any knowledge either of navigation or of war, and the King could have no object in forcing him to continue in a service from which the state could derive no possible advantage. He begged that he might be thought of no more in connection with the navy, and that, since the Lord had not been pleased to call him to the vocation, he might not be compelled to return in a situation of which he could not, as he had many times explained, conscientiously discharge the duties. His Majesty, he said, could not surely wish the destruction of a faithful subject. With sea affairs he neither could nor would meddle any further, though it should cost him his head.[1] Better so than fail in an office of the duties of which he was ignorant, and where he had to be guided by the advice of others, in whose honesty of intention he could feel no confidence.

The last allusion was of course to Diego Florez, on whom, since it was necessary to punish someone, the blame was allowed to fall. In justice, if justice was to have a voice in the matter, the person really guilty was Don Philip. Of the subordinates, Diego Florez was probably the most in fault, and he was imprisoned in the Castle of Burgos. For the rest, Philip was singularly patient, his conscience perhaps telling him that if he was to demand a strict account he would have to begin with himself. The popular story of the composure with which he heard of the fate of the Armada is substantially true, though rather too dramatically pointed. The awful extent of the catastrophe became known to him only by degrees, and the end of Alonzo de Leyva, which distressed him most of all, he only heard of at Christmas.

To the Duke's letter he replied quietly and affectionately, without a syllable of reproach. Philip ordered clothes, food, medicine, everything that was needed, to be sent down in haste to Corunna and Santander. The widows and orphans of the dead sailors and soldiers were pensioned at the cost of the state. To Medina Sidonia he sent the permission which the Duke had asked for, to leave the fleet and go home. He could

---

1. 'En las cosas de la mer, por ningun caso ni por alguna via trataré dellas, aunque me costase la cabeza.'

not in fairness have blamed the commander-in-chief for having failed in a situation for which he had protested his incompetence. The fault of Philip as a king and statesman was a belief in his own ability to manage things. In sending out the Armada he had set in motion a mighty force, not intending it to be used mightily, but that he might accomplish with it what he regarded as a master-stroke of tame policy. He had selected Medina Sidonia as an instrument who would do what he was told and would make no rash experiments. And the effect was to light a powder-magazine which blew to pieces the naval power of Spain.

It is to his credit, however, that he did not wreak his disappointment upon his instruments, and endured patiently what had befallen him as the will of God. Philip's formal piety provided a solution, and on the October 13 the following letter was addressed by him to the bishops and archbishops throughout his dominions:

MOST REVEREND, – The uncertainties of naval enterprises are well known, and the fate which had befallen the Armada is an instance in point. You will have already heard that the Duke of Medina Sidonia has returned to Santander, bringing back with him part of the fleet. Others of the ships have reached various ports, some of them having suffered severely from their long and arduous voyage. We are bound to give praise to God for all things which He is pleased to do. I on the present occasion have given thanks to Him for the mercy which He has shown. In the foul weather and violent storms to which the Armada has been exposed, it might have experienced a worse fate; and that the misfortune has not been heavier is no doubt due to the prayers which have been offered in its behalf so devoutly and continuously.

These prayers must have entailed serious expense and trouble on those who have conducted them. I wish you, therefore, all to understand that while I am, so far, well pleased with your exertions, they may now cease. You may wind up in the cathedrals and churches of your dioceses with a solemn Thanksgiving Mass on any day which you may appoint, and for the future I desire all ecclesiastics and other devout persons to continue to commend my actions to the Lord in their secret devotions, that He may so direct them as shall be for His own service, the exaltation of His Church, the welfare and safety of Christendom, which are the objects always before me.

From the Escurial: October 13, 1588.[1]

---

1. Duro, vol. ii, p. 314.

Medina Sidonia reconsidered his resolution to have no more to do with ships and fighting. He continued in his office of Lord High Admiral; he was again appointed governor of Cadiz, and he had a second opportunity of measuring himself against English seamen, with the same result as before. Essex went into Cadiz in 1596, as Drake had gone in 1587. The Duke acted in the same manner, and withdrew to Seville to seek for reinforcements. He ventured back only after the English had gone, and was again thanked by his master for his zeal and courage. As if this was not enough, Philip, in 1598, raised him to the rank of Consejero altísimo de Estado y Guerra, Supreme Councillor in Politics and War.

The people were less enduring. Clamours were raised that he had deserted the fleet at Santander, that he had shown cowardice in action, that he had neglected the counsels of his wisest admirals, that he was as heartless as he was incapable, and that, leaving the seamen and soldiers to die, he had hastened home to his luxuries at San Lucar. In reality he had gone with the King's permission. He was accused of having carried off with him a train of mules loaded with ducats. He had told Philip that he had not brought home a maravedi.

But nothing could excuse him to Spain. Every calumny found credit. He had shown 'cobardia y continual pavor y miedo de morir, avaricia, dureza y crueldad' – cowardice, constant terror and fear of death, avarice, harshness, and cruelty. His real faults were enough without piling others on him of which he was innocent. With or without his will, he had been in the thickest and hottest parts of the hardest engagements, and the *San Martin* had suffered as severely as any ship in the fleet. He knew little of the work which he was sent to do; that is probably the worst which can justly be said of him; and he had not sought an appointment for which he knew that he was unfit. But an officer who tried to defend him was obliged to admit that it would have been happy for his country if the Duke had never been born; that he threw away every chance which was offered him, and that he talked and consulted when acts and not words were wanted.

His journey home across Castile was a procession of ignominy. The street boys in Salamanca and Medina del Campo pelted him with stones; crowds shouted after him 'A las gallinas, á las almadradas' – 'To the hens and the tunnies' – the tunnies being the fattest and the most timid of fish, and the tunny fishing being a monopoly of his dukedom. History does not record the reception which he met with from his wife when he reached his palace.

Index

Albert, Archduke, 14
Almenara, Marquis of, 191, 193, 195
Alva, Duke of, 91, 112, 176, 182, 190; in Low Countries, 43–5, 60, 163; Ridolfi conspiracy, 61–2, 65–6, 207;
America, discovery of, 30, 31
Antwerp, 66
Aragon, 5, 190, 193, 195–6
Aranda, Don Martin de, 244
Arica, 75
Ark Raleigh, 69, 134, 139, 141, 230, 232, 235
Armada, 21, 68; compared with English fleet, 11–12; composition and leaders, 3–4, 219–21; delayed by gales, 222; Drake's exploits in Cadiz, 117–18, 211; effects of defeat, 150–1; engagements, 132–5, 226–8; English accounts, 201; English preparations, 130; escape northwards, 146, 239; fate of remaining ships, 148–50; fire-ship attack, 140–1, 234–5; in Calais Roads, 137–44, 233–7; in Tagus, 120–1, 211, 221; Philip's involvement in detail, 214–16; Philip's orders, 109, 127, 216–17; popular support, 126, 136–7, 147, 202; preparations, 116-17, 126, 203, 210, 218; provisioning, 137, 217–18, 221–2, 223–4, 240; remnant returns to Spain, 251–2; sets sail, 127, 131, 218–19, 224; ships lost in first engagement, 229; Spanish account, 9, 156; standard, 204–5; tactics of English fleet, 226–7; wrecked on Irish coast, 243–51
Arundel, Earl of, 87, 91
Ashantee, 47
Autos-da-fé, 36
Avila, Christobal de, 241
Azores, 36

Babington, Anthony, 113–14
Baçan, Alvarez de, 42, 56–9
Bacon, Francis, 91, 199

Ballard, John, 113–14
Bassano, Emilia (Mrs Lanier), 7
Bayona, Isles of, 99
Bear, 130
Bedford, Duke of (Francis Russell), 54
Bemandero, Don Pedro, 99–100
Bobadilla, Don Francisco de, 238–9, 241–2, 244
Bretandona, Martin de, 142, 230, 235
Brille, 66–7
Bromley, Sir Thomas, 82
Brussels, 163
Buonaventure, 117–18
Burboroata, 51, 52
Burghley, Lord (William Cecil), 43, 50, 60–1, 85, 99, 124; and Mary Queen of Scots, 63–5, 115, 116; on Drake's Cadiz raid, 80, 82; support for Protestant League, 91; supporting naval development, 38

Cabot, John, 30–1
Cabot, Sebastian, 31
Cacafuego, 75–7, 106
Cadiz, 17, 42; Armada preparations, 210–11; Drake's raid, 10, 117–19, 211; Essex's capture, 256
Calais, 12, 135, 137–44, 233–7
Calatayud, 191
California, 78
Calvinism, 92, 93, 250
Campion, Edmund, 85
Canary Islands, 46, 48, 49, 51, 55, 101
Cape de Verde Islands, 101
Cape St Vincent, 128, 221
Capitana, 132–3, 141, 228, 234–5
Carew family, 38
Carey, Sir George, 134
Caribs, 102
Carlile, Christopher, 99, 100, 101, 103, 105
Carlyle, Thomas, 24
Carnarvon, Lord, 25

257

Index

Pérez, Doña Gregoria, 159, 189
'Perpetual Edict', 166, 167
Philip II of Spain, 4–5, 9, 28, 155; and
   Don John of Austria, 162; and Drake's
   Cadiz raid, 123; and Mary Stuart's execution, 115–16; and Pérez, 173, 185–6,
   188–9, 191–3; Armada, 9, 13, 137,
   207, 211, 214–17, 232–3, 254–5; attitude to Papacy, 205–6; basis of negotiations with Elizabeth, 112–13, 124–5,
   209–10; desire for peace, 112, 209;
   expectations from Armada, 214; Hawkins' approach, 62–6; instructions to
   Parma, 123–4; moves against Aragon's
   'Liberties', 197–8; relationship with
   Elizabeth I, 98, 112; on aid to English
   Catholics, 111–12; on right of kings
   over subjects lives, 169–70, 187–8; on
   trade to West Indies, 51; Peruvian gold
   and silver, 70–1; prepares to attack
   England, 53; Princess of Eboli, 173–7,
   177n, 180–1n, 200, 212–13; takes pos-
   session of Portugal, 182, 202, 223; titu-
   lar King of England, 163, 206, 209
Pilgrimage of Grace, 33
Pirates and piracy, 32–3, 36, 39, 67
Pius V, Pope, 162
Plymouth, 32, 43–4, 53, 130–2, 135, 226
Port St Julian, 73, 74
Portland, 133
Portsmouth, 34
Portugal, 182, 202, 205, 223
Privateers, 32, 33; actions against
   Spanish, 112, 164; join to repel
   Armada, 134; under Elizabeth I, 39, 98
Protestants and Protestantism: attacked
   in France and Flanders, 53; English
   support in Europe, 93; European
   League, 91, 111
Puritans, 30, 89

Raleigh, Sir Walter, 54, 107
Rata Coronada, 131, 220, 229, 252
Recalde, Martinez de, 202; Armada, 127,
   131–3, 142, 145, 149–50; background,
   220; death, 251; in Calais Roads,
   228–9, 232, 235, 237–40; reaches
   Ireland, 250–1
Reformation, 28, 35, 93, 95, 159, 205
Revenge, 14, 129
Ridolfi conspiracy, 60–1 65–6, 111, 164
Rio de la Hacha, 52, 55
Rochelle, 38, 93

Roman Catholics: at time of Armada,
   29; conspiracies against Elizabeth I, 84,
   94, 98, 111–14, 164, 206; effect of
   Mary Stuart's execution, 115; invasions
   of England planned, 207; Parsons on
   condition of England, 86–90; reactions
   to Drake's exploits, 107–9; support for
   Spain in England, 36, 202; under Elizabeth, 92

St Domingo, 46, 49, 102–5, 208
St Helen's, 10, 135
St Kitts, 102
St Sebastian, 251
San Juan de Ulloa, 3, 12, 55–9, 61, 70, 81
San Lorenzo, 12
San Martin, 12, 127, 131, 133–4, 138–41,
   143–5, 147–9, 219, 222, 225, 230–2,
   234–8, 241–2, 256
San Matteo, 12, 144
San Salvador, 12, 14
Sandwich, 33, 34
Santiago, 101, 103
Santa Aña, 12, 137, 220, 225
Santa Catalina, 132, 228
Santa Cruz, Marques de (Alonzo de
   Bazan), 10, 100–1, 108, 116, 120, 124,
   207, 211–12; death, 125, 212
Santander, 149, 150, 168, 253
Saragossa, 198
Scilly Isles, 32, 36, 37
Scotland: Armada wreckage, 15–16,
   146; Reformation, 94
Sebastian of Portugal, 46
Señora de la Rosa, 220, 229
Seymour, Lord Henry, 12, 129–30,
   138–9, 233–4
Seymour, Sir Thomas, 37, 45
Shakespeare, William, 7–8
Sheffield Castle, 63–4, 163
Shetland, 148
Shrewsbury, Earl of, 64, 89
Sidney, Sir Philip, 99
Sierra Leone, 49, 80
Silva, Ruy Gomez de (Prince of Eboli),
   15–16, 52–3, 61, 160–1, 171, 176, 212
Simancas, 4, 169, 201
Sixtus V, Pope, 14, 209
Slave trade, 46–52, 55, 69
Sligo Bay, 244
Soto, Juan de, 161–2
Southampton, Earl of, 6–8, 87
Spain: action against Hawkins, 50;

261

Index

attacks by Protestant ships, 60–1; Drake's harassment, 99–100, 107–9; relations with English sailors, 35; sea power, 27–8; secret executions, 169–70; support for Pope against England, 94–5; withdrawal from Low Countries, 163
Stanley, Sir William, 91
Story, Dr, 61, 66
Stourton, Lord, 87
Strangways family, 38, 39
Stukely, Thomas, 45–6

Tagus, River, 120–1, 211, 221
Tavistock, 54
Thorne, Robert, 31
Tierra del Fuego, 74
Toledo, Archbishop of, 166
Treasure fleets, 43–4, 101
Tremayne family, 38, 39
Tremayne, Edmund, 80–1
Trent, Council of, 111
Tunis, 162

Valdez, Don Diego de, 126, 220
Valdez, Don Pedro de, 12, 14, 127–8, 132–3, 202, 220, 223, 228, 232
Valparaiso, 74–5

Vargas, Don Alonzo de, 197–8
Vargas Mexia, Juna de, 168–9
Vasquez Matteo, 175, 178–80, 180–1n, 181–2
Vasquez, de Arce, Rodrigo, 158, 183–4, 186, 188
Vega, Lope de, 68
Velez, Marques de los, 166, 170–1, 177–8
Vigo, 99–100, 108
Virginia, 107

Wales, 86
Walsingham, Sir Francis, 80, 82, 91, 116, 214
Wars of religion, 131, 206
West Indies, 112; disappearance of Caribs, 46; Drake's expedition, 99, 101–7; introduction of black races, 47; slave trade, 50–1
Westmorland, Earl of, 87
Willoughby, Sir Hugh, 35
Winchester, Marquis of, 88
Winter, Captain, 72, 74, 80
Winter, Edward, 99
Winter, Sir William, 14
Worcester, Earl of, 87

FROUDE THE HISTORIAN
Victorian Man of Letters

A. L. Rowse

Froude is the last of the great Victorian historians to be resuscitated and placed in his proper place among them. It is odd that this has not been done before. In the Victorian age he was the only historian to compare with Macaulay in achievement, force and style as a writer, and in the response of the public to his work. His books sold in hundreds of thousands, he was read all over the English-speaking world, he was a public figure.

Beginning as a radical – much in sympathy with his brother-in-law, Charles Kingsley – Froude became a prophet of Empire, though a highly critical one of its record in Ireland, South Africa and the West Indies. Of the two outstanding figures who dominated (and polarised) the late Victorian scene, Gladstone and Disraeli, Froude was critical of both: he disliked the humbug of the one, and suspected charlatanism in the latter, admiring the writer in Disraeli rather than the politician. Indeed Froude had little opinion of party-politicians, and none of humbug – a defect in the Victorian world. Though a famous figure in society he was regarded as 'enigmatic'. Yet the leader of the Oxford school, Bishop Stubbs, admitted in the end: 'Froude was a man of genius, and he has been treated abominably.'

136pp   216mm × 135mm
ISBN 0 86299 384 9 (case) £9.95

THE LITTLE LAND OF CORNWALL

A.L. Rowse

This book by A.L. Rowse, whose autobiography, *A Cornish Childhood*, was highly acclaimed, celebrates and illustrates the diversity and variety of Cornwall. Its main theme is to establish its separate identity, its difference from an ordinary county. Hence the title – a Little Land on its own.

The author's subjects are wide ranging – all the way from the Age of the Saints through the Middle Ages, Tudor times, and the Industrial Revolution, to the present day. Fascinating and idiosyncratic personalities are described. Literature, folklore and legend, as well as history, are drawn upon to describe the creation of a markedly individual people and a familiar and beautiful landscape that still has many secrets to reveal.

The result is a feast for all who love this unique land.

320pp   198mm × 127mm
ISBN 0 86299 265 6 (paper) £5.95